Paston Letters

PASTON LETTERS.

ORIGINAL LETTERS,

WRITTEN DURING THE REIGNS OF

HENRY VI., EDWARD IV., AND RICHARD III.

BY

VARIOUS PERSONS OF RANK OR CONSEQUENCE:

CONTAINING MANY

CURIOUS ANECDOTES, RELATIVE TO THAT TURBULENT AND BLOODY,
BUT HITHERTO DARK, PERIOD OF OUR HISTORY;

AND ELUCIDATING NOT ONLY

PUBLIC MATTERS OF STATE, BUT LIKEWISE THE PRIVATE MANNERS OF THE AGE.

WITH

NOTES HISTORICAL AND EXPLANATORY;

AND AUTHENTICATED BY ENGRAVINGS OF AUTOGRAPHS AND SEALS.

By Sir JOHN FENN, M.A., F.A.S.

A NEW EDITION,

IN WHICH THE LESS IMPORTANT LETTERS ARE ABRIDGED; THE WHOLE SERIES IS DIGESTED IN
CHRONOLOGICAL ORDER, AND ADDITIONS MADE TO THE NOTES OF THE ORIGINAL EDITOR:

By A. RAMSAY.

IN TWO VOLUMES.

VOL. II.

LONDON:
CHARLES KNIGHT & CO., LUDGATE STREET.
MDCCCXLI.

LONDON :
Printed by WILLIAM CLOWES and Sons,
Stamford Street.

CONTENTS.

CONTENTS.

CONTENTS. v

CONTENTS.

CONTENTS.

PASTON LETTERS.

EDWARD IV.—1460 TO 1483.

LETTER CCXLIX.—(LXVIII. vol. iv p. 267.)

I have given this letter to show the great desire which the relations and other connexions of a deceased man of property always expressed to get possession of his estates, in prejudice to the minor and widow, and of the steps they took to obtain it. This letter likewise makes us acquainted with the process the lady wished to pursue, through the means of Sir John Paston, to regain her property. Elizabeth Poynings, the writer of this letter, and the daughter of John Paston, married Robert Poynings, a younger son of Robert Lord Poynings, by whom she had her son Edward here mentioned. He was Lord Deputy of Ireland, and during his administration in 1494, 10 H. VII , those statutes called Poynings' Laws were passed, by which the power of the Irish parliament was restrained, and their Acts subjected to the revisal of the Privy Council of England. He died of a pestilential fever in 1522, 14 H VIII., aged about sixty-two years. These, with other Acts enacting the dependency of Ireland on this kingdom, were repealed in 1785, 25 Geo. III. [We need hardly point out Fenn's magical deduction of "always" drawn from this single letter. We believe there is no want of alacrity shown even now by the relations and connexions of a deceased man of property in taking advantage of any point of law in their favour.]

To the worshipful Sir John Paston, Knight, be this delivered in haste.

WORSHIPFUL and with all mine heart entirely well-beloved nephew, I recommend me to you, desiring to hear of your prosperity and welfare, which I pray Almighty God maintain and increase to his pleasure and your heart's desire, thanking God of your amending and health. Furthermore certifying you that Sir Robert Fynes[1] hath done great hurt in the livelihood which pertained to my husband and me in the shire of Kent, wherein William Keene and other persons are enfeoffed, and greatly troubleth it, and receiveth the issues and profits of great part of them, and as of my said husband's livelihood as well in the same shire as in other shires.

Beside mine jointure my said husband, when he departed towards the field of St. Alban's, made and ordained his will that I should have the rule of all his livelihood, and of Edward his son and mine, and to take the issues and profits of the said livelihood to the finding of his and mine said son, to pay his debts, and to keep the right and title of the same livelihood, which I might not ac-

cordingly occupy for Sir Edward Poynings mine said husband's brother; and so, since my said husband's departing, I assigned that the said Sir Edward for certain years should have and take the revenues of the manors of Westwood, Eastwell, Loneland, Horsemonden, Totingdon, Eccles, Standon, and Combesden, parcel of the said livelihood, which are clearly yearly worth 76l. 13s. 4d., to the intent that the said Sir Edward should pay mine husband's debts, for he would not suffer me to be in rest without that he might have a rule in the livelihood; and after the said assignment made, the said Robert Fynes, contrary to truth, and without cause of right, interrupted me and the said Sir Edward, as well of and in the said manors as of other manors underwritten, whereupon the same Sir Edward sued unto the king's highness, and had the king's honourable letters under his signet directed to the said Sir Robert Fynes, the tenour whereof I send unto you herein enclosed: and as for residue of the livelihood of mine said husband's and mine within the same shire of Kent, wherein the said William Keene and other are enfeoffed, that is to say, the manors of Tyrlingham, Wolverton, Halton, Newington, Bartram,

---

[1] This was a knightly family, of great worth and worship, and a branch of it became Barons Dacre of Gillesland.

Rokesley and Northcray, with the appurtenances, I of them, by mine said husband's
will, should have residue, and take the issues
and profits of them, contrary to right and
conscience taking away my right, and breaking my said husband's will, the said Robert
Fynes hath done great waste and hurt there,
and long time hath taken up the revenues
and profits of the same, where thorough I
have not my right, and the said will may
not be performed.

Wherefore I heartily pray you that ye will
labour unto the king's highness that it liketh
him (to) address his honourable letters to be
directed to the said Robert Fynes, discharging
him utterly of the menurance, occupation,
and receipt of the revenues of the said manors
of Tyrlingham and other, according to the
tenour of the letters laboured by Sir Edward,
for the manors assigned to him from the king's
highness directed to the same Robert Fynes,
or straiter if it may be, and that I and mine
assigns may peaceably re-enjoy them; and if
any person would attempt to do the contrary,
that a commandment, if it please the king's
highness, by him might be given to my Lord
Chancellor to seal writings sufficient with
his great seal in aiding and assisting me and
mine assigns in the same.

And as for the manors of Easthall, Faulkham,

Asslie, and Chelsfield, with the appurtenances
in the said shire of Kent, whereof my husband
at his departure was seised, and my son sithen
(since), unto the time that the Earl of Kent,[1]
without any inquisition or title of right for
the king, by colour of the king's letters
patent, entered into them, and him thereof
put out, and now my Lord of Essex[2] occu-
pieth them in like manner and form; if any
remedy therein will be had I pray you
attempt it.

Also, furthermore I heartily pray you that
if any general pardon be granted, that I may
have one for John Dane, my servant, whom
the said Robert Fynes of great malice hath
indicted of felony, and that ye secretly labour
this, and send me an answer in writing in as
goodly haste as ye may; as soon as it may
please you to send me parcels of costs and
expenses ye bear and pay for the said causes,
I will truly content you it of the same, and
over that reward you to your pleasure; by
the grace of Jesu, who have you in his blessed
keeping. Written in Southwark, the 15th
day of December,

By your aunt,

ELIZABETH POYNINGS.

Southwark, 15th December,
    between 1465 and 1471.
    5 and 11 E. IV.

LETTER CCL.—(XX. vol. i. p. 289.)

This letter, though without any name, was written by Sir John Paston to his brother John Paston, and the
mention of oil for sallads shows us that at this time vegetables for the table were still cultivated here; for
the common opinion has been that most of our fruits and garden productions were so entirely neglected during
these civil wars, as to have been almost totally destroyed. [And oil was used in dressing sallads as
now.]

To Master John Paston, or to my mistress his mother, be this letter delivered in haste.

BROTHER, I commend me to you (*then follows
an order for making out an account, and receiving some rents, &c.*)

By Juddy I sent you a letter by Corby
within four days before this; and therewith
two pots of oil for sallads, which oil was
good as might be when I delivered it, and

shall be good at the receiving, if it be not
mishandled nor miscarried.

Item, as for tidings, the Earl of Northumberland[3] is home into the north, and my

---

[1] Edmund Grey, Lord Grey of Ruthin, and Baron
Hastings, was created Earl of Kent in 1465; he died
in 1489.

[2] Henry Viscount Bourchier, &c., uncle to King
Edward IV., was created Earl of Essex in 1461; he
was succeeded by his son Henry in 1483.

[3] John Nevile was created Earl of Northumberland in 1463, but resigned this title in 1469 to the
family of Percy, the ancient possessors of it.

Lord of Gloucester [1] shall after as to-morrow, men say. Also this day Robert of Ratclyff wedded the Lady Dymock at my place in Fleet-street, and my lady and yours, Dame Elizabeth Bourchier, [2] is wedded to the Lord Howard's son and heir. Also Sir Thomas Walgrave is dead of the sickness that reigneth on Tuesday, now (*q. no*) cheer for you. Also my Lord Archbishop [3] was brought to the Tower on Saturday at night; and on Monday, at midnight, he was conveyed to a ship, and so into the sea, and as yet I cannot understand whither he is sent nor what is fallen (*become*) of him; men say that he hath offended; but, as John Forter saith, some men say nay; but all his meny [*household*] are disparbled (*dispersed*), every man his way; and some that are great clerks and famous doctors of his go now again to Cambridge to school.

As for any other tidings I hear none. The Countess of Oxford [4] is still in St. Martin's; I hear no word of her.

The queen had child, a daughter, [5] but late at Windsor, thereof I trow ye had word. And as for me, I am in like case as I was; and as for my Lord Chamberlain [6] he is not yet come to town, when he cometh then shall I weet what to do. Sir John of Parr is your friend and mine, and I gave him a fair arming sword within this three days. I heard somewhat by him of a back friend of yours; ye shall know more hereafter.

Written the last day of April.

30th of April,
1466. 6 E. IV.

LETTER CCLI.—(LXIX. vol. iv. p. 273.)

This letter is endorsed in an ancient hand, as follows, " A very good Lre moving Sir J P. to be carefull for his wrytings and evidence and how much his ffather did esteme of them." The disputes concerning Sir John Fastolf's will being undetermined at John Paston's death, his widow was fearful lest, by taking the management of his affairs, she should bring both herself and her son into trouble, she therefore cautions him against interfering Her admonitions to Sir John respecting his attention to his writings and evidences show us the value our ancestors set upon their title-deeds, &c The whole letter is replete with good advice to a young man just become his own master by the death of his father, and convinces us that the writer knew mankind, and wished her son to profit by her experience. The date may be later than I have placed it, but the reasons for giving the letter remain the same.

To my right worshipful master, Sir John Paston, Knight, be this letter delivered in haste.

I GREET you well, and send you God's blessing and mine; desiring you to send me word how that ye speed in your matters, for I think right long till I hear tidings from you; and in alwyse (*by all means*) I advise you for to beware that ye keep wisely your writings that be of charge, that it (*they*) come not in their hands that may hurt you hereafter; your father, whom God assoil in his trouble's season! set more by his writings and evidence than he did by any of his moveable goods: remember, that if they were had from you, ye could never get no more such as they be for your part, &c.

Item, I would ye should take heed that if any process come out against me, or against any of those that were indicted afore the co-

---

[1] Richard Plantagenet, afterwards King Richard III.

[2] Thomas Howard, son of John Lord Howard, was created Earl of Surrey by Richard III., and Duke of Norfolk by Henry VIII He married Elizabeth, daughter and heir of Sir Frederick Tilney, Kt , and widow of Humphrey Bourchier, Lord Berners; she died about 1507 Their son Thomas, afterwards Duke of Norfolk, was born about 1470.

[3] I suppose this means George Nevile, Archbishop of York, and brother to Richard Nevile, Earl of Warwick, who at this time was greatly discontented with the proceedings of the king, and perhaps had drawn his brother the Archbishop into the commission of some act disagreeable to Edward.

[4] Margaret, wife of John de Vere, Earl of Oxford, was daughter of Richard Nevile, Earl of Salisbury, and sister of Richard Earl of Warwick This lady suffered much, both from poverty and distress, during the imprisonment and exile of her husband

[5] Elizabeth, afterwards Queen Consort of Henry VII ; she was born in February, 1465.

[6] William Lord Hastings.

B 2

roner, that I might have knowledge thereof, and to purvey a remedy therefore.

Item, as for your father's will, I would ye should take right good counsel therein, as I am informed it may be proved though no man take no charge this twelvemonth; ye may have a letter of administration to such as ye will, and administer the goods, and take no charge; I advise you that ye in no wise take no charge thereof till ye know more than ye do yet, for ye may verily know by that your uncle William said to you and to me, that they will lay the charge upon you and me for more things than is expressed in your father's will, the which should be too great for you or me to bear, but as for me I will not be too hasty to take it upon me I assure you; and at the reverence of God speed your matters so this term that we may be in rest hereafter, and let not for no labour for the season, and remember the great cost and charge that we have had hithertoward, and think verily it may not long endure. Ye know what ye left

when ye were last at home, and weet it verily there is no more in this country to bear out no charge with. I advise you to inquire wisely if ye can get any more there as (*where*) ye be, for else by my faith I fear else it will not be well with us; and send me word in haste how ye do, and whether ye have your last deeds that ye failed [*wanted*], for plainly they are not in this country. It is told me in counsel that Richard Calle hath nigher conquered your uncle William with fair promise touching his livelihood and other things, the which should prevail him greatly as he saith; beware of him and of his fellow by mine advice. God send you good speed in all your matters. Written at Caister, the morrow next after Simon and Jude, whereas I would not be at this time but for your sake, so might I choose.

By your mother,

MARGARET PASTON.

Caister, Wednesday,
29th of October, 1466.   6 E. IV.

LETTER CCLII.—(LXX. vol. iv. p. 277.)

On the back of this letter in an ancient hand is written, "Testes idonei ad negandā veritatem, ut patet infra." The disposal of Sir John Fastolf's large property occasioned many long and expensive contests, some claiming by heirship, some by gift, and others by different titles under his will. The present dispute seems to have been relative to the estate intended for the foundation of his college at Caister. The account of the characters of those who were going to London to be examined on this occasion is curious. This letter has neither subscription nor date, but by the contents it appears to have been written to Sir John Paston by his brother, and not till after the death of their father, it could not be written therefore before 1466.

John Paston to Sir John Paston, Knight.

SIR, it is so that this Saturday John Russe sent me word by Robert Butler that William Yelverton hath been this three days in Yarmouth for to get new witnesses up to London, and it is thought by the said John Russe and Robert Butler, their witnessing is for to prove that it was Sir John Fastolf's will that there should be amortised 300 marks (200*l.*) by year to the college; and also that such estate as my father took here at Caister, at Lammas next before that Sir John Fastolf died, was delivered to my father to the intent for to perform the said will.

Bartholomew Ellis, John Appleby and John Clerk are the witnesses: and as for Bartholomew Ellis he is outlawed; and also men say

in Yarmouth that he is bawd betwixt a clerk of Yarmouth and his own wife. And as for John Appleby he is half frentyk (*crazy*) and so taken in the town, notwithstanding he is an attorney, as Bartholomew Ellis is, in the bailiff's court of Yarmouth; and as for John Clerk of Gorleston, he is outlawed at Sir John Fastolf's suit, and at divers other men's, notwithstanding he is thorough with Sir Thomas for Sir John Fastolf, for this cause that the said clerk was one of Sir Thomas Howys's last witnesses before this. I trow John Loer shall be another witness. As for Bartholomew Ellis and John Appleby, they lie this night at Blighborough onward on their way to London ward; make good watch on them.

I pray you send us some good tidings.

Written the Saturday late at night next after Candlemas-day. I pray you remember John Grey and John Burgess ; we have home the most part of your barley save from Winterton, and that I trust to have the next week, or else we will strait (*q. distrain*) for it by the grace of God, whom I beseech make you good.

I think their coming up is for to disprove your witnesses that ye had into the Chancery.

JOHN PASTON.

February, after 1466.
6 E IV

LETTER CCLIII.—(LXXI. vol. iv. p. 281.)

The various matter treated of in this letter gives it a claim to be inserted in this collection, especially as it discovers the characters and views of many persons mentioned in this work. It has no date, nor can we clearly ascertain how long after 1466 it must have been written, 'tis probably not a great while. William Wainfleet, the founder of Magdalen College in Oxford, was at this time Bishop of Winchester, his partiality for this university is therefore easily to be accounted for.

To my right worshipful mistress, Margaret Paston, widow.

RIGHT worshipful mistress, after due recommendation, please your good mistress-ship to weet that I communed late with your entirely well-beloved son, Sir John Paston, if the foundation of my master Fastolf's college might be at Cambridge in case it shall not be at Caister, neither at St. Benet's, because that university lieth near the country of Norfolk and Suffolk ; for albeit [*although*][1] my Lord of Winchester is disposed to found a college in Oxford for my said master to be prayed for, yet with much less cost he might make some other memorial also in Cambridge, and (*if*) it were of two clerks and three or four scholars, founded at least with the value of good benefices and rich parsonages that might be purchased the advowsons with much less goods than lordships or manors may ; and I found your son well disposed to move and excite my said lord. Also now the Christmas week next before the feast at London, my Lord Winchester called me to him in presence of Sir John, and desired him effectually to be my good willer ; and master would have no words rehearsed on my behalf, and he said, full well, would Jesu, mistress, that my good master that was some time your husband in my said master Fastolf's life days, as he showed to me there could have found in his heart to have trusted and loved me as my master Fastolf did, and that he would not have given credence to the maliciously contrived tales that Friar Brackley, W. Barker and others imagined untruly, saving your reverence, of me. And now ye may openly understand the sooth, and your son Sir John also; and yet for all that, I put never my master Fastolf's livelihood in trouble, for all the unkindness and covetousness that was showed me, as I have declared to the bearer hereof, that I know ye trust well, to whom in this ye may give credence at this time.

God amend J. Russe, I would he had been at Ireland for one day's sake.

Your

WILLIAM WORCESTER.

And I thank you heartily for my poor woman, she should come to you at your commandment late or rathe (*early*), but for jealousy and misdeeming of people that have me in great await (*that mean to do me mischief*) ; and ye know well, mistress, better is a friend unknown than known ; the world is so misdeeming and ready to make division and debate ; that cometh of an envious disposition. And I am right glad that Caister is and shall be at your commandment, and yours in especial, a rich jewel it is at need for all the country in time of war ; and my master Fastolf would rather he had never builded it than it should be in the governance of any sovereign that will oppress the country. And I find the religious of St. Benet's full unkindly took away a chamber the elder abbot had put me

[1] [In the original *albe it*. Fenn translates "for all be it, my Lord of Winchester," &c]

in possession for my solace, when I might come thither and desport me, and took that chamber to master John Smyth, that Sir Thomas Howys said to me was none wholesome counseller in the reformation of the last testament made, but two executors to have the rule alone; I would he had never meddled of it, that counsel made much trouble; I pray you keep this letter close to yourself, as I trust you and Sir James, and also in R. Toly, that I understand him close and just.

I had no time to speak within now late, when I was but one day at Norwich. W. Barker slandered me in certain matters of good to the sum of 500 marks (333*l.* 6*s.* 8*d.*) that

Reynold Harneys should keep and take one half; would Jesus Barker had said true, it might have done me much good; and, mistress, as I dare desire you, I pray you recommend me to my best mistress your mother Agnes, for she favoured me and did me great charity, to be the better disposed to her son master John. And by my soul it made me the heartier to save the livelihood from trouble or from claims, as I report me to all the world, I put never manor nor livelihood of my master Fastolf's in trouble, nor entitled no creature to no place, and ye may speak to her hereof when ye be alone.

After 1466. 6 E. IV

LETTER CCLIV.—(LXXII. vol. iv. p. 287.)

In the proposals of marriage here preserved of this distant age, we find the care and attention paid by our ancestors to the endowment of the lady; most proposals being accompanied with terms for that purpose The Strangers or L'Estranges here mentioned, were of the ancient and knightly family of L'Estrange of Hunstanton, in Norfolk.

To my right worshipful and good master, Sir John Paston, Knight.

RIGHT worshipful Sir, after due recommendation, please it you to understand the cause of my writing is for a marriage for my mistress Margery your sister; for my nephew John Straunge would make her sure of forty pounds jointure, and two hundred marks (133*l.* 6*s.* 8*d*) by year of inheritance; and if ye and your friends will agree hereto, I trust to God it shall take a conclusion to the pleasure of God and worship to both parties.

Moreover, and it pleaseth you to weet, I am sore troubled with Bedston, as well by the way of attachments out of the Chancery as

otherwise; I must beseech you of your good mastership and help in secret manner, as Sir Thomas Lynes the bringer of this shall inform you. I shall be at London in the beginning of this term by the grace of God, which preserve you. Written at Norwich, in haste, the Monday after Twelfth-day.

By your

J. STRANGE.

Norwich, January, between 1466 and 1469. 6 and 9 E. IV.

LETTER CCLV.—(XXI. vol. i. p. 293.)

This letter of Sir John Paston, to his mother, appears to have been written between the years 1466 and 1469, after King Edward's marriage, and the consequent displeasure of the Earl of Warwick, but as it has no date the precise time cannot be ascertained, nor have our histories mentioned any public entry of the king into London, on his coming from York, about this period. Here is no mention of any of the queen's relations as attendant on the king, who is said to speak of the Duke of Clarence, the Earls of Warwick and Oxford, and the Archbishop of York as his best friends, though those of his household knew he regarded them in a very different light.

To Mistress Margaret Paston be this delivered.

RIGHT worshipful mother, I commend me to you and beseech you of your blessing and

God's; thank you for your tenderness and help both to me, my brother, and servants. (*Then follows an account of money, debts, &c., a dispute with his uncle William, and a desire to defer his sister Margery's marriage with Richard Calle till Christmas, &c.*)

The king is come to London, and there came with him, and rode again (*and rode to meet*) him the Duke of Gloucester, the Duke of Suffolk,[1] the Earl of Arundel,[2] the Earl of Northumberland,[3] the Earl of Essex ;[4] the Lords Harry and John of Buckingham,[5] the Lord Dacre,[6] the Lord Chamberlain,[7] the Lord Montjoy[8] and many other knights and esquires; the mayor of London, twenty-two aldermen in scarlet, and of the craftsmen of the town to the number of two hundred all in blue.

The king came thorough Cheap, though it were out of his way, because (*if he had not*) he would not be seen; and he was accompanied in all people with one thousand horse, some harnessed and some not.

My Lord Archbishop[9] came with him from York, and is at the Moor,[10] and my Lord of Oxford[11] rode to have met the king, and he is with my Lord Archbishop at the Moor ; and

came not to town with the king. Some say that they were yesterday three miles to the king wards from the Moor ; and that the king sent them a messenger that they should come when that he sent for them. I wot (*know*) not what to suppose therein.

The king himself hath good language of the Lords of Clarence, of Warwick, and of my Lords of York and of Oxford, saying, they be his best friends; but his household men have other language, so what shall hastily fall I cannot say. My Lord of Norfolk[12] shall be here this night. I shall send you more when I know more.

Item, if Ebesham[13] come not home with my uncle William, that then ye send me the two French books, that he should have written, that he may write them here.

JOHN PASTON, *Knight.*

The seal has here a circle of fleur de lys, they usually adopted but one.

LETTER CCLVI.—(LXXIII. vol. iv. p. 289.)

The date of this letter from Margaret Paston does not appear, but it seems to have been written within a few years after her husband's death, though as the age of her daughter Anne at her father's decease is not known we cannot exactly ascertain it. Anne was now grown tall, and becoming a woman. The endeavouring to educate young women in the houses of their superiors or of their friends and relations at a distance from home has been before noticed (see Letter cvii. v. i. p. 82.), and was certainly a very proper method of having them instructed [There appears, notwithstanding, a great want of affection between mother and daughters; a consequence, we think, of such estrangement.]

To John Paston, the younger, be this delivered in haste.

I GREET you well, and send you God's blessing and mine; letting you weet that since ye departed my cousin Calthorpe sent me a

letter complaining in his writing that forasmuch as he cannot be paid of his tenants as he hath been before this time, he proposeth

---

[1] John de la Pole, Duke of Suffolk, he married Elizabeth, sister of Edward IV.

[2] William Fitzalan, Earl of Arundel, married Joan, daughter of Richard Nevile, Earl of Salisbury.

[3] John Nevile, Earl of Northumberland, from 1463 to 1469.

[4] Henry Bourchier, Earl of Essex, he married Cecily, aunt to Edward IV.

[5] These two lords were of the family of Stafford, Duke of Buckingham.

[6] Richard Fynes, Lord Dacre.

[7] William Lord Hastings.

[8] Walter Blount, created Lord Montjoy in 1465.

[9] George Nevile, Archbishop of York.

[10] The Moor, a seat of the Archbishop's in Hertfordshire.

[11] John de Vere, Earl of Oxford.

[12] John Mowbray, Duke of Norfolk.

[13] Ebesham was a transcriber of books, an employment much patronised before the invention of printing.

to lessen his household, and to live the staitlier, wherefore he desireth me to purvey for your sister Anne; he saith she waxeth high (*grows tall*), and it were time to purvey her a marriage; I marvel what causeth him to write so now, either she hath displeased him, or else he hath taken her with default; therefore I pray you commune with my cousin Clere at London, and weet how he is disposed to her ward, and send me word, for I shall be fain to send for her, and with me she shall but lose her time, and without she will be the better occupied she shall often times move me and put me in great inquietness; remember what labour I had with your sister, therefore do your part to help her forth, that may be to your worship and mine.

Item, remember the bill that I spake to you of to get of your brother of such money as he hath received of me since your father's decease; see your uncle Maultby if ye may, and send me some tidings as soon as ye may; God keep you. Written the Friday next before Saint Thomas of Canterbury, in haste (*29th of December*).

By your mother,

MARGARET PASTON.

Friday, December,
between 1466 and 1470. 6 and 10 E. IV.

LETTER CCLVII.—(LXXIV. vol. iv. p. 291.)

I have printed this letter as showing not only the friendly and just disposition of the writer, evident from the advice which he gives Sir John Paston, but to show the duty and respect of children then continued annually to the memory of their deceased parents The year-day or anniversary of any person's death was called the Obit, and to observe such day with prayers and alms, or other commemoration, was called keeping the Obit. We find that Hugh Fenne strictly fulfilled this observance of filial duty to his deceased mother The device on his seal is a flourishing tree, having the initial letters of his names, one on each side, it alluded perhaps to his own happy and flourishing situation in respect to his fortune, family, and friends. [The advice seems very strongly to tend to his own interest, or his client's]

To the right worshipful Sir John Paston, Knight.

RIGHT worshipful Sir, I recommend me to you; like you (*to*) weet a distress was taken in Caister, by Thomas Peacock, I trow your servant, a busy man called, of a full true soul, John Hadynet of Heringsby, a poor man, his plough hath lain ever since he saith; I understand it is for Catts' land. I sent my clerk to my mistress your mother, and the said John with him therefore; and my mistress would him come again another day, for Peacock was not then at home; so he did, and cannot have it as he saith, but that ye would I should speak with you at Caister thereof and of other matters he told me this day; and because of my mother s year-day holden this day, God have her soul, and tomorrow shall be a good day, I would by God s grace dispose me to his mercy against Thursday, as I have used, therefore I pray you pardon my coming; in the week after Easter, I intend to see you and my said mistress certainly; it is long since I saw her meseemeth,

and if ye be not then at Caister I pray you send me word that I may come sooner to you to commune with you in this matter, and in all other that ye will, and so depart to London from thence, and therefore I will abide with you a good while.

Sir, as to Catts, ye be remembered what I said to you at London at two times, I am the same man; I have since I came gotten the evidences into my hands, and I am ready to show them what learned man here that ye will assign, the matter is clear to my thinking. Titteshale that sold it to Sir John Fastolf might as well have sold him your land or mine; and if the sale be lawful, I shall leave my hands at the first, as I said at London, the distress to be kept for that I wiss it need not, and it was unlawfully taken; like it you to do deliver the poor man his goods again, I am ready to answer you for old and new as right will; I shall break no day to be assigned for to leave all other things.

By the Blessed Lady I believe that ye will dispose you well, and so I pray God ye do, and have you in his blessed governance.

Written at the head town of Norfolk, this Tuesday. Your own

HUGH at FENNE.

Norwich, Tuesday, March or April, between 1467 and 1469. 7 and 9 E IV.

LETTER CCLVIII.—(XXIII. vol. ii. p. 3.)

We have in this letter a most curious and authentic account of the marriage of Charles the Bold, Duke of Burgundy, with Margaret, daughter of Richard Plantagenet, Duke of York, and sister of Edward IV., and of the subsequent diversions exhibited at Bruges in honour of it, written by John Paston, an eye-witness, who, with his brother Sir John Paston, Knight, attended in the retinue of a princess. The description here given affords us a high idea of the splendour of the court of the duke, and of the politeness of the courtiers.

To my right reverend and worshipful mother, Margaret Paston, dwelling at Caister, be this delivered in haste.

RIGHT reverend and worshipful mother, I recommend me unto you as humbly as I can think, desiring most heartily to hear of your welfare and heart's ease, which I pray God send you as hastily as my heart can think.

Please it you to weet, that at the making of this bill, my brother, and I, and all our fellowship, were in good heele (*health*), blessed be God.

As for the guiding here in this country, it is as worshipful as all the world can devise, and there were never Englishmen had so good cheer out of England that ever I heard of.

As for tidings here, but if (*unless*) it be of the feast, I can none send you; saving, that my Lady Margaret[1] was married on Sunday last past at a town that is called The Dame,[2] three miles out of Bruges, at five of the clock in the morning; and she was brought the same day to Bruges to her dinner; and there she was received as worshipfully as all the world could desire; as with procession with ladies and lords, best beseen of any people that ever I saw or heard of. Many pageants were played in her way in Bruges to her welcoming, the best that ever I saw; and the same day my Lord, the Bastard,[3] took upon him to answer twenty-four knights and gentlemen within eight days at justs of peace; and when that they were answered, they twenty-four and himself should turney with other twenty-five the next day after, which is on Monday next coming; and they that have justed with him into this day have been as richly beseen, and himself also, as cloth of gold, and silk, and silver, and goldsmith's work, might make them; for of such gear, and gold, and pearl, and stones, they of the Duke's court, neither gentlemen, nor gentlewomen, they want none; for without (*unless*) that they have it by wishes, by my truth I heard never of so great plenty as here is.

This day my Lord Scales[4] justed with a

[1] Margaret Plantagenet, sister of Edward IV., according to this account, was married on Sunday the 3rd of July, 1468. 8 E.IV.

[2] [Damme.]

[3] Anthony Count de la Roche, called the Bastard of Burgundy, was a natural son of Duke Philip the Good, by Johanna of Prulles, famous for his wit, courage, and polite accomplishments. He was born in 1421, and died in 1504.

[4] Anthony Widville, or Woodville, Lord Scales, &c., and afterwards Earl Rivers, son of Sir Richard Widville, by Jaqueline of Luxemburgh, Duchess Dowager of Bedford, and brother of Elizabeth, queen of Edward IV., was born about 1441, and became the most distinguished warrior, statesman, and most learned gentleman of his time. In the 7 Edward

lord of this country, but not with the Bastard; for they made (a) promise at London, that none of them both should never deal with other in arms; but the Bastard was one of the lords that brought the Lord Scales into the field; and of misfortune a horse struck my Lord Bastard on the leg, and hath hurt him so sore that I can think he shall be of no power to accomplish up his arms; and that is great pity, for by my truth I trow (think) God made never a more worshipful knight.

And as for the Duke's court, as of lords, ladies, and gentlewomen, knights, esquires, and gentlemen, I heard never of none like to it, save King Arthur's court. And by my troth, I have no wit nor remembrance to write to you half the worship that is here; but what lacketh, as it cometh to mind I shall tell you when I come home, which I trust to God shall not be long tofore. We depart out of Bruges homeward on Tuesday next coming, and all folk that came with my Lady of Burgoyn (Burgundy) out of England, except such as shall abide here still with her, which I wot (know) well shall be but few.

We depart the sooner, for the Duke[1] hath word that the French king[2] is purposed to make war upon him hastily, and that he is within four or five days' journey of Bruges, and the Duke rideth, on Tuesday next coming, forward to meet with him; God give him good speed and all his; for by my troth they are the goodliest fellowship that ever I came amongst, and best can behave them, and most like gentlemen.

Other tidings have we none here, but that the Duke of Somerset[3] and all his bands departed well beseen out of Bruges a day before that my lady the Duchess came thither, and they say here that he is to Queen Margaret that was, and shall no more come here again, nor be holpen by the Duke.

No more, but I beseech you of your blessing as lowly as I can, which I beseech you forget not to give me every day once; and, mother, I beseech you that ye will be good mistress to my little man, and to see that he go to school.

I sent my cousin Daubeney five shillings by Calle's man for to buy for him such gear as he needeth: and, mother, I pray you this bill may recommend me to my sisters both, and to the master, my cousin Daubeney, Sir James, Sir John Stylle, and to pray him to be good master to little Jack,[4] and to learn him well; and I pray you that this bill may recommend me to all your folks, and to my well-willers; and I pray God send you your heart's desire.

Written at Bruges the Friday next after St. Thomas.[5]

Your son and humble servant,

J. PASTON, *the younger.*

Bruges,
Friday, 8th of July,
1468. 8 E. IV.

IV. he challenged and vanquished the Bastard of Burgundy in a grand and solemn just in Smithfield; at which time the promise mentioned in this letter was made. This accomplished nobleman was beheaded at Pomfret, in June 1483, by the command of the Protector, Richard Duke of Gloucester.

[1] Charles the Bold, Duke of Burgundy, was born in 1433, and was slain in battle, near Nancy, in Lorrain, in 1477.

[2] Charles VII. It is worthy of remark how cautious the writers of these times were not to give the title of King of France to the ruler of that kingdom, but to style him the French King. In this place (and I have observed it in others) the word "Kyng" (intending to go on with, of France) was written without consideration, and then, on observing it, immediately crossed out, and "Frenshe Kyng" put in its place.

[3] Edmund Beaufort, Duke of Somerset, an adherent to Henry VI. and his queen Margaret, commanded at the battle of Tewkesbury, in 1471; which being lost, he fled to sanctuary, whence he was taken and beheaded.

[4] This little John, whose school education J. Paston seems so anxious about, must have been born before 1464, and most probably died under age, if he was his son, as Sir William Paston, knight, who, as some pedigrees state, was born in 1464, stands in the pedigree as heir to his father; but I rather think that J. Paston had not been married at this time, and that this "lytyll man" was not his son.

[5] This must mean either the 3rd or 7th day of July, the one being the translation of St. Thomas the Apostle, the other of St. Thomas à Becket. I believe it means the latter.

LETTER CCLIX.—(LXXV. vol. iv. p. 295.)

The exact date of this letter is not easily determined, nor is it of any consequence, it only shows that one of the family of Fastolf of Suffolk pretended a claim to Caister, and intended coming to assert that claim with a large fellowship: whether this was Thomas Fastolf, the son of the lady who had some time before applied to J. Paston for his assistance towards regaining the livelihood of her son out of the hands of those who had the wardship of him, does not appear. I have ventured to fix the date of this letter to 1468, as it most probably was written about that time. Relic Sunday is the Sunday fortnight after Mid-summer-day.

To Sir John Paston, Knight, be this delivered in haste.

I GREET you well, and send you God's blessing and mine; letting you weet that Blickling of Heylesdon came from London this week, and he is right merry, and maketh his boast that within this fortnight at Heylesdon should be both new lords and new officers; and also this day was brought me word from Caister, that Rysing of Fretton should have heard said in divers places there, as he was in Suffolk, that Fastolf of Conghawe maketh all the strength that he may, and proposeth him to assault Caister, and to enter there if he may, insomuch that it is said that he hath a five score men ready, and sendeth daily spies to understand what fellowship keep the place; by whose power, or favour, or supportation, that he will do this I know not, but ye wot well that I have been affrayed (*frightened*) there before this time, when that I had other comfort than I have now; and I cannot well guide nor rule soldiers, and also they set not by a woman as they should set by a man; therefore I would ye should send home your brothers or else Daubeney to have a rule, and to take in such men as were necessary for the safe-guard of the place, for if I were there, without I had the more sadder (*graver*) or worshipful persons about me, and there come a meny [1] of knaves and prevailed in their intent, it should be to me but a villainy. And I have been about my livelihood to set a rule therein, as I have written to you, which is not yet all performed after mine

desire, and I would not go to Caister till I had done; I will no more days make thereabout if I may, therefore in any wise send somebody home to keep the place, and when that I have done and performed that I have begun, I shall purpose me thither-ward if I should do there any good, and else I had lever (*rather*) be thence.

I have sent to Nicholas and such as keep the place, that they should take in some fellows to assist and strength them till ye send home some other word, or some other man to govern them that be therein, &c.

I marvel greatly that ye send me no word how that ye do, for your elmyse (*enemies*) begin to wax right bold, and that putteth your friends both in great fear and doubt, therefore purvey that they may have some comfort that they be no more discouraged, for if we lose our friends it shall (*be*) hard in this troublesome world to get them again.

The blessed Trinity speed you in your matters, and send you the victory of your elmyse [*enemies*], to your heart's ease and their confusion.

Written at Norwich, the Saturday next before Relic Sunday, in haste.

I pray you remember well the matters that I wrote to you for in the letter that ye had by James Gresham's man, and send me an answer thereof by the next man that cometh, &c.

By you mother,
MARGARET PASTON.

Norwich, Saturday, 9th of July, 1468. 8 E. IV.

---

[1] [*Meny*—a following Penn translates *many*.]

LETTER CCLX.—(LXXVI. vol. iv. p. 299.)

On the back of this letter is the following memorandum :—" Sir T. Howys agreith to sell the manuor of
Caister to the Duke of Norfl and mouith thereto my Lord Cardenall " It was in consequence of this
agreement with Sir Thomas Howys, one of the executors of Sir John Fastolf, that the Duke of Norfolk, I
suppose, claimed the manor and castle of Caister, and in pursuit of that claim undertook to besiege it in
the manner explained in the following letters. What Sir Thomas Howys says of J. Paston must be
believed with caution, as they had disagreed concerning the executorship of Sir John Fastolf's will.

To my most honourable Lord Cardinal [1] and Archbishop of Canterbury.

MOST reverend and my right good lord, I recommend me to your gracious lordship in my most humble wise; please your lordship to weet that my Lord (of) Norfolk's counsel hath now late moved Sir William Yelverton, knight, and me, to be proffered for to purchase the manor of Caister and certain other lordships that were my master Fastolf's, whom God pardon! out excepted the manor of Gunton that your lordship desireth to purchase, and other certain manors that my master Fastolf's friends have desired to be proffered;[2] and because the pretens (pretended) bargain that John Paston in his lifetime surmitted (*surmised*),[3] by colour of which he intended to have all my master Fastolf's lands in Norfolk and Suffolk for nought, saving the high reverence of your estate, was not just nor true ; and because that I, with other of my master Fastolf's executors, may have whereof to dispose in charityful deeds to do for his soul, I have condescended the rather that my said Lord of Norfolk shall be proffered to the purchase of the said manor of Caister and other manors that may be spared to the increase of his livelihood in this land, and these covenants to be engrossed up within short time as by All Halowaunce[4] in case your lordship be agreed and pleased withall, whereupon I would beseech your noble lordship to let me weet your good pleasure and advice in this behalf.

And because my said Lord (of) Norfolk is so near of blood to your highness knitted, that moved me to be the more willing to condescend to the foresaid purchase, and so trusting your lordship would be right well pleased withall. Written at Norwich the 10th day of October, in the eighth year of the reign of Edward IV.

Your poor chaplain,

THOMAS HOWYS.

Norwich, Monday,
10th of October, 1468 8 E. IV.

LETTER CCLXI.—(LXXVII. vol. iv. p. 303.)

This letter informs us of the preparations for the defence of Caister, and gives us a very minute account of
the several merits of the four warlike men sent down to be useful when it should be attacked

*To my right well-beloved brother, John Paston, Esq , being at Caister, or to John Daubeney
there, be this letter delivered.*

RIGHT well-beloved brother, I commend me to you ; letting you weet that I have waged, for to help you and Daubeney to keep the place at Caister, four well assured and true men to do all manner of thing what that they be desired to do in safeguard or inforcing (*strengthening*) of the said place; and moreover they be proved men, and cunning (*expert*) in the war and in feats of arms, and they can well shoot both guns and cross-bows, and amend and string them, and devise bulwarks, or any things that should be a strength

---

[1] Thomas Bourchier, Bp. of Ely, was translated to
Canterbury in 1454. He died an old man, in 1486.
[2] [Fenn reads *preferred*.]
[3] [*Surmised* cannot be the meaning of the word

Procured or *fraudulently procured* seems the sense
here required]
[4 In orig. *all Halowaunce*, Allhallows, Nov. 1.
Fenn omits all]

to the place, and they will as need is keep watch and ward, they be sad (*serious*) and well-advised men, saving one of them, which is bald, and called William Peny, which is as good a man as goeth on the earth saving a little, he will, as I understand, be a little copschotyn [1] (*high-crested*), but yet he is no brawler but full of courtesy, much upon (*much like*) James Halman; the other three be named Peryn Sale, John Chapman, Robert Jack's Son (*Jackson*), saving that as yet they have none harness come, but when it cometh it shall be sent to you, and in the mean while I pray you and Daubeney to purvey them some.

Also a couple of beds they must needs have, which I pray you by the help of my mother to purvey for them till that I come home to you; ye shall find them gentlemanly comfortable fellows, and that they will and dare abide by their tackling, and if ye understand that any assault should be towards; I send you these men, because that men of the country there about you should be frayed (*frightened*) for fear of loss of their goods; wherefore if there were any such thing towards, I would ye took of men of the country but few, and that they were well assured men, for else they might discourage all the remanent.

And as for any writing from the king, he hath promised that there shall come none, and if there do his unwarys [2] (*with his privity*), your answer may be this how the king hath said, and so to delay them till I may have word, and I shall soon purvey a remedy.

I understand that ye have been with my Lord of Norfolk now of late, what ye have done I wot not; we see that he shall be here again this day. Moreover I trow John Alford shall not long abide with my lord; I shall send you tidings of other things in haste, with the grace of God, who, &c. Written on Wednesday next before St. Martin.

JOHN PASTON.

I fear that Daubeney is not all there (*altogether*) best stored to continue household long; let him send me word in haste, and I will relieve him to my power, and ere long too I hope to be with you.

Roger Ree is sheriff of Norfolk, and he shall be good enough. The escheator I am not yet ascertained of

Also, that these men be at the beginning entreated as courteously as ye can.

Also, I pray you to send me my flower [3] by the next messenger that cometh.

Also, as for my Lord Fitzwalter's obligation I know none such in mine adward as yet.

Also, the obligation of the Bishop of Norwich's obligation, I never saw it that I remember, wherefore I would and pray my mother to look it up

Also, as for the Bible [4] that the master hath, I wend the utmost price had not past five marks (3*l*. 6*s*. 8*d*.) and so I trow he will give it, weet I pray you.

Also, as for Sir William Darber and Sir William Falgate, I would, if they can purvey for themselves, full fain be discharged of them.

London, Wednesday,
9th November, 1468. 8 E IV.

---

[1] *Copschotyn* is *cup-shotten*, apt to get a little drunk]

[2] I do not understand this sentence, perhaps it means, "unless they take him unexpectedly." [We think "his unwarys" means *without* his privity]

[3] This may mean flour for household use; or it may signify his flower, his device or cognisance.

[4] This must mean some MS copy, for at this time there was only one printed edition of the Bible, which would have sold even then for a much greater sum than is here mentioned. I mean "Biblia Latina. Mogunt per J Fust and P Schöffer, 1462."

LETTER CCLXII.—(LXXVIII. vol. iv. p. 309.)

At a time when his keeping possession of Caister was doubtful, it was a stroke of policy in Sir John Paston to gain the goodwill of the queen by presenting her chaplain to the free chapel at Caister, though his intention had been to have united it to the mastership of his college there, and this he does not now despair of accomplishing, as it was probable that the queen's chaplain would soon have such preferment as would induce him to resign this. The difference of opinion between the parson who was to receive the money, and him who was to pay it, is a curious anecdote, and the cautious determination of Sir John likewise is worthy observation, that this priest " must have it as it was hadde befor " The following entry is taken from the institution books of the Bishop of Norwich.—

" Cantaria in Cayster-hall.

Lib xi. p. 170.   21 Mar 1468.   Mr. Iohes Yetton S T. P. ad col. Epī pr. laps " "

By which it appears that Sir John Paston's presentation either was not allowed, or was not made out in time, and that the bishop presented by a lapse.

To my well-beloved brother, John Paston, or to John Daubeney, in his absence.

RIGHT worshipful and well-beloved brother, I commend me to you, letting you weet that Sir Thomas Howes had a free chapel in Caister whereof the gift belongeth to me, which chapel as I understand should be in the old time, ere the place at Caister were built, within the moat, wherefore I am but the better pleased; and so it is now that at the special request of the queen and other especial good lords of mine, I have given it to the bearer hereof called Master John Yotton, a chaplain of the queen's; nevertheless in time past I purposed that the master of the college should have had it, and so ere long to I hope he shall, wherefore I think he must take possession, and that is the cause of his coming; wherefore I pray you make him good cheer; he is informed that it should be worth an hundred shillings by year, which I believe not: I think it dear enough (*at*) forty shillings by year; he must have it as it was had before.

Item, this day I understand that there be come letters from my mother, and you, and Daubeney, wherein I shall send you answer when I have seen them.

No more at this time, for within this three days I shall let you have knowledge of other matters.

Written the 17th day of March.

Whither he needeth induction, or institution, or none, I wot not; if it need, brother, ye may seal any such thing as well as I. Master Stephen can tell all such things.

JOHN PASTON, *knight.*

London,
Friday, 17th of March,
1468.   9 E. IV.

LETTER CCLXIII.—(LXXIX. vol. iv. p. 311.)

The curiosity of this letter consists in the cautions given by W. Paston to the bailiff for the safe and secret conveyance of the money, and in his attention to the good keeping of his horse Bayard   William Paston was brother to John Paston, and uncle to Sir John, and probably wrote this letter in the reign of Edward IV.   Edward IV. was in Norfolk in 1469, and again in 1474.

To the bailiff of Mautby.

MASTER bailiff I recommend me unto you; praying you that ye will send me by William Cocks, bearer hereof, four nobles in gold, put into the same box that this bill is in as though it were evidence, for I have told the messenger that he should bring me nothing but evidence, for he is in a manner departing out of my service, wherefore I would not he knew so much of my counsel, and as for the remanent I would ye should keep it till I come myself.

And if Bayard be unsold, I pray you let him be made fat against the king come into the country, whatsoever I pay for the keeping of him, and I shall weet how good a courser I shall be myself at my coming into the country, by the grace of God, who have you in keeping.   Written at Heveningham.

By your WILLIAM PASTON.

Heveningham. Suffolk.

Perhaps 1469. 9 E. IV.

LETTER CCLXIV.—(XXIV. vol. ii. p. 11.)

Before the invention of printing, the number of writers and copiers was very great; most monasteries and religious houses having an office called a scriptorium, wherein several writers were almost constantly employed in copying books on various subjects, missals and books of psalms, &c. richly and elegantly adorned with illuminations, &c. Men of fortune and learning likewise occasionally employed copiers to transcribe books for their libraries. W. Ebesham was one of those who pursued this employment and wrote a good hand; he complains of poverty, and petitions to have his account discharged. One of the articles in the bill is dated 30th of October, 1468, 8 E. IV.: what follows therefore was done after that day; so that perhaps the bill was not delivered, nor this letter written, before the next year, 1469.

To my most worshipful master, Sir John Paston, Knight.

My most worshipful and most special master, with all my service most lowly I recommend (*me*) unto your good mastership, beseeching you most tenderly to see me somewhat rewarded for my labour in the great book which I wrote unto your said good mastership; I have oftentimes written to Pampyng, according to your desire, to inform you how I have laboured in writings for you, and I see well he spake not to your mastership of it; and God knoweth I lie in sanctuary[1] at great costs and amongst right unreasonable askers.

I moved this matter to Sir Thomas (*Lewis*) lately, and he told me he would move your mastership therein, which Sir Thomas desired me to remember well what I have had in money at sundry times of him.

(*Then comes the account, as stated more at large in the following bill.*)

And in especial I beseech you to send me for alms one of your old gowns, which will countervail much of the premises I wot well; and I shall be yours while I live, and at your commandment; I have greatly missed[2] of it God knows, whom I beseech preserve you from all adversity; I am somewhat acquainted with it.

Your very man,
WM. EBESHAM.

About 1469,
9 E. IV.

Following appeareth, parcelly, divers and sundry manner of writings, which, I, William Ebesham, have written for my good and worshipful master, Sir John Paston, and what money I have received, and what is unpaid.[3]

	s.	d.
" First, I did write to his mastership a little book of physic, for which I had paid by Sir Thomas Lewis, in Westminster.		20
" Item, I had for the writing of half the Privy Seal, of Pampyng . .		8
" Item, for the writing of the said whole Privy Seal,[4] of Sir Thomas .		2
" Item, I wrote eight of the witnesses[5] in parchment but after 14*d.* a-piece, for which I was paid of Sir Thomas		10
" Item, while my said master was over the sea in midsummer term, Calle set me at work to write two times the Privy Seal in paper, and then after clearly in parchment . . .	4	8
And also I wrote at the same time one more of the longest witnesses, and other diverse and necessary writings, for which he promised me 10*s.* (whereof I had of Calle but 4*s.* 8*d.*) due 5*s.* 4*d.*	5	4
Carried forward. . . .	21	4

[1] Why he was in sanctuary I know not, but it appears that it was expensive being there. [Most likely for debt.]

[2] [*threte myst* in orig. Probably *great want.*]

[3] We are here furnished with a curious account of the expenses attending the transcribing of books previous to the noble art of printing. At this time the common wages of a mechanic were, with diet, 4*d.*, and without diet 5½*d.* or 6*d.* a day; we here see that a writer received 2*d.* for writing a folio leaf, three of which he could with ease finish in a day, and I should think that many quick writers at that time would fill four, five, or even six in a day: if so, the pay of these greatly exceeded that of common handicraft men.

[4] Some grant, or other matter, which was to pass the Privy Seal.

[5] The depositions of witnesses.

	s.	d.
Brought forward	24	4
" Item, I received of Sir Thomas at Westminster 30th October,[1] 8 E. IV. 1468	3	4
" Item, I did write two quires of paper of witnesses, every quire containing 14 leaves after 2d. a leaf .	4	8
" Item, as to the Great Book :—[2] . .		
" First, for writing of the Coronation; and other Treatises of Knighthood, in that quire which containeth a 12 leaves and more, 2d. a leaf. . .	2	2
" Item, for the Treatise of War in four books, which containeth 60 leaves, after 2d. a leaf	10	
" Item, for Othea,[3] an epistle, which containeth 43 leaves	7	2
Carried forward	51	8

[1] This exactly ascertains the date of this receipt to be the 30th of October, 1468. 8 E. IV.

[2] This Great Book seems to have contained various treatises.

[3] Othea means a Treatise on Wisdom.

[4] De Regimine Principum.—A Treatise Concerning the Government of Princes, and by being written for a penny each leaf, I suppose it was in quarto.

[5] This either means ornamenting the whole with red capital letters, or writing the heads of the several treatises or chapters in red letters. [Rubricking.]

[6] " Und p'o m° libro script' xxvijs cu' diu' chal." This in the original follows "Sum' non sol. 41s. 1d."

The following account of payments for writing, &c. is extracted from an original quarto MS. in the editor's possession, containing the various expenses of Sir John Howard, knight, of Stoke by Nayland, in Suffolk, (afterwards Duke of Norfolk).

Item the vijth yere of Kynge Edward y⁰ iiijth and y⁰ xxviij day of July (1467). My mast' rekened wt Thomas Lympnor of Bury, and my mast' peid hym—

	s.	d.
For viij hole vynets,* p'se y⁰ vynett xijd .	viij	
I{tm}. for xxj dī vynets, p'se y⁰ dī vynett, iiijd	vij	
It' for Psalmes lettres, xv⁰† and dī, y⁰ p'se, of C iiijd	v	ij
Carried forward . . xx	ij

* Borders, flowers, or flourishes at the beginning of a book, chapter, &c.—[vignettes.]
† xv⁰ and dī=1500 and an half.

	s.	d.
Brought forward	51	8
" Item, for the Challenges and the Acts of Arms, which is 28 leaves . .	4	8
" Item, for De Regimine Principum,[4] which containeth 45 leaves, after 1 penny a leaf, which it is right well worth	3	9
" Item, for rubrishing[5] of all the book	3	4
	63	5

	£.	s.	d.
Sum received . . .	0	22	4
Sum unpaid . . .	0	41	1[6]
Sum total. .	3	3	5

WILLIAM EBESHAM.

	s.	d.
Brought forward . .	xx	ij
It' for p'ms lettres, lxiijᶜ, ‡ p'se of a Cj¹ . .	v	iᵕj
It' for wrytynge of a quare and dī, p'se y⁰ quayr xxd	ij	vi
It' for wrytynge of a Calender		xij
It' for iij quayres of velym, p'se y⁰ quayr xxd	v	
It' for notynge of v quayres and ij leves, p'se of y⁰ quayr) viiij	iij	vij
It' for capital drawynge iijᶜ and dī y⁰ p'se		iij
It' for floryshynge of capytallis v⁰ . . .		v
It' for byndynge of y⁰ boke‖		xij

| The wyche p'cellis my mastr paid hȳ yis day and he is content. . . . . . | 1 | ij |

This is an account of a limner or illuminator of manuscripts, who resided at Bury.

‡ lxiijᶜ=6300.

§ A quire of vellum from this entry seems to consist of four leaves, and his receiving only 3d. for noting two leaves might be accounted for, by the last leaf not being full ; the drawing and flourishing of the capital letters seems very cheap.

‖ 12s. appears a great price for binding a book, but it is so stated in the original account.

LETTER CCLXV.—(LXXX. vol. iv. p. 313.)

The reader cannot help being interested in the family scenes here laid before him; the pleasure his mother expresses at her son's engagement, and the good and prudent advice she gives him relative to his marriage shows her anxiety for his future happiness. The desire which she has to have her daughter (Margery, I suppose) introduced into the family of some noble lady, shows her concern for her education, at the same time that it hints at their not being comfortable together. The handsome character given of Sir John Paston by my Lord Scales, and repeated to him by his mother, shows her satisfaction at hearing so good a report of him.

To Sir John Paston.

I GREET you well, and send you God's blessing and mine, thanking you for my seal that ye sent me, but I am right sorry that ye did so great cost thereupon, for one of forty pence should have served me right well; send me word what it cost you and I shall send you money therefor; I sent you a letter by a man of Yarmouth, send me word if ye have it, for I marvel ye sent me none answer thereof by Juddy.

I have none very (certain or true) knowledge of your insurance (engagement), but if ye be insured, I pray God send you joy and worship together, and so I trust ye shall have if it be as it is reported of her;[1] and anempts (before) God ye are as greatly bound to her as ye were married, and therefore I charge you upon my blessing that ye be as true to her as she were married unto you in all degrees, and ye shall have the more grace and the better speed in all other things.

Also I would that ye should not be too hasty to be married till ye were sure of your livelihood, for ye must remember what charge ye shall have, and if ye have not to maintain it it will be a great rebuke; and therefore labour that ye may have releases of the lands, and be in more surety of your land or than (before) ye be married.

The Duchess of Suffolk[2] is at Ewelm, in Oxfordshire, and it is thought by your friends here, that it is done that she might be far and out of the way, and the rather feign excuse because of age or sickness if that the king would send for her for your matters.

Your enemies be as bold here as they were

before, wherefore I cannot think but that they have some comfort;[3] I sent to Caister that they should be wary[4] in keeping of the place as ye did write to me; haste you to speed your matters as speedily as ye can that ye may have less fellowship at Caister, for the expenses and costs be great, and ye have no need thereof, and [if] ye remember you well what charges ye have beside, and how your livelihood is despoiled and wasted by your adversaries.

Also I would ye should purvey for your sister[5] to be with my Lady of Oxford,[6] or with my Lady of Bedford[7] or in some other worshipful place whereas ye think best, and I will help to her finding, for we be either of us weary of other: I shall tell you more when I speak with you; I pray you do your devyr (endeavour) herein as ye will my comfort and welfare and your worship, for divers causes which ye shall understand afterward, &c.

I spake with the Lord Scales at Norwich, and thanked him for the good lordship that he had showed to you, and desired his lordship to be your continual good lord; and he swore by his troth he would do that he might do for you, and he told me that Yelverton the justice had spoken to him in your matter, but he told me not what; but I trow and (if) ye desired him to tell you he would. Ye are beholden to my lord of his good report of you

---

[3] [Comfort is here meant for support.]
[4] [Fenn translates beware. In orig be u ar]
[5] This was most probably Margery Paston, with whom the whole family were very soon after the writing of this letter so much displeased for having without their consent contracted herself in marriage to Richard Calle.
[6] Elizabeth, the daughter of Sir John Howard, knight, and widow of John de Vere, Earl of Oxford.
[7] Jacqueline, the widow of John Plantagenet, Duke of Bedford, was at this time the wife of Richard Widville, Earl Rivers, by whom she was the mother of Anthony Widville, Lord Scales, the nobleman mentioned in this letter. she died in 1472.

---

[1] Who the lady is does not appear in this letter, but it most probably meant Anne Hault.
[2] Alice, widow of William de la Pole, Duke of Suffolk, was the daughter and heir of Thomas Chaucer, Esq. of Ewelm, and grand-daughter of our famous poet, Geoffrey Chaucer.

in this country, for he reported better of you than I trow ye deserve. I felt by him that there hath been proffered him large proffers on your adversaries' part again you.

Send me word as hastily as ye may after the beginning of the term how ye have sped in all your matters, for I shall think right long till I hear some good tidings.

Item, I pray you recommend me to the good master[1] that ye gave to the chapel of Caister, and thank him for the great cost that he did on me at Norwich; and if I were a great lady he should understand that he should fare the better for me, for me seemeth by his demeaning he should be right a good man.

Item, I send you the ouch[2] with the diamond, by the bearer hereof. I pray you forget not to send me a kersche of cr'melle[3] for neckerchiefs for your sister Anne, for I am scheut (blamed) of the good lady that she is with because she hath none, and I can none get in all this town.

I should write more to you but for lack of leisure; God have you in his keeping, and send you good speed in all your matters. Written in haste on Easter Monday.

By your mother,

MARGARET PASTON.

Norwich, Monday,
3d of April, 1469.
9 E. IV.

LETTER CCLXVI.—(LXXXI. vol. iv. p. 319.)

Edward IV. came into Norfolk in the spring of the year in 1469. We see the desire which noblemen had to be honourably attended on such occasions, and the interest they employed to procure a respectable retinue when they came to meet their sovereign. John Paston in this case applied to the lady to find out her husband's intentions, and it appears that his application was successful.

To Master Sir John Paston.

SIR, I pray you recommend me to my Lord Scales's good lordship, and to let him weet that in like wise as his lordship gave me in commandment I have inquired what the gentleman's answer was that my Lord of Norfolk sent to await upon him at the king's coming into this country; his answer was to my Lord of Norfolk's messenger, that he had promised my Lord Scales to await upon him at the same season, and inasmuch as he had promised my Lord Scales, he would not false his promise for no man on live (alive). I found the means that the said gentleman's wife moved her husband with the same matter

as though she had asked him of her own head, and he told her that he had given this answer; this gentleman is Sir William Calthorpe,[4] but I pray you tell my Lord Scales that ye understand not who it is, for he prayed me to be secret therein.

I pray with all my heart hie you home in haste, for we think long till ye come; and I pray you send me word whether ye shall be made a Christian[5] man ere ye come home or not; and if so be that ye send any man home hastily, I pray you send me an hat[6] and a bonnet by the same man, and let him bring the hat upon his head for (fear of) mis-

---

[1] Dr. John Yotton, to whom Sir John Paston had given the chapel in Caister in 1468.

[2] An ouch is a collar of gold, formerly worn by women : a gold button, set with some jewel, is likewise so called, and that most probably was the ornament here mentioned to be sent to Sir John by his mother ; we may suppose it was intended as a present to his betrothed bride.

[3] A kersche of er'melle, perhaps means a kerchief of cremell, crewel or worsted, to be made into neck-handkerchiefs for her daughter Anne, who appears to have been with some lady of consequence for education and board.

[4] Sir William Calthorpe, knight, had been High Sheriff of Norfolk and Suffolk, both in this and the preceding reign, and died very old in 1494. His second wife was Elizabeth, daughter and co-heir of Sir Miles Stapleton, knight, of Ingham.

[5] If this mean that Sir John Paston was now to be christened it appears somewhat extraordinary, and what else it can mean I know not, unless we may infer from this expression an entrance into some religious society.

[6] We have here a proof of the early introduction of hats; and J. Paston's care that his might not be put out of shape, is worthy a beau of the present age.

fashioning of it; I have need to both, for I may not ride nor go out at the doors with none that I have, they be so lewd (*shabby*); a murrey bonnet, and a black or a tawney hat; and God send you your desire; written at Caister, the 7th day of April. Your

Caister, Friday,   JOHN PASTON.
7th of April, 1469.   9 E IV

LETTER CCLXVII.—(LXXXII. vol. iv. p. 323.)

A copy of this and the following letter are written upon the same piece of paper, but without signature or address The following memorandum on the back of the paper, however, ascertains both " Copea Literz Dm de Scales ad concilu Duc Norff et alys (*alios*) in favore J Paston mil eò quod maritaret Cognatā suam Anna Hawte " The contents of these letters sufficiently ascertain the advantages arising from forming connexions with families of consequence; no sooner was an alliance proposed, but both the father and son take Sir John Paston and his affairs under their protection ; the Duke of Norfolk's counsel (of which Lord Scales was one) were immediately to take care that no further injuries were to be committed upon his property, and the servants and dependants of these powerful noblemen are to do all in their power to give him every assistance This marriage never took effect, and the manner in which this affair is several times mentioned, serves only to involve it in mystery. It appears here that the lady's connexions were great, and that she must have been nearly related to the queen.

WORSHIPFUL and my right good friend, I commend me to you; and whereas I am informed that my Lord of Norfolk pretendeth title to certain lands of Sir John Paston's which were late of Sir John Fastolf, it is said that by the commandment and supportation of my said lord certain his servants felleth wood, maketh great waste, and distrained the tenants of the said lands, to the great damage of the said Sir John Paston and his said tenants; and also that my said lord intendeth to enter certain places of the same; and forasmuch as marriage is fully concluded betwixt the said Sir John Paston and one of my nearest kinswomen, I doubt not that your reason well conceiveth that nature must compel me the rather to show my good will, assistance, and favour unto the said Sir John in such things as concern his inheritance; and because I am one of my said lord's counsel, and must and will tender his honour, I heartily pray you that it may like you to advertise and advise my said lord and yours that all such entries, felling of wood, distraining of tenants, and all such matters like, touching the said lands or any part of them, be ceased unto such time as a reasonable mean may be found by my said lord's counsel, my lord my father's, and other cousins and friends of my said kinswoman this next term, as may be to my said lord's honour, and and to the saving of the right title of the said Sir John Paston.

Over this I pray you that ye will inform my good friend James Hobart of the premisses, that he may advertise my said lord in likewise; and that ye will give credence unto William Paston, and I shall be well willed to do that may be to your pleasure, with God's mercy.

From Westminster, the 10th day of April.

SCALES.

Westminster, Monday, 10th of April,
1469   9 E IV.

LETTER CCLXVIII.—(LXXXIII. vol. iv. p. 325)

RIGHT trusty and well-beloved, I greet you well; and forasmuch as a marriage is fully concluded betwixt Sir John Paston and my right near kinswoman Hawte, I will that ye and all other my servants and tenants understand that my lord my father, and I, must of nature and reason show unto him our good assistance and favour in such matters as he shall have a do, wherefore I pray you heartily that ye will take the labour to come to Norwich to commune with William Paston, and to give credence unto him in such matters as he shall inform you of mine intent, and of certain persons with whom ye shall commune by the advice of the said William Paston, of such matters as touch the said Sir John Paston, praying you to tender this matter as ye would do mine own.

From Westminster, the 10th day of April.

SCALES.

Westminster,
Monday, 10th of April, 1469.
9 E. IV.

c 2

LETTER CCLXIX.—(LXXXIV. vol. iv. p. 327.)

This letter must have been written in 1469, as the thanks to his brother here given by Sir John Paston related to his proper and spirited conduct at Caister Place. His attention to whose success in his marriage with the daughter of Lady Boleyn shows his good nature, and his brotherly regard for him; and the advice which he gives him, respecting his behaviour both to the lady and her daughter, shows Sir John to be a man who not only knew the world, but likewise one who understood the passions and prejudices of individuals. He seemed to think too that a handsome young man could not fail of pleading his own cause successfully with a young lady. Sir Godfrey, or Sir Jeffery Boleyn, was Lord Mayor of London about 1457 or 1458. He died in 1463, leaving Anne, the daughter of Thomas Lord Hoo and Hastings, his widow, by whom he had three daughters, Isabel, Anne, and Alice; the last of these was the lady to whom J Paston wished to pay his addresses, and who afterwards married Sir John Fortescue, knight. The elder married William Cheyney, Esq., and the other became the wife of Sir Henry Heydon, of Baconsthorp, knight, and all were great aunts to Queen Anna Boleyn, the mother of our sovereign Elizabeth.

To my brother, John Paston.

Right worshipful and verily well-beloved brother, I heartily commend me to you, thanking you of your labour and diligence that ye have in keeping of my place at Caister so surely, both with your heart and mind, to your great business and trouble; and I again ward have had so little leisure that I have not sped but few of your errands, nor cannot before this time.

As for my Lady Boleyn's disposition to you ward, I cannot in no wise find her agreeable that ye should have her daughter for all the privy means that I could make, insomuch I had so little comfort by all the means that I could make that I disdained in mine own person to commune with her therein; nevertheless I understand that she sayeth, "what if he and she can agree I will not let it, but I will never advise her thereto in no wise." And upon Tuesday last past she rode home into Norfolk; wherefore as ye think ye may find the mean to speak with her yourself, for without that in mine conceit it will not be; and as for Crosby, I understand not that there is no marriage concluded between them,

nevertheless there is great language that it is like to be; ye be personable, and, peradventure, your being once in the sight of the maid, and a little discovering of your good will to her, binding her to keep it secret, and that ye can find in your heart with some comfort [*support*] of her to find the mean to bring such a matter about as shall be her pleasure and yours, but that this ye cannot do without some comfort of her in no wise; and bear yourself as lowly to the mother as ye list, but to the maid not too lowly, nor that ye be too glad to speed, nor too sorry to fail; and I always shall be your herald both here, if she come hither, and at home when I come home, which I hope hastily, within forty days at the farthest; my mother hath a letter which can tell you more, and ye may let Daubeney see it.

JOHN PASTON, *knight.*

I suppose and (*if*) ye call well upon R. Calle he shall purvey you money. I have written to him enough.

London, April,
1469. 9 E. IV.

LETTER CCLXX.—(LXXXV. vol. iv. p. 331.)

This curious letter furnishes us with the solemn declarations of a sick man on his death bed, relative to the authenticity of the will of Sir John Fastolf, which was proved by John Paston, and which was reported not to have been the real will of that knight. The Pastons had many long and expensive suits at law on this account, which were not finished either in the life-time of John Paston or in that of his son Sir John Paston. These solemn assertions of a priest, and a man of learning and character, thus conscientiously declared, must have had great weight in clearing the character of J Paston from these foul aspersions, especially as they came from so respectable a man as Friar Mowth or Mowght, who was a brother of consequence in the monastery at Norwich (see Letter xxix. p 20).

John Paston, to his brother Sir John Paston.

Sir, please it you to weet that my mother and I communed this day with Friar Mowght,

to understand what his saying shall be in the court when he cometh up to London, which

is in this wise · he sayeth that at such time as
he had shriven Master Brackley[1] and how-
selled him both, he let him weet that he was
informed by divers persons that the said
Master Brackley ought for to be in great
conscience for such things as he had done
and said, and caused my father, whom God
assoil, for to do and say, also, in proving of
Sir John Fastolf's will; to whom the said
Master Brackley answered thus again; "I am
right glad that it cometh to you in mind for
to move me with this matter in discharging of
my conscience against God," saying furthermore to the said Friar Mowght, by the way
that his soul should to, that the will that
my father put into the court was as verily
Sir John Fastolf's will as it was true that he
should once die. This was said on the Sunday when the said Brackley wend (thought)
to have died then; on the Monday he revived
again, and was well amended till on the Wednesday, and on the Wednesday he sickened
again, supposing to have died forthwith, and
in his sickness he called Friar Mowght, which
was confessor unto him, of his own motion,
saying unto him in this wise, "Sir, whereas
of your own motion ye moved me the last
day to tell you after my conscience of Sir
John Fastolf's will likewise as I knew; and
now of mine own motion, and in discharging
of my soul, for I know well that I may not
escape but that I must die in haste, wherefore
I desire you that (you) will report after my
death that I took it upon my soul at my
dying that that will that John Paston put in
to be proved was Sir John Fastolf's will;" and
the said Brackley died the same Wednesday.

And whereas ye would have had Richard
Calle to you as on Sunday last past, it was this
Tuesday ere I had your letter; and whereas
it pleaseth you for to wish me at Eltham, at
the tourney,[2] for the good sight that was
there, by truth I had lever (rather) see you
once in Caister-hall than to see as many
king's tourneys as might be betwixt Eltham
and London.

And, Sir, whereas it liketh you to desire to
have knowledge how that I have done with
the Lady Boleyn, by my faith I have done nor
spoken nought in that matter, nor nought
will do till time that ye come home, and (if)
ye come not this seven year; notwithstanding
the Lady Boleyn was in Norwich in the week
after Easter, from the Saturday till the Wednesday, and Heydon's wife and mistress Alice
both, and I was at Caister and wist not of it;
her men said that she had none other errand
to the town but for to sport her, but so God
help me, I suppose that she wend (thought) I
would have been in Norwich for to have seen
her daughter. I beseech you with all my
heart hie you home though ye should tarry
but a day, for I promise you your folk think
that ye have forgotten them, and the most
part of them must depart at Whitsuntide at
the furthest, they will no longer abide; and
as for R. Calle we cannot get half a quarter
the money that we pay for the bare household
beside men's wages. Daubeney nor I may
no more without coinage.

Your
JOHN PASTON.

April, 1469   9 E. IV.

LETTER CCLXXI.—(LXXXVI. vol. iv. p. 335.)

As King Edward often made excursions, and by his insinuating manner and address conciliated the minds of
his subjects, and induced them to bestow liberal gifts upon him, it cannot be certainly known whether this
visit to Norwich was merely to raise money, or whether, having intimations of the discontent of the Earl
of Warwick, the king was endeavouring to make himself popular, the better to encounter and defeat any
designs of that nobleman. His manner of travelling, his attendants, and the familiar conversations which
are drawn in this letter with ease and precision, interest the reader as well as delineate the manners of the
times. We find the Duke of Gloucester accompanied the king, but we hear nothing of the Duke of Cla-

---

[1] The meaning of this is, after he had heard his
confession and administered the extreme sacrament
to Master Brackley

[2] Sir John Paston is said to have been the king's
champion at this tournament at Eltham.

rence; he most probably was at this very instant with the Earl of Warwick, forming those plans which soon after for a time replaced Henry upon the throne.—Edward's conversation with William Paston was certainly very proper and becoming a king desirous that justice should be done according to the law; for what can show this intention more strongly than the following words, "I will neither treat nor speak for him, but I will let the law proceed." His conversation likewise with Brandon was both manly and spirited.

To Sir John Paston, Knight.

To begin, God yeld (*shield or preserve*) [1] you for my hats. The king hath been in this country, and worshipfully received into Norwich, and had right good cheer and great gifts in this country, wherewith he holdeth him so well content that he will hastily be here again, and the queen also, with whom by my poor advice ye shall come, if so be that the term be done by that time that she come into this country; and as for your matters here, so God help me, I have done as much as in me was, in labouring of them, as well to my Lord Rivers [2] as to my Lord Scales, [3] Sir John Wydville, Thomas Wingfield and others about the king. And as for the Lord Rivers, he said to my uncle William, Fairfax, and me, that he should move the king to speak to the two Dukes of Norfolk and Suffolk that they should leave of their titles of such land as were Sir John Fastolf's, and if so be that they would do nought at the king's request, that then the king should command them to do no waste, nor make none assaults nor frays upon your tenants nor places, till such time as the law hath determined with you or against you; this was said by him the same day in the morning that he departed at noon; whether he moved the king with it or not I cannot say, my uncle William thinks nay; and the same afternoon following I told my Lord Scales that I had spoken with my lord his father in like form as I have rehearsed, and asked him whether that my lord his father had spoken to the king or not, and he gave me this answer, that whether he had spoken to the king or not that the matter should do well enough.

Thomas Wingfield told me, and swore unto me, that when Brandon moved the king, and besought him to show my lord favour in his matters against you, that the king said unto him again "Brandon, though thou canst beguile the Duke of Norfolk and bring him about the thumb as thou list, I let thee weet thou shalt not do me so; for I understand thy false dealing well enough." And he said unto him, moreover, that if my Lord of Norfolk left not of his hold of that matter that Brandon should repent it, every vein in his heart, for he told him that he knew well enough that he might rule my Lord of Norfolk as he would, and if my lord did anything that were contrary to his laws, the king told him he knew well enough that it was by nobody's means but by his, and thus he departed from the king.

Item, as by words, the Lord Scales and Sir John Wydville took tender your matters more than the Lord Rivers

Item, Sir John Wydville told me, when he was on horseback at the king's departing, that the king had commanded Brandon of purpose to ride forth from Norwich to Lynn, for to take a conclusion in your matter for you; and he bade me that I should cast no doubts but that ye should have your intent, and so did the Lord Scales also; and when that I prayed them at any time to show their favour to your matter, they answered that it was their matter as well as yours, considering the alliance betwixt you. [4]

Commune with Jakys Hawte, and he shall tell you what language was spoken between the Duke of Suffolk's counsel, and him, and me; it is too long to write, but I promise you ye are beholden to Jakys, for he spared not to speak.

Item, the king rode through Heylesdon Warren towards Walsingham, and Thomas Wingfield promised me that he would find

---

[1] [*Yeld* is rather *thank.* It has occurred in these volumes already more than once in that sense.]

[2] Richard Wydville, Earl Rivers, father to the queen, was at this time Lord Treasurer. This nobleman and his eldest son Sir John Wydville, were in August following both beheaded at Northampton, by a riotous mob headed by one Robert of Riddesdale.

[3] Anthony Wydville, Lord Scales, was second son to the Earl Rivers.

[4] This refers to the contract between Sir John Paston and Anne Hawte.

the means that my Lord of Gloucester,[1] and himself both should show the king the lodge[2] that was broken down, and also that they would tell him of the breaking down of the place.

Contrary to these matters and all the comfort that I had of my Lord Scales, Sir John Wydville, and Thomas Wingfield, my uncle William saith that the king told him (*with*) his own mouth, when he had ridden forth by the lodge in Heylesdon Warren, that he supposed as well that it might fall down by the self as be plucked down, for if it had been plucked down he said that we might have put in our bills of it when his judges sat on the oyer and determiner in Norwich, he being there; and then my uncle saith how that he answered the king, that ye trusted to his good grace that he should set you thorough with both the dukes by mean of treaty, and he saith that the king answered him that he would neither treat nor speak for you, but for to let the law proceed, and so he saith that they departed; and by my troth and (*if*) my Lord Treasurer encourage you not more than he did us here, ye shall have but easy help as on that party, wherefore labour your matters effectually, for by my troth it is needy; for, for all their words of pleasure, I cannot understand what their labour in this country hath done good, wherefore be not over swift till ye be sure of your land, but labour sore the law, for by my troth till that be passed with you ye get but easy help as I can understand.

I had with me one day at dinner in my mother's place, she being out, the Lord Scales, Sir John Wydville, Sir John Howard, Nichol-as Howard, John of Parr, Thomas Garnet, Festus Cheyney, Trussel the knight's son, Thomas Boleyn, qua propter (*in short*) Brampton, Bernard, and Broom, Peise Howse, W. Tonstal, Lewis de Bretayl, and others, and made them good cheer, so as they held them content.

Item, my Lord of Norfolk gave Bernard, Broom, nor me no gowns at this season, wherefore I awaited not on him; notwithstanding I offered my service for that season to my lady, but it was refused, I wot by advice; wherefore I purpose no more to do so. As for Bernard, Barney, Broom, and W. Calthorpe are sworn my Lord of Gloucester's men, but I stand yet at large notwithstanding my Lord Scales spoke to me to be with the king, but I made no promise so to be, for I told him that I was not worth a groat without you, and therefore I would make no promise to nobody till they had your good will first, and so we departed.

It was told me that there was out a privy seal for you to attend upon the king northward; and if it be so, I think verily it is done to have you from London by craft, that ye should not labour your matters to a conclusion this term, but put them (*in*) delay. I pray you purvey you on it to be at home as soon as the term is done, for by God I take great hurt for mine absence in divers places, and the most part of your men at Caister will depart without abode and (*if*) ye be not at home within this fortnight. I pray you bring home points and laces of silk for you and me.

JOHN PASTON.

1469. 9 E IV.

LETTER CCLXXII.—(LXXXVII. vol. iv. p. 345.)

On the back of this letter is written, "pro marritag. intr Riem Call and Margtam Paston." "A pleasant lre to Sir J. Paston, from his brother J. Paston, wherein the stoutness of Sir John is somewhat declared." The stoutness, or rather family pride, both of Sir John Paston and his brother, are discovered in this letter, in the behaviour of the one to the Duke of Norfolk, and in the disdain which the other showed to the idea of his sister s marriage with a person in trade. Richard Calle has been often mentioned in the course of these letters, and he seems to have been a confidential friend of the family. This, however, seems in the opinion of J Paston by no means to have been sufficient to have authorised his pretensions to become the husband of his sister [This, however, seems strangely in contradiction with Letter cclv p 7, where, according to Fenn, Sir John had agreed to the marriage, but only wished it deferred] We here see the origin of the Duke of Norfolk's claim to Caister to have arisen from his supposed purchase of it from two of Sir

---

[1] Richard Duke of Gloucester, afterwards King Richard III.

[2] For a full account of the mischief here done, see Letter ccxxxviii. vol. i. p. 191.)

John Fastolf's executors · this claim he pursued, and in a few months after the writing of this letter, besieged the place in form, having been, I presume, refused a peaceable entry by John Paston, who defended
it for his brother, and in which defence Daubeney and others lost their lives The letter is curious, and
written in such an easy and familiar style as greatly to interest the reader in its contents. [It is, however,
strangely stuffed with the needless oaths, which were too customary at the time Fenn says "Daubeney
and others lost their lives;" the others were two men of the Duke of Norfolk's party.]

To Sir John Paston, Knight.

SIR, pleaseth it to understand, that I conceive, by your letter which that ye sent me by Juddy, that ye have heard of Richard Calle's labour which he maketh by our ungracious sister's assent, but whereas they write that they have my good will therein, saving your reverence, they falsely lie of it, for they never spake to me of that matter, nor none other body in their name. Lovell asked me once a question whether that I understood how it was betwixt Rd Calle and my sister; I can think that it was by Calle's means, for when I asked him whether Calle desired him to move me that question or not, he would have gotten it away by hums and by haas, but I would not so be answered; wherefore at the last he told me that his eldest son desired him to spere (*inquire*) whether that Richard Calle were sure of her or not, for he said that he knew a good marriage for her, but I wot he lied, for he is whole with Richard Calle in that matter; wherefore to that intent that he nor they should pick no comfort of me, I answered him that and (*if*) my father, whom God assoil! were alive, and had consented thereto, and my mother, and ye both, he should never have my good will for to make my sister to sell candle and mustard in Framlingham, and thus, with more which were too long to write to you, we departed [*parted*].

And whereas it pleaseth you in your letter to cry me mercy for that ye sent me not such gear as I sent you money for; I cry you mercy that I was so lewd (*rude*) to encumber you with any so simple a matter, considering the great matters and weighty that ye have to do; but need compelled me, for in this country is no such stuff as I sent to you for.

Also, whereas it pleaseth you to send to Richard Calle to deliver me money, so God help me I will none ask him for myself, nor none had I of him, nor of none other man but of mine own since ye departed, but that little that I might forbear (*spare*) of mine own I have delivered to Daubeney for household, and paid it for you in men's wages, and there-

fore whoever sendeth you word that I have spent you any money since ye went hence, they must give you another reckoning, saving in meat and drink, for I eat like an horse, of purpose to eat you out at the doors, but that needeth not for you come not within them, wherefore so God help me, the fellowship here thinks that ye have forgotten us all, wherefore and (*if*) anything be ill ruled when ye come home wyte (*blame*) it yourself for default of oversight.

Also, I understand for very certain, and it is sent me so word out of my lord's house, that this Pentecost (*Whitsuntide*) is my lord's counsel at Framlingham, and they purpose this week and the next to hold courts here at Caister, and at all other manors that were Sir John Fastolf's, purchased of Yelverton and of Sir Thomas Howys, whom God assoil, and how that my demeaning should be it is too late to send to you for advice, wherefore and (*if*) I do well I ask no thank, and if I do ill I pray you lay the default on over little wit, but I purpose to use the first point of hawking, to hold fast and (*if*) I may; but so God help me, and (*if*) they might pull down the house on our heads I wyte (*blame*) them not, which I trust to God to keep them from; for by God that bought me, the best earl in England would not deal so with my lord and my lady as ye do, without making of some means to them; so God help me, whosoever advise you to do so he is not your friend; and I may I trust to God to see you about Midsummer or before, for in good faith I ween ye purpose you that it shall be Easter ere ye come home, for all your servants here ween that ye purpose no more to deal with them, but to leave them here in hostage to my Lord of Norfolk.

Also, Sir, I pray you purvey what inn[1] that my brother Edmund shall be in, for he loseth sore his time here I promise you; I pray you send me word by the next messenger that

---

[1] [The inn to be purveyed was an inn of court no doubt But Edmund became a soldier, and was in garrison at Calais in 1473]

cometh, and I shall either send him or bring him up with me to London.

Also, Sir, we poor sans deniers (*moneyless men*) of Caister have broken three or four steel-bows, wherefore we beseech you and there be any maker of steel-bows in London which is very cunning, that ye will send me word, and I shall send you the bows that be broken, which be your own great bow, and Robert Jackson's bow, and John Pampyng's bow; these three have cast so many calvys that they shall never cast quarrels (*square-headed arrows*) till they be new made.

I pray you find the means that my lord may have some reasonable mean proffered, so that he and my lady may understand that ye desire to have his good lordship, I promise you it shall do you ease and your tenants both, and God preserve (*you*).

JOHN PASTON.

Caister, Whitsuntide,
May, 1469. 9 E. IV
Whitsunday was on the 21st May, in 1469.

LETTER CCLXXIII.—(LXXXVIII vol. iv. p. 351.)

On the back of this letter is the following memorandum, " Lrä Ricï Calle Margerie Paston filie Johïs Paston a'ri quä p̃ea duxit in uxrem." We cannot read this letter without entering into the private family-concerns of the Pastons, and however we may think with them that their daughter may have made, without their knowledge and consent, an improper contract, yet we must pity the lover In ancient times families intermarried more amongst those of their own rank than at present; the gentry considered those in trade as moving in a different sphere to them , they dealt with them and required their attendance, but they scorned to intermarry. The extension of commerce and the large fortunes raised by the merchants and men of business have however broken down those barriers of distinction , and not only the gentleman but the nobleman, now often select their wives from the city, and introduce into their families the daughters of those, who, by their honourable and extensive dealings in various branches of traffic, have enriched themselves, and trained up their children to become that elevated situation which their beauty, their education, and their good qualities, enables them to adorn The picture drawn in this letter is a true one, and gives us a much better idea of ancient family matters than the most laboured disquisition of a dry historian.

To Mistress Margery Paston.

MINE own lady and mistress, and before God very true wife, I with heart full sorrowful recommend me unto you, as he that cannot be merry, nor nought shall be till it be otherwise with us than it is yet, for this life that we lead now is neither pleasure to God nor to the world, considering the great bond of matrimony that is made betwixt us, and also the great love that hath been and as I trust yet is betwixt us, and as on my part never greater; wherefore I beseech Almighty God comfort us as soon as it pleaseth him, for we that ought of very right to be most together are most asunder, meseemeth it is a thousand year ago since that I spake with you, I had lever (*rather*) than all the good in the world I might be with you ; alas, alas! good lady, full little remember they what they do that keep us thus asunder, four times in the year are they accursed that let (*hinder*) matrimony; it causeth many men to deem in them they have large conscience in other matters as well as herein; but what lady suffer as ye have done, and make you as merry as ye can, for I wis, lady, at the long way, God will of his righteousness help his servants that mean truly, and would live according to his laws, &c.

I understand, lady, ye have had as much sorrow for me as any gentlewoman hath had in the world, as would God all that sorrow that ye have had had rested upon me, and that ye had been discharged of it, for I wis, lady, it is to me a death to hear that ye be entreated otherwise than ye ought to be ; this is a painful life that we lead. I cannot live thus without it be a great displeasure to God.

Also like you to weet that I had sent you a letter by my lad from London, and he told me he might not speak with you, there was made so great await upon him and upon you both : he told me John Thresher came to him in your name, and said that ye sent him to my lad for a letter or a token which I should have sent you, but he trust him not, he would not deliver him none; after that he brought him a ring, saying that ye sent it him, commanding him that he should deliver the letter or token to him, which I conceive since by my lad it was not by your sending, it was by my mistress and Sir James's advice;[1] alas! what mean they? I suppose they deem we be not ensured together, and if they so do I marvel, for then they are not well advised, remembering the plainness that I brake to my mistress at the beginning, and I suppose by you, both,[2] and ye did as ye ought to do of very right, and if ye have done the contrary, as I have been informed ye have done, ye did neither conciensly (*conscientiously*) nor to the pleasure of God, without ye did it for fear and for the time, to please such as were at that time about you; and if ye did it for this cause, it was a reasonable cause, considering the great and importable [3] calling upon that ye had, and many an untrue tale was made to you of me, which, God know it, I was never guilty of.

My lad told me that my mistress your mother asked him if he had brought any letter to you, and many other things she bare him on hand, and among all other at the last she said to him that I would not make her privy to the beginning, but she supposed I would at the ending; and as to that God knoweth, she knew it first of me and none other; I wot not what her mistress-ship meaneth, for by my troth there is no gentlewoman alive that my heart tendereth more than it doth her, nor is loather to displease, saving only your person, which of very right I ought to tender and love best, for I am bound thereto by the law of God, and so will do while that I live whatsoever fall of it; I suppose and (*if*) ye tell them sadly (*seriously*) the truth, they will not damn their souls for us; though I tell them the truth they will not believe me as well as they will do you, and therefore, good lady, at the reverence of God be plain to them and tell the truth, and if they will in no wise agree thereto, betwixt God, the devil, and them be it, and that peril that we should be in I beseech God it may lie upon them and not upon us; I am heavy and sorry to remember their disposition. God send them grace to guide all things well, as well (*as*) I would they did; God be their guide, and send them peace and rest, &c.

I marvel much that they should take this matter so heedely (*cautiously*)[4] as I understand they do, remembering it is in such case as it cannot be remedied, and my desert upon every behalf it is for to be thought there should be none obstacle against it; and also the worshipful that is in them is not in your marriage, it is in their own marriage, which I beseech God send them such as may be to their worship and pleasure to God, and to their hearts' ease, for else were it great pity. Mistress, I am afraid to write to you, for I understand ye have showed my letters that I have sent you before this time; but I pray you let no creature see this letter, as soon as ye have read it let it be burnt, for I would no man should see it in no wise; ye had no writing from me this two year,[5] nor I will not send you no more, therefore I remit all this matter to your wisdom; Almighty Jesu preserve, keep, and (*give*) you your heart's desire, which I wot well should be to God's pleasure, &c.

This letter was written with as great pain as ever wrote I thing in my life, for in good faith I have been right sick, and yet am not verily at ease, God amend it, &c.

1469. 9 E. IV.   RICHARD CALLE.

LETTER CCLXXIV.—(XXV. vol ii. p. 17.)

Humphrey Lord Stafford was created Earl of Devonshire in May 1469, and beheaded at Bridgewater, the 17th of August following, by command of the king, for abandoning the Earl of Pembroke before the battle of Banbury; by which means the rebels were victorious.

To my worshipful brother, Sir John Paston, be this bill delivered in haste.

RIGHT worshipful brother, I recommend me unto you, letting you to weet that my Lord Stafford was made Earl of Devonshire upon Sunday; and as for the king, as I understand,

---

[1] [Probably Sir James Gloys.]
[2] [The construction is rather obscure here, but we think he means to speak of the plainness with which I and (I suppose) you, both, brake the matter to my mistress, if ye did as ye ought to have done, &c.]
[3] [*Importable*—unbearable.]

[4] [We rather think *headily*—angrily, madly—is here meant.]
[5] [This would seem to put letter celv. at least as far back as 1466, and is scarcely reconcileable with Letter cclxxii., where the marriage seems spoken of as recent.]

he departyt (*departs*) to Walsingham[1] upon Friday come sev'night, and the queen also, if God send her hele (*health*). And as for the king, (*he*) was appointed for to go to Calais, and now it is put off.

And also as for the goiug to the sea, my Lord of Warwick's ships go to the sea, as I understand None other tidings I can none write unto you, but Jesu have you in his keeping.

Written at Windsor on Monday after Whitsunday in haste, &c.

By your brother,[2]

JAMES HAWTE.

Whitsun Monday,
22nd of May, 1469.   9 Ed. IV

LETTER CCLXXV.—(XXVI. vol. ii. p. 19.)

This letter shows the attention which the city of Norwich wished to pay to the queen on her reception, and during her residence there. Henry Spelman married Ela, daughter and coheir of William de Narburgh, and was the first of that family that settled at Narborough in Norfolk.

To the right reverend Sir Henry Spelman, recorder of the city of Norwich, be this letter delivered.

RIGHT reverend Sir, I recommend me to you. Please it you to know this same day came to me the sheriff of Norfolk[3] himself, and told me that the queen[4] shall be at Norwich upon Tuesday[5] come sev'night surely. And I desired to have know of him, because this should be her first coming hither, how we should be ruled, as well in her receiving as in her abiding here. And he said he would not occupy him therewith, but he counselled us to write to you to London, to know of them that been of counsel of that city, or with other worshipful men of the same city, that been knowing in that behalf; and we to be ruled thereafter as were according [*fitting*] for us; for he let me to weet that she would desire to be received and attended as worshipfully as ever was queen afore her.[6] Wherefore I, by the assent of my brethren aldermen, &c., pray you heartily to have this labour for this city, and that it please you, if it may be, that at that day ye be here in proper person. And I trust in God, that either in rewards or else in thankings both of the king's coming and in this, ye shall be pleased as worthy is. Written in haste at Norwich, the 6th day of July anno 9° Regis Edw[di] quarti.

By your well-willer,

JOHN AUBRY,[7] &c.

Norwich,
Thursday, 6th of July,
1469.   9 E IV.

LETTER CCLXXVI.—(XXVII. vol. ii. p. 23.)

There is no date to this letter, whether it refers therefore to the coming of the king into Norfolk, in 1469 or in 1474, is uncertain and of little consequence; the chief reason for inserting it was to show the preparations expected to be made for the attending upon and receiving him The peculiarity of the Duke of Norfolk's liveries is worthy notice, being to be made party-coloured of blue and tawny, having the left side of the former, and the right of the latter colour. Dresses of this kind may be seen in various illuminated manuscripts of this age. [From the time of Richard II there had been many enactments against the practice of keeping large bands of liveried retainers. The prohibition was renewed 8 Edward IV. c 2, and the penalty was one hundred shillings for every person, "other than his menial servant, officer, or man learned in the one law or the other," so retained by any one "of what estate, degree, or condition that he be;" the fine to be repeated for every month "that any such person is so retained by him, by oath, writing, indenture, or promise," and a like penalty on the person retained. The exceptions, however, are numerous. "Provided

---

[1] This must have been on a pilgrimage to our Lady of Walsingham in Norfolk.

[2] I do not know why he calls Sir John Paston his brother; for Sir John certainly never married Anne Hawte, who possibly might be the sister of James.

[3] Roger Ree was sheriff of Norfolk in 1469

[4] Elizabeth, queen of Edward IV.

[5] 18th of July, 1469.

[6] [A necessary caution, perhaps, on account of her birth]

[7] John Aubry was mayor of Norwich in 1469.

also, that this ordinance do not extend to any livery given or to be given at the king's or queen's coronation, or at the stallation of an archbishop or bishop, or erection, creation, or marriage of any lord or lady of estate, or at the creation of knights of the Bath, or at the commencement of any clerk in any university, or at the creation of serjeants in the law, or by any guild, fraternity, or mystery corporate, or by the mayor and sheriffs of London, or any other mayor, sheriff, or other chief officer of any city, borough, town, or port of this realm of England for the time being, during that time, and for executing their office or occupation; nor to any badges or liveries to be given in defence of the king and of this realm of England: nor to the constable and marshal, nor to any of them for giving any badge, livery, or token for any such feat of arms to be done within this realm; nor to any of the wardens toward Scotland for any livery, badge, or token of them to be given from Trent northward, at such time only as shall be necessary to levy people for defence of the said marshes, or any of them." We should think that now, at least, a coach and four might be driven through an act like this, although the Earl of Oxford could not escape; but to be sure he was taken by surprise, and entrapped by a powerful antagonist. But, as Hallam remarks, ('State of Europe during the Middle Ages,' vol. iii. p. 246,) "it appears that, far from these acts being regarded, it was considered as a mark of respect to the king" (and he cites this letter as a proof) "for the noblemen and gentry to meet him with as many attendants in livery as they could muster. Sir John Paston was to provide twenty men in their livery gowns, and the Duke of Norfolk two hundred. This illustrates the well-known story of Henry VII. and the Earl of Oxford, and shows the mean and oppressive conduct of the king in that affair, which Hume has pretended to justify."]

To my mother, and to my brother John Paston.

BROTHER, it is so that the king shall come into Norfolk in haste, and I wot (*know*) not whether that I may come with him or not; if I come, I must do make a livery of twenty gowns, which I must pick out by your advice; and as for the cloth for such persons as be in that country, if it might be had there at Norwich or not I wot not; and what persons I am not remembered.

If my mother be at Caister, as there shall be no doubt, for the keeping of the place while the king is in that country, that I may have the most part at Caister.[1]

And whether ye will offer yourself to wait upon my Lord of Norfolk or not, I would ye did that best were to do; I would do my lord pleasure and service, and so I would ye did, if I wist (*thought*) to be sure of his good lordship in time to come. He shall have two hundred in a livery blue and tawny,[2] and blue on the left side, and both dark colours.

I pray you send me word and your advice by Juddy of what men, and what horse I could be purveyed of, if so be that I must needs come; and of your advice in all things by writing, and I shall send you hastily other tidings. Let Sorrell[3] be well kept.

JOHN PASTON, *knight.*

LETTER CCLXXVII.—(LXXXIX. vol. iv. p. 359.)

We find by the conversation here given us between the Bishop of Norwich, Agnes Paston, and Margaret Paston, that a contract of marriage had been made between Margery Paston, the daughter of the latter, and Richard Calle, and that her family wished to have a hearing in the Bishop's Court, either to disprove it, or, if proved, to set it aside. The young lady's behaviour, and the account which both she and Richard Calle give of the contract, seem to confirm it, and obliged the bishop to take time to consider of the matter before any sentence could be pronounced; though he seemed to wish to have it in his power to adjust the matter to the satisfaction of the family. The expressions of Margaret Paston respecting her daughter must be read with some allowance; we must construe some of them as words of passion and resentment, arising from her avowal of her intentions to fulfil the contract, &c. [The bishop was still Walter Lyhert, or Hart, who died in 1472.]

To Sir John Paston, Knight.

I GREET you well, and send you God's blessing and mine; letting you weet that on Thursday last was, my mother and I were with my Lord of Norwich, and desired him that he would no more do in the matter touching your sister till that ye and my

---

[1] [This sentence is not clear. Perhaps "the most part" may mean the strongest party.]

[2] Tawny colour appears to have been a yellowish dusky brown orange colour, and much worn at this time.

[3] A horse so called.

brother and others that were executors to your father might be here together, for they had the rule of her as well as I; and he said plainly that he had been required so often to examine her, that he might not nor would no longer delay it, and charged me in pain of cursing that she should not be deferred, but that she should appear before him the next day; and I said plainly that I would neither bring her nor send her; and then he said that he would send for her himself, and charged that she should be at her liberty to come when he sent for her; and he said by his troth that he would be as sorry for her, and (*if*) she did not well, as he would be and (*if*) she were right near of his kin, both for my mother's sake and mine, and other of her friends, for he wist well that her demeaning had sticked sore at our hearts.

My mother and I informed him that we could never understand by her saying, by no language that ever she had to him, that neither of them were bound to other, but that they might choose, both; then he said that he would say to her as well as he could before that he examined her; and so it was told me by divers persons that he did as well and as plainly as (*if*) she had been right near to him, which were too long to write at this time, hereafter ye shall weet, and who were labourers therein; the chancellor[1] was not so guilty therein as I wend (*thought*) he had been.

On Friday the bishop he sent for her by Ashfield and other that are right sorry of her demeaning, and the bishop said to her right plainly, and put her in remembrance how she was born, what kin and friends that she had, and should have more if she were ruled and guided after them; and if she did not, what rebuke, and shame, and loss should be to her if she were not guided by them, and cause of forsaking[2] of her for any good, or help, or comfort that she should have of them;

and said that he had heard say that she loved such one that her friends were not pleased with that she should have, and therefore he bade her be right well advised how she did; and said that he would understand the words that she had said to him whether it made matrimony or not, and she rehearsed what she had said, and said if those words made it not sure, she said boldly that she would make it surer ere than she went thence, for she said she thought in her conscience she was bound whatsoever the words were; these lewd words grieveth me and her grandam as much as all the remanent; and then the bishop and the chancellor both said that there was neither I nor no friend of hers would receive (*her*).

And then Calle was examined apart by himself, that her words and his accorded, and the time, and where it should have been done; and then the bishop said that he supposed that there should be found other things against him that might cause the letting thereof, and therefore he said he would not be too hasty to give sentence thereupon, and said that he would give over day till the Wednesday or Thursday after Michaelmas, and so it is delayed; they would have had her will performed in haste, but the bishop said he would none otherwise than he had said.

I was with my mother at her place when she was examined, and when I heard say what her demeaning was, I charged my servants that she should not be received in my house: I had given her warning, she might have been aware afore if she had been gracious; and I sent to one or two more that they should not receive her if she came; she was brought again to my place for to have been received, and Sir James told them that brought her that I had charged them all and she should not be received; and so my Lord of Norwich hath set her at Roger Best's, to be there till the day before said, God knoweth full evil against his will and his wife's if they durst do otherwise; I am sorry that they are cumyred (*cumbered, or troubled*) with her, but yet I am better paid (*satisfied*) that she is there for the while than she had been in other place, because of the sadness (*seriousness*) and good disposition of himself and his wife, for she shall not be sou'd

---

[1] Dr. John Saresson, otherwise Wigenhale, was chancellor to the bishop from 1435 to 1471, and had other church preferment in the diocese.

[2] [And *be the* cause of *their* forsaking, &c. Many instances of this concise style will have been already noticed in these letters, and was by no means uncommon among our best writers to a much later period.]

(*suffered ?*) there to play the brethel (*frail one*); I pray you and require you that ye take it not pensily (*heavily*), for I wot well it goeth right near your heart, and so doth it to mine and to others, but remember you, and so do I, that we have lost of her but a brethel, and set it the less to heart, for and (*if*) she had been good, wheresoever she had been, it should not have been as it is, for and (*if*) he were dead. at this hour, she should never be at mine heart as she was. As for the divorce that ye write to me of, I suppose what ye meant, but I charge you upon my blessing that ye do not, nor cause none other to do, that should offend God and your conscience, for and (*if*) ye do, or cause for to be done, God will take vengeance

thereupon, and ye should put yourself and others in great jeopardy, for wot it well she shall full sore repent her lewdness hereafter, and I pray God she might so. I pray you for mine heart's ease be ye of a good comfort in all things; I trust God shall help right well, and I pray God so do in all our matters; I would ye took heed if there were any labour made in the court of Canterbury for the lewd matter aforesaid.

But if the duke[1] be purveyed for, he and his wise counsel shall leave this country; it is told me that he saith that he will not spare to do that he is purposed for no duke in England. God help at need.[2]

Norwich, before Michaelmas,
1469. 9 E. IV.

LETTER CCLXXVIII.—(XC. vol. iv. p. 367.)

The dispute concerning the possession of Caister now becoming a matter of great consequence, and the siege of it being determined upon by the Duke of Norfolk if some conciliatory plan could not be devised, Margaret Paston informs Sir John of the different schemes proposed; these she wishes him thoroughly to consider, and, if none should be adopted, at all events to succour his friends there. Sir John Heveningham though engaged against the Pastons, shows himself not only a friend to them, but a faithful officer to his commander the Duke of Norfolk.

To Sir John Paston, be this delivered in haste.

I GREET you well, and send you God's blessing and mine; letting you weet that Sir John Heveningham was at Norwich this day, and spake with me at my mother's, but he would not that it should be understood, for my lord hath made him one of the captains at Caister of the people that should keep the watch about the place that no man should succour them, if my lord departed. I desired him to favour them if any man should come to them from me or you, and he would not grant it, but he desired me to write to you to understand, if that my lord might be moved to find surety to recompense you all wrongs, and [*if*] ye would suffer him to enter peaceably, and the law after his entry would deem it you; be ye advised what answer ye would give.

Item, since that I spake with him and the same day, a faithful friend of ours came unto me and moved me if that my lord might be intreated to suffer indifferent men to keep the place, and take the profits for both parties

till the right be determined by the law; and my lord for his part, and ye for your part, to find sufficient surety that you neither should vex, let, nor trouble the said indifferent men to keep peaceably the possession of the said place, and to take the profits unto the time it be determined by the law to his behoof that the law deemeth it; and the said persons that so indifferently keep possession, before their entry into the said place, to find also sufficient surety to answer the party that the law deemeth it to of the profits during their possession, and to suffer him peaceably

---

[1] This I suppose relates to the Duke of Norfolk; the other duke most probably means either the Duke of Clarence or of Suffolk.

[2] On the back of the letter in an ancient hand is written, " A Lré to Sr. Io. Paston from his mother, touching the good-will between hir daughter Margery P. and Ric. Call, who were after maryed together." It seems from this memorandum that the contract of marriage was proved and confirmed, and that in consequence of it a marriage took place between the parties.

to enter, or any in his name, whensoever they be required by the party to whom the right is deemed of all these premises; send me word how ye will be demeaned by as good advice as ye can get, and make no longer delay, for they must needs have hasty succour that be in the place, for they be sore hurt and have none help, and if they have hasty help it shall be the greatest worship that ever ye had, and if they be not holpen it shall be to you a great disworship; and look never to have favour of your neighbours and friends but if (*unless*) this speed well; therefore prend (*consider*)[1] it in your mind, and purvey

therefore in haste; howsoever ye do, God keep you, and send you the victory of your enemies, and give you and us all grace to live in peace. Written on St. Giles's even, at nine of the bell at night.

Robin came home yester even, and he brought me neither writing from you, nor good answer of this matter, which grieveth me right ill that I have sent you so many messengers and have so feeble answers again.

By your mother,
MARGARET PASTON.

Norwich, Friday,
1 September, 1469. 9 E. IV.

LETTER CCLXXIX. (XCI. Vol. iv. p. 371.)

Master Writtill, or Wrettell, the person to whom this letter is addressed, was a servant of the Duke of Clarence, and appears to have been sent down to endeavour at an accommodation between the besiegers and the besieged, during the truce which was then taken. Sir John Paston, however, seems fearful lest any appointment should be taken detrimental to his interest, though at the same time he would submit to anything rather than that his brother's and his servant's lives should be endangered. John Duke of Norfolk claimed this manor and castle of Caister under an agreement for a purchase, which had passed between him and Sir William Yelverton and Thomas Howys, two of Sir John Fastolf's executors. It does not appear that they could legally convey this estate, as, by Sir John Fastolf's will, it had been left for charitable uses, and towards founding and endowing a college, &c. &c. [What was Sir John Paston's right? It is nowhere clearly stated.]

To Master Writtill.

MASTER WRITTILL, I recommend me to you, beseeching you heartily, as mine whole trust is in you, that ye do your devoir to continue truce till Friday or Saturday in the morning, by which time I hope the messenger shall come, and that ye be not driven to take an appointment if ye can understand by any likelihood that it be able to be abydyn[2] and resisted, and that ye feel my brother's disposition therein as my trust is in you, praying you to remember that it resteth, as God help me, on all my weal; for, as God help me, I had lever (*rather*) the place were brenned (*burnt*), my brother and servants saved, than the best appointment that ever ye and I communed of should by my good-will be taken, if this message from the king may rescue it; and if it be so that my lord be removed by the king's commandment, which resteth with his honour, I may in time to come do him

service as shall recompense any grudge or displeasure that he ever had or hath to me or mine, and ye, if it the rather by your wisdom and policy the mean above written may be had, shall be as sure of the service of my true brother and servants and me as ye can devise by my troth; for in good faith this matter sticketh more nigh mine heart and me than I can write unto you, and to my brother and servants more near than, as God knoweth, they wot of; wherefore, master Writtill, all our welfare resteth in you, beseeching you to remember it, for this matter is to all us either making or marring.

Item, as for Arblaster or Lovell, I cannot think that they or any of them may be with you, wherefore in you is all; and God have you in keeping.

Written at London, the next day after your departing; I shall send you more knowledge to-morrow, with God's grace.

Yours,
JOHN PASTON, knight.

London, September.
1469 9 E IV.

---

[1] [*Pretend* in original; perhaps an error for *perpend*]
[2] [So in original] Abydin is to be *delayed* Fenn translates *avoided*]

LETTER CCLXXX.—(XCII. vol. iv. p. 373.)

Sir John Paston in this letter gives further directions to Master Writtill, and informs him of what had passed at London, between the lords and himself, &c.; he appears likewise to rely much on his wisdom and discretion.

To Master Writtill.

RIGHT worshipful Sir, I recommend me to you, thanking you of your great labour which I have not as yet but I shall deserve to my power; and furthermore like you to weet that I have thought right long after you; nevertheless I remember well that ye dealt with right delayous people, my lord archbishop and other of my lords, and I dempt (*deemed*) because of your long tarrying that by your sad (*sage*) discretion all had been set thorough; nevertheless I understand by your writing that my Lord of Norfolk's counsel thinketh that his intent, which ye certified me by your writing, should be more to his worship than the appointments and rule made by the lords of the king's council, which be to my said Lord of Norfolk ner kyne (*nothing kind*), which appointments since your departing hath been largely remembered among the said lords here, thinking it in themselves so honourable to my Lord of Norfolk, that there should none of my lords counsel well advised (*have*) moved to the contrary.

James Hobart[1] was sent from my (*Lord*) of Norfolk hither, and spake with my lord archbishop,[2] and answer he had of my said lord and how my lord tendered the matter yet and will; I trow he hath told you, and if he have not the bringer hereof shall inform you; and he brought this same appointment from my lord, that my lord was well agreed that I should occupy; for my part, if I should take no other appointment but according to your letter, it were hard for me and for my title to put my lord in that possession, for there is things in erthe (*scarcely*) to mine ease in your letter, [*or*] good for me in that appointment, saving the surety of my brother s

life and my servants, which ye think doubtful if so be that they lack stuff, shot, and victuals; marvelling sore, and think it impossible in this short season, or in four times the season hithertowards, that they should lack either, without it so be that my lord s men have entered ought (*somewhat*) the place, and so had their stuff from them, which I cannot think. Also, Sir, for the time of your coming to my Lord of Norfolk, servants of my lord's were with my mother at Norwich, moving to send to my brother her son to deliver the place under such a form as your letter specifieth, and so I cannot understand what regard my lord's counsel taketh to my lords' letter and to your labour in this behalf, but that they offered as largely afore; ye writeth in your letter that ye durst not pass your credence, please you to remember that [*you*] said your credence afore the lords was right large, and as large as might well be in this matter, both to my lord's counsel of Norfolk to withdraw the siege, with more other matter as ye know, and to the justice of the peace, and to the sheriff and his officers, your authority was great enough to each of them.

Wherefore, Master Writtill, I never for this nor yet will take appointment in this matter but as my lords will and my lord archbishop, which, as well as I myself, have wholly put our trust to your discreet direction; and my said lord since your going, thinking you as meet a man in executing their commandment as could be chosen; nevertheless for answer to you at this season, my lord archbishop is northwards towards the king; howbeit, it is said, upon a meeting with my Lord of Clarence my lord shall return again; and as yester even he sent a servant of his to me, weening to his lordship (*his lordship thinking*) that Sir Humphrey[3] and

---

[1] This most probably was James Hobart, who, in 1478, was Lent-reader at Lincoln's Inn, and in 1487 attorney-general. He died in 1516, and lies buried in Norwich Cathedral; from him the present Earl of Buckinghamshire is lineally descended

[2] George Nevile was translated from Exeter to York in 1464.

[3] Sir Humphrey Talbot was a captain at this siege, under the Duke of Norfolk.

ye were in Caister as was appointed, and ye should send to his lordship answer of the guiding there by writing, commanding me that, if any such writings came from you, if his lordship were not past twenty miles from London to come to his lordship with the same; understanding for certain that he is not yet so far; wherefore I will in all the haste possible ride night and day till I see his lordship, and after communication had with his lordship, as soon as is possible that a man may go betwixt, ye shall have an answer of his disposition; for his interest is such that, as I have written, I shall never do therein without him, as my cousin, bringer hereof, more plainly shall inform you; for I can think right well that, as ye writeth to me, my brother will not deliver the place to none earthly person but if (*unless*) he see writing from my lord.

It seemeth by your writing that my Lord of Norfolk's counsel intend not that my lord archbishop should deal in this matter, for he is not named in your letter, whereof I marvel; for it was moved to you at your departing hence the king's council should have taken direction in this matter, or else my lord cardinal,[1] my Lord of Clarence, my lord archbishop, and my Lord of Essex,[2] &c. Nevertheless, Master Writtill, all profit, manor, or livelihood laid apart, if it be so that through recklessness my brother and servants be in such jeopardy as ye have written to me, which should be half impossible in my mind that they should misuse so much stuff in four times the space, and that ye have evident knowledge by my said brother himself thereof; I will pray you to see him and them in surety of their lives, whatsoever shall fall of the livelihood, howbeit, I would not that my brother and servants should give up the place not for a thousand

pounds if they might in any wise keep it and save their lives; and therefore, at the reverence of God, since it is so that my lord archbishop, and my lords all, and I, have put our trust in you, that ye will do your devoir to have the very knowledge of my brother himself, and not of my lord's men, whether he stand in such jeopardy as your letter specifieth or not, for I doubt not upon the sight of this letter, and of the letter that ye had before, that my brother will put no mistrust in you, considering that he knoweth that ye come from my lords and my lord archbishop and have my writing; and as for my lord archbishop's writing and answer, such as it shall be, ye shall have it in all haste possible, but I think verily that my lord escheweth to tell you anything without that he might speak with you alone, and methinketh verily that they ought not to let (*hinder*) you to speak with him alone, considering that ye have authority and writing from the lords so to do; and as for the justification of entering the place, and siege laying to the same, and the commandment of the justice of the peace and the sheriff to assist my lord in this guiding, I wot ye understand that the lords know all that matter, and ye heard it communed, and how they took it in their conceits.

There is no more, Master Writtill, but I commit all this writing unto your discretion, and as ye think best according to such men's desire as have intreated you therein and for my most avail, I pray you, Sir, so do, and I shall see unto your business, and labour that ye shall have cause to do for me in time coming, and as the bringer hereof shall tell you, and I pray God have you in his keeping.

Written at London, the 10th day of September.

By your friend for ever,
JOHN PASTON, *knight*.

London, Sunday,
10th of September,
1469. 9 E. IV.

---

[1] Thomas Bourchier, Archbishop of Canterbury, and Lord Cardinal.
[2] Henry Bourchier, Earl of Essex.

LETTER CCLXXXI.—(XCIII. vol. iv. p. 383.)

My readers I make no doubt will be equally pleased with myself, in having so authentic an account of the manners of the times placed before them, wherein a disputed title to an estate is not contested in the courts of law, but by a regular and well conducted siege laid to the castle claimed by the besiegers. Every warlike preparation is made by both parties, and the assault and defence is carried on with the greatest military skill The number of the besiegers is said by Blomefield to have amounted to three thousand, while the number of those who defended the place did not exceed thirty persons ; a proof of the strength of the fortress attacked, which, with this handful of men, held out some time. The anxiety of Margaret Paston for the safety of her son and his companions interests us in her favour, and her advice to Sir John to apply to the Earl of Oxford for his assistance to raise the siege, though, if attended with success, he should enjoy the manor of Caister for his life, is a curious circumstance, and throws light upon the manners and politics of the times [This was in fact a *legal* proceeding; and even at present, as we have before remarked, the holding or acquiring possession of premises by force is by no means unfrequent. " Disseisin, or forcible dispossession of freeholds," says Hallam ('Middle Ages,' vol iii.), "makes one of the most considerable articles in our law books." He also adds in a note ;—" If a man was disseised of his land, he might enter upon the disseisor and reinstate himself without course of law In what cases this right of entry was taken away, or tolled, as it was expressed, by the death or alienation of the dis-seisor, is a subject extensive enough to occupy two chapters of Littleton. What pertains to our inquiry, is that, by *an entry* in the old law-books, we must understand an actual repossession of the disseisee, not a suit in ejectment, as it is now interpreted, but which is a comparatively modern proceeding. The first remedy, says Britton, of the disseisee is to collect a body of his friends (recoiller amys et force), and with-out delay to cast out the disseisors, or at least to maintain himself in possession along with them—c 44. This entry ought indeed, by 5 Ric. II., stat 1 c 8, to be made peaceably , and the justices might assemble the posse comitatus to imprison persons entering on lands by violence (15 Ric. II , cap. 2), but these laws imply the facts that made them necessary " The law, as far as regards freeholds, is now rather modified than altered " the entry must be made peaceably,"—and, as the law has now more vigour, any open breach of the public peace is no longer permitted, and the entry is usually made by a forcible surprise. Even as regards leasehold or yearly tenancies, it was only by the 1 & 2 Victoria, c 74, that magistrates were em-powered to give possession to landlords of premises of not more than 20/. a-year rent, where the tenant refused to give up possession Unroofing the house, stopping the chimneys, and other means were occasionally resorted to in order to eject a refractory tenant In the case of Caister, the right on either side appears very doubtful Sir John Paston held it as executor to Sir J. Fastolf; but from the complaints of Howys, Worcester, the Abbot of Langley, and others, it would seem he was very dilatory in fulfilling the directions of the will, and, in fact, was treating it as his own property. On the other hand, Yelverton and Howys sold it to Norfolk, probably under the pretext of paying the bequests of the will, or at least their own ; but the act of these two executors only could clearly convey no legal title. That these pro-ceedings were customary, and considered not illegal, accounts also for the absence of any personal ani-mosity The Duke of Norfolk's party well knew that J. Paston could never be convicted of the murder, with which he was accused, but the charge would take an active opponent out of their way ; while J. Paston, equally aware of the real state of the case, would not thereby be prevented from taking service under the Duke]

To Sir John Paston, Knight.

I GREET you well, letting you weet that your brother and his fellowship stand in great jeopardy at Caister, and lack victuals, and Daubeney[1] and Berney[2] be dead, and divers other greatly hurt; and they fail gunpowder and arrows, and the place (*is*) sore broken with guns of the other party, so that but (*unless*) they have hasty help they be like to lose both their lives and the place, to the greatest rebuke to you that ever came to any gentleman, for every man in this country marvelleth greatly that ye suffer them to be so long in so great jeopardy without help or other remedy.

The duke hath been more fervently set [*determined*] thereupon, and more cruel, since that Writtill, my Lord of Clarence's man, was there, than he was before : and he hath sent for all his tenants from every place, and others, to be there at Caister on Thursday next coming, that there is then like to be the greatest multitude of people that came there yet; and they purpose then to make a great assault, for they have sent for guns to Lynn and other places by the sea's side, that, with their great multitude of guns with other shot and ordnance, there shall no man dare appear in the place, they shall hold them so busy with their great (*number of*) people that it

---

[1] John Daubeney, Esq., whose death is here mentioned, was a gentleman of a good family in the county of Norfolk

[2] Osbert Berney, the other person here mentioned as dead, was not killed at this siege : he survived, and died without issue some years after, when he was buried in Bradeston Church in Norfolk, there being a brass-plate in the chancel to his memory.

shall not lie in their power within to hold it against them without God help them or (*they*) have hasty succour from you; therefore, as ye will have my blessing, I charge you and require you that ye see your brother be holpen in haste, and if ye can have none mean rather desire writing from my Lord of Clarence if he be at London, or else of my Lord Archbishop of York, to the Duke of Norfolk, that he will grant them that be in the place their lives and their goods, and in eschewing of insurrections with other inconveniences that be like to grow within the shire of Norfolk, this troublous werd (*tumultuous world*), because of such conventicles and gatherings within the said shire, for cause of the said place, they shall suffer him to enter upon such appointment or other like, taken by the advice of your counsel there at London if ye think this be not good, till the law hath determined otherwise, and let him write another letter to your brother to deliver the place up on the same appointment; and if ye think, as I can suppose, that the Duke of Norfolk will not agree to this because he granted this afore, and they in the place would not accept it, then I would the said messenger should with the said letters bring from the said Lord of Clarence, or else my lord archbishop, to my Lord of Oxford other letters to rescue them forthwith, though the said Earl of Oxford should have the place during his life for his labour; spare not this to be done in haste if ye will have their lives, and be set by (*esteemed*) in Norfolk, though ye should lose the best manor of all for the rescue [*rescue*]. I had lever (*rather*) ye lost the livelihood than their lives; ye must get a messenger of the lords, or some other notable man, to bring these letters; do your devoir now, and let me send you no more messengers for this matter, but send me by the bearer hereof more certain comfort than ye have done by all other that I have sent before; in any wise let the letters that shall come to the Earl of Oxford, come with the letters that shall come to the Duke of Norfolk, that if he will not agree to the one, that ye may have ready your rescue that it need no more to send, therefore God keep you.

Written the Tuesday next before Holy Rood day, in haste.

By your mother,
MARGARET PASTON.

Norwich, Tuesday,
12th of September,
1469. 9 E. IV.

LETTER CCLXXXII.—(XCIV. vol. iv. p. 387.)

Sir John Paston here seems hurt at his mother's suspecting him of not exerting himself to the utmost in endeavouring either to accommodate matters, or to assist his brother and friends within the place. He shows himself likewise both a man of spirit in coming with a few to their relief if he had a place in Norfolk for their reception, and of feeling for the distress of those shut up in his castle at Caister. [We do not doubt that Sir John Paston was a man of courage and of feeling, but this is but a slight proof of either, particularly as he neither came nor sent any effective assistance. He does not, in fact, appear to attach much importance to his mother's news.]

To Margaret Paston.

MOTHER, upon Saturday last was Daubeney and Berney were alive and merry, and I suppose there came no man out of the place to you since that time that could have ascertained to you of their deaths; and as touching the fierceness of the Duke or of his people, showed since that time that Writtill departed, I trow it was concluded that truce and abstinence of war should be had ere he departed, which shall endure till Monday next coming; and by that time I trow that truce shall be taken till that day sev'nnight after, by which time I hope of a good direction [*that*] shall be had; and whereas ye write to me that I should sue for letters from my Lords of Clarence and York, they be not here, and if they wrote to him as they have done two times, I trow it would not avail; and as for to labour those letters and the rescue together, they be two sundry things, for when the rescue is ready, that the cost thereof is done, for if I be driven thereto to rescue it, ere they come there that should do it, it shall cost a thousand escutys, and as much after, which way were hard for

D 2

me to take while that I may do it otherwise: but as to say that they shall be rescued if all the lands that I have in England and friends may do it, they shall and (*if*) God be friendly, and that as shortly as it may goodly and well be brought about; and the greatest default earthly is money and some friends and neighbours to help, wherefore I beseech you to send me comfort with what money ye could find the means to get or chevise (*borrow upon interest*), upon surety sufficient or upon livelihood to be in mortgage or yet sold, and what people by likelihood your friends and mine could make upon a short warning, and to send me word in all the haste as it is needful; but, mother, I feel by your writing that ye deem in me I should not do my devoir (*endeavour*) without ye wrote to me some heavy tidings, and, mother, if I had need to be quickened with a letter in this need I were of myself too slow a fellow; but, mother, I ensure (*assure*) you that I have heard ten times worse tidings since the siege began than any letter that ye wrote to me, and sometimes I have heard right good tidings both; but this I assure you that they that be within have no worse rest than I have, nor casteth more jeopardy; but whether I had good tidings or ill, I take God to witness, that I have done my devoir as I would be done for in case like, and shall do till there be an end of it.

I have sent to the king to York, and to the lords, and hope to have answer from them by Wednesday at the furthest, and after that answer shall I be ruled, and then send you word, for till that time can I take none direction; and to encomfort you, despair you not for lack of victuals nor of gunpowder, nor be not too heavy nor too merry therefore; for and (*if*) heaviness or sorrow would have been the remedy thereof, I knew never matter in my life that I could have been so heavy or sorry for, and with God's grace it shall be remedied well enough, for by my troth I had lever (*rather*) lose the manor of Caister than the simplest man's life therein if that may be his salvation; wherefore I beseech [1] you to send me word what money and men ye think that I am like to get in that country; for the hasty purchase of money and men shall be the getting and rescue of it, and the salvation of most men's lives, if we take that way.

Also, this day I purpose to send to York to the king for a thing, which same only may by likelihood be the salvation of all; ye must remember that the rescue of it is the last remedy of all, and how it is not easy to get; and also ye send me word that I should not come home without that I come strong, but if I had had one other strong place in Norfolk to have come to, though I had brought right few with me, I should with God's grace have rescued it by this time, or else he should have been fain to have besieged both places ere yet, and (*if*) the duke had not kept Yarmouth out: but, mother, I beseech you send me some money, for by my troth I have but ten shillings; I wot not where to have more; and moreover I have been ten times in like case, or worse, within this ten weeks.

I sent to Richard Calle for money, but he sendeth me none; I beseech you to guide the evidence that Peacock can tell you of, and to see it safe, for it is told me that Richard Calle hath had right large language of them; I would not they come in his fingers: I have no word from you of them, nor whether ye have yet in your keeping the evidence of East Beckham out of his hands, nor whether ye have sent to my manors that they should not pay him no more money or not; also that it like you to give credence to Robin in other things.

Written the Friday next after Holy Rood day.

JOHN PASTON, *knight.*

London, Friday,
15th of September,
1469. 9 E. IV.

---

[1] The original word, in this and some similar cases, is *savacion*,—a better word for the purpose though long obsolete.]

LETTER CCLXXXIII.—(XCV. vol. iv. p. 395.)

This letter is written by Sir John Paston to his brother John Paston, to encourage him to hold out Caister Castle as long as he has hopes of relief he tells him of the good opinion which is entertained of the courage and conduct of those in the place, but that those who besiege it are mentioned in a very different manner. The letter is curious, and written in a style to give both spirits and hope to the besieged.

To John Paston, and to none other.

I RECOMMEND me to you, and promise you that I have and shall labour and find the mean that ye shall have honour of your dealing, as ye have hithertowards, as all England and every man reporteth; and moreover I am in way for it by many divers ways, whereof there shall be one executed by this day fortnight at the furthest, and peradventure within seven days; and if ye may keep it so long I would be glad, and after that if ye have not from me other writing, that then ye do therein for your safeguard and your fellowship only and to your worships; and as for the place, no force therefore; ye know this hand, therefore needeth no mention from whom it cometh; and moreover they that be about you be in obloquy of all men; and moreover they have been written to by as special writing as might be, after the world that now is, and promise you that the Duke's counsel would that they had never begun it, and moreover they be charged in pain of their lives that though they get the place they should not hurt one of you, there is neither ye nor none with you, but, and (*if*) he knew what is generally reported of him, he or ye, and God fortune you well, may think him four times better in reputation of all folk than ever he was.

Beware whom ye make a counsel to this matter.

Also, I let you weet that I am in much more comfort of you than I may write, and they that be about you have cause to be more feide (*afraid*) than ye have; and also beware of spending of your stuff of quarrels (*square-headed arrows*), powder, and stone (*stone bullets*), so that if they assault you ere we come that ye have stuff to defend you of over, and then of my life ye get no more; and that your fellowship be ever occupied in renewing of your stuff.

Written the Monday next after Holy Rood day.

I trow, though ye be not privy thereto, there is taken a truce new till this day sev'nnight.

Monday, 18th of September, 1469   9 E IV.

LETTER CCLXXXIV.—(XCVI. vol. iv. p. 397.)

This well-written letter of Margaret Paston to Sir John Paston gives us a high opinion of her good sense and prudent conduct; she is justly displeased with him for supposing that she should knowingly send him false information the good advice she gives him flows from her own reliance upon God, and from her knowledge of mankind, she laments her own inability to assist him with money, and recommends proper methods for the increase of his livelihood

To Sir John Paston in haste, a matre.

I GREET you well, and send you God's blessing and mine, letting you weet that me-think by the letter that ye sent me by Robin that ye think that I should write to you fables and imaginations, but I do not so, I have written as it have been informed me, and will do. it was told me that both Daubeney and Berney were dead; but for certain Daubeney is dead, God assoil his soul! whereof I am right sorry, and it had pleased God that it might have been otherwise.

Remember you, ye have had two great losses within this twelvemonth of him and of Sir Thomas. God visiteth you as it pleaseth him in sundry wises: he would ye should know him and serve him better than ye have done before this time, and then he will send you the more grace to do well in all other things; and for God's love remember it right well, and take it patiently, and thank God of his visitation, and if anything have been amiss, any otherwise than it ought to have been before this, either in pride, or in lavish expenses, or in any other thing that have offended God, amend it, and pray him of his grace and help, and intend well to God and to your neighbours; and though your power hereafter be to acquit [*requite*] them of their malice, yet be merciful to them, and God shall send you the more grace to have your intent in other things. I remember these clauses because of the last letter that ye sent me. I have sent to Harry Halman, of Sporle, to help to get as ye desired me, and he cannot get past five or eight at the most, and yet it will not be but if (*unless*) he come that [*they*] ye trust upon that should come, for they long (*belong*) apart to him; and Richard Sharman hath assayed on his part, and he cannot get past five; for those that long to us, they long also to our adversaries, and they have been desired by them, and they would nought do for them, and therefore they think to have magery (*q. manage-ment*)[1] of the other part.

As for the gentleman that ye desired me to speak with, I spake with his wife, and she told me he was not in this country nor nought wist when he should be here; and as for the other man, he has bought him a livery[2] in Bromholm priory, and have given up the world, &c.

Item, as for money I could get but ten pounds upon pledges, and that is spent for your matters here, for paying of your men that were at Caister, and other things, and I wot not where to get none, neither for surety

nor for pledges; and as for mine own liveli-hood, I am so simply paid thereof that I fear me I shall be fain to borrow for myself or else to break up household; or both.

As for the yielding of the place at Caister, I trow Writtill hath told of the pawntements (*appointments*) how it is delivered. I would that had been so ere this time, and then there should not have been done so mickle hurt as there is in divers ways, for many of our well-willers are put to loss for our sakes, and I fear me it shall be long ere it be recompensed again, and that shall cause others to do the less for us hereafter.

I would ye should (*send*) your brother word, and some other that ye trust, to see to your own livelihood to set it in a rule, and to gather thereof that may be had in haste; and also of Sir John Fastolf's livelihood that may be gathered in peaceable wise, for as for Richard Calle he will no more gather it but if (*unless*) ye command him, and he would fain make his account, and have your good mastership, as it is told me, and deliver the evidence of Beckham and all other things that longeth to you, that he trusteth that ye will be his good master hereafter; and he saith he will not take none new master till ye refuse his service.

Remember that your livelihood may be set in such a rule that ye may know how it is, and what is owen to you, for by my faith I have holpen as much as I may and more, saving myself, and therefore take heed ere it be worse.

This letter was begun on Friday was sev'nnight, and ended this day next after Michaelmas day. God keep you, and give you grace to do as well as I would ye did, and I charge you beware that ye set no land to mortgage, for if any advise you thereto they are not your friends; beware betimes mine advice, &c.: I trow your brother will give you tidings in haste.

MARGARET PASTON.

Begun Friday, 22nd of September, ended Saturday, 30th September, 1469. 9 E IV.

---

[1] [We do not know the word *magery*, but it seems used in the sense of neutrality—the services of the tenantry are claimed by both parties, and having refused to do aught for the one part, they link it right to hold a neutrality as to the other part.]

[2] It was usual in these times for persons growing into years to procure by purchase or gift a retreat in some religious society, where, giving up all concern in worldly matters, they passed the remainder of their time in prayer and confession: some did it to finish a pure and unspotted life in a place set apart for religion, where they should be free from every worldly engagement, others undertook it as an atonement for their former evil deeds, with a hope that it might insure their eternal welfare.

LETTER CCLXXXV. (CXVII. vol. iv. p. 405.)

This is the only letter written to the besiegers which appears in this collection, and the writer of this cannot be ascertained. he seems however to be a well-wisher to the Pastons by what he says in his letter of the opinion of the lords on this business, who likewise appear favourable to them. He seems to hint that the extremity to which things are carried is more the fault of these captains to whom the letter is addressed than that of the Duke of Norfolk, who "is noted so well disposed."

(*To*) *Sir John Hevengham*[1] *Thomas Wingfield*,[2] *Gilbert Debenham*,[3] *William Brandon*,[4] *and every of them severally in others absence.*

It is so that, according to such direction as was moved to be desired of my lords being here as for such as here be, they marvel greatly thereof, thinking and remembering in themselves that such offer as was made by my credence to my lord, and tofore you reported, should have sounded more to his pleasure and honour than this his desire; nevertheless my lords think, whereas they wrote and desired jointly that such credence, as ye remember, might be observed and taken, and by you refused; now if they should assent to the desire of this direction, it is thought in them not so to do, for it is so fortuned that divers of my lords, from whom I brought both writing and credence, be at the king's high commandment hastily departed unto his highness; trusting in God to have hearing in brief time of their hasty again coming, at which time my lords that here be, and they that shall come again, shall commune and speak together of this desire and direction, and such answer as they give and make shall be sent unto you then with haste possible. Over this me thinketh for your excuse of burden and charge, such as I hear will be laid unto you concerning the great works that daily be and are at the manor of Caister, if ye think that God should have pleasure, and also the king our sovereign lord, and that my said lords should think in you good advice or sad, and that ye intended to avoid the shedding of Christian blood and the destruction of the king's liege people, that at your politic labour and wisdom ye might bring my lord to the abstinence of war, and a truce to be had and continued unto time of the return of my said lords, or else knowledge of their intent; certifying you for truth that there be messengers sent unto my said lords with letters of such answer as I had of you and your desire together, knowing certainly that there shall be hasty relation of their intents in the premises; which answers ye shall have at furthest by Monday cometh sev'nnight. Furthermore letting you weet that I understand for certain that my lords that be here eschew, for such inconvenience that might fall, to conclude any answer by themselves, considering that my credence was given by all the lords, praying you, as shall be done to the continuance of this truce aforesaid, that I may be ascertained; or if at this hour ye could yet think my credence reasonable and honourable to be accepted and taken, send me word in writing from you by my servant, bringer of this, all delays laid apart; for I ascertain [*assure*] you as he that owe you service, I was and yet am greatly blamed for my long tarrying with you, for divers of my lords tarried here for me, by the assent of all my lords, longer than they would have done, to know my answer and guiding from you; and over this I certify you that ye cannot make my lords here to think that if there be inconvenience or mischief, murder or manslaughter, had or done, but and (*if*) your wills and intents were to the contrary, my lord is noted so well disposed, that without your great abetment he neither will do nor assent to none such thing; praying you, therefore, as your friend, to remember well

[1] Sir John Heveningham, knight and banneret, was a descendant of an ancient family situated at the towns of Heveningham, in Suffolk; his son Thomas became owner of the estate at Ketteringham, in Norfolk, where this family continued for several generations.

[2] Sir Thomas Wingfield was a younger son either of Sir Robert or Sir John Wingfield, of Letheringham, in Suffolk.

[3] Sir Gilbert Debenham, knight, was descended of an ancient family in the county of Suffolk.

[4] Sir William Brandon married Elizabeth, daughter of Sir Robert Wingfield, and was ancestor to Charles Brandon, afterwards Duke of Suffolk.

yourself, and so to rule you as my lords may have in time to come knowledge of your more sad (*grave*) disposition than as yet I feel they think in you; and how that my lords note some of you, James Hobart, being of my lord's counsel, can inform you, wherefore for God's sake remember you, and deliver my servant, and if ye think my first credence or this advertisement shall be

taken to effect, then I pray you that my servant, bringer hereof, may have sure conduct to speak with John Paston, and to report to him these directions, and upon that to deliver him a bill certifying the same.

London,
September, 1469.
9 E. IV.

LETTER CCLXXXVI.—(XXVIII. vol. ii. p. 25.)

This letter is endorsed in an ancient hand "The Duke of Norff' Lr'e upon his entrie into Caister A⁰ E. 4. ix⁰ " This is given to show the regal style used by the nobility of these times. In Blomefield's ' History of Norfolk,' vol v. p. 1552, a particular account of the siege of Caister Castle is given, with the names of the principal persons engaged on both sides. The mark of the signet remains, but the impression is defaced. It is likewise signed with the Duke's own hand.

THE DUKE OF NORFOLK.

WHERE(**as**) John Paston, Esquire, and other diverse persons have, against the peace, kept the manor of Caister with force, against the will and intent of us the Duke of Norfolk to our great displeasure; which notwithstanding, at the contemplation of the writing of the most worshipful and reverend father in God the Cardinal of England, and our most trusty and entirely-beloved uncle the Archbishop of Canterbury, the right noble prince my Lord of Clarence, and other lords of our blood, and also at the great labour and instance of our most dear and singular-beloved wife, we be agreed that the said John Paston, and his said fellowship, being in the said manor, shall depart and go out of the said manor without delay, and make thereof deliverance to such persons as we will assign, the said fellowship having their lives and goods, horse

and harness, and other goods being in the keeping of the said John Paston; except guns, cross-bows, and quarrels, and all other hostlements (*warlike implements*) to the said manor annexed and belonging. and to have fifteen days respite after their said departing out to go into what place shall like them, without any actions or quarrel to be taken or made by us or in our name to them or any of them, within our franchise or without, during the said time.

Given under our signet at Yarmouth the 26th day of September, the 9th year of King Edward the IVth.

NORFOLK.

Yarmouth,
Tuesday, 26th of September,
1469. 9 E. IV.

LETTER CCLXXXVII.—(XCVIII. vol. iv. p. 411.)

Caister yielded. J. P.

On reading this letter no one can withhold the praise due to John Paston as a brave soldier and a kind and generous master, and at the same time wishing that he and his companions had been able to have kept possession of Caister · the noble manner in which he speaks of his companions interests us both in his and their favour; these are the same four soldiers that his brother Sir John had so particularly recommended to him in his letter dated November 9, 1468

To Sir John Paston, Knight.

RIGHT worshipful Sir, I recommend me unto you; and as for the certainty of the deliver-

ance of Caister, John Chapman can tell you how that we were enforced thereto as well as myself; as for John Chapman and his three fellows I have purveyed that they be paid each of them forty shillings with the money that they had of you and Daubeney; and that is enough for the season that they have done you service; I pray you give them their thank, for by my troth they have as well deserved it as any men that ever bore life; but as for money ye need not to give them without ye will, for they be pleased with their wages.

Wryttill promised me to send you the certainty of the appointment, we were for lack of victuals, gunpowder, men's hearts, lack of surety of rescue, driven thereto to take appointment.[1]

If ye will that I come to you send me word and I shall purvey me for to tarry with you a two or three days; by my troth the rewarding of such folks as hath been with me during the siege, hath put me in great danger for the money; God preserve you, and I pray you be of good cheer till I speak with you, and I trust to God to ease your heart in some things.

JOHN PASTON.

September, 1469. 9 E. IV.

LETTER CCLXXXVIII —(XCIX. vol. iv. p. 413.)

The advice given to Sir John Paston by his brother relative to his servants, who had faithfully served him during the siege, &c shows the goodness of his heart, and interests the reader in wishing that he had been of ability to have retained them himself. It seems odd that a man who had so lately commanded a garrison against the forces of the Duke of Norfolk, should, so immediately after the surrender of the place, have any thoughts of engaging himself in his grace's service, as it fully appears by this letter that J. Paston had. We learn from it, however, that, in disputes of this kind, whenever the cause of dispute was ended all animosity ceased, and the different parties forgot they had so lately been enemies We find a great deal of similar behaviour between the partisans of the White and Red Rose during the civil wars of this distant period [This is true, but very contradictory of Sir J. Fenn's opinions expressed in other places]

To my master, Sir John Paston, in Fleet-street.

RIGHT worshipful Sir, I recommend (*me*) unto you; praying you that ye will in all haste send me word how that ye will that Sir John Styll, John Pampyng, William Milisent, Nicholas Maudent, (*and*) T. Tomson shall be ruled, and whether that they shall seek them new services or not; and Matthew Bedford also, for he hath been with me this season, and is from my mother; and if so be that ye will have these to abide with you, or any of them, send word which that they be, for betwixt this and Hallowmas my mother is agreed that they shall have meat and drink of her for such a certain weekly as my mother and ye and I can accord when we meet, notwithstanding if ye could get Berney, or any of these said fellows which that ye will not keep, any service in the mean season, it were more worship for you than to put them from you like masterless hounds, for by my troth they are as good men's bodies as any alive, and specially Sir John Still and John Pampyng; and (*if*) I were of power to keep them and all these before rehearsed, by troth they should never depart from me while I lived.

If ye send me word that I shall come to you to London for to commune with you of any matter, so God help me, I have neither money to come up with nor for to tarry with you when I am there, but if (*unless*) ye send me some; for by my troth these works have caused me to lay out for you better than ten or twelve pounds,b esides

---

[1] [The original has—" we wer sor (with a long *s*, probably a typographical error) lak of vetayl gonepoudyr menys herts lak of suerte of rescwe dreuyn therto to take apoyntement" Fenn translates it thus " we were sore lack of victuals (*and*) gunpowder, men's hearts lack of surety of rescue (*were*), driven thereto to take appointment." Two words are here driven in, and the sentence is made nonsense. With the correction of *sor* into *for* we think the meaning is quite clear Lack of men's hearts means, that the hearts of the men, having done all they could, had at length given way—they were no longer manly.]

that money that I had of my mother, which is about an eight pound; God amend defaults, but this I warrant you, without that it be Matthew which ye sent word by John Thresher that ye would have to await on you, there is no man that was hired for the time of this siege that will ask you a penny.

Also, I pray you send down a commandment to Statevylle, or to some auditor, to take accounts of Daubeney's bills, for his executors are sore called upon for to administer by the bishop, or else he saith that he will sequester; Daubeney set in his debts that ye owed him twelve pounds and ten shillings; whether it be so or not his bills of his own hands will not lie, for he made his bills clear or then (*before*) the siege came about us. As for the evidence of Beckham, my mother sent to Calle for them, and he sent her word that he would make his accounts and deliver the evidence and all together.

My mother hath sent to him again for them this day; if she speed they shall be sent to you in all haste, or else and (*if*) ye send for me I shall bring them with me. Send my mother and me word who ye will that (*shall*) have the rule of your livelihood here in this country, and in what form that it shall be dealt with. I will not make me masterfast with my Lord of Norfolk nor with none other till I speak with you; and ye think it be to be done get me a master.

Deal courteously with the queen and that fellowship, and with mistress Anne Hawte for wappys[1] till I speak with you. Written on St. Faith's even.

JOHN PASTON.

By Saint George I and my fellowship stand in fear of my Lord of Norfolk's men, for we be threatened sore, notwithstanding the safeguards that my fellowship have; as for me I have none, nor none of your household men, nor none will have; it were shame[2] to take it.

Thursday, 5 October,
1469. 9 E. IV.

LETTER CCLXXXIX.—(C. vol. iv. p. 417.)

Two men having been killed during the siege at Caister, the Duke of Norfolk's counsel instigate their widows to lodge an appeal for the murder against John Paston and others. An appeal is an accusation of a murderer by a person who had interest in the person killed, as the wife had interest in the life of her husband, and must be brought within a year and day after the fact committed; and in this appeal of death the king cannot pardon the defendant. The latter part of this letter contains Latin, French, and English, by which we may judge how liberally J. Paston had been educated. He seems likewise in good spirits though threatened with this appeal. [The appeal in cases of murder is now abolished.]

To Master Sir John Paston, Knight.

RIGHT worshipful Sir, I recommend me to you, &c.; it is so that this day there came a good fellow to me which may not be discovered, and let me weet that my Lord of Norfolk's counsel hath this Christmas gotten the two widows, whose husbands were slain at the siege of Caister, and have them bounden in a great sum that they shall sue an appeal against me and such as were there with me within the place, and they be bound also that they shall release no man within the appeal named till such time as my Lord of Norfolk will license them.

Item, the cause is this, as it is told me by divers, that ye make no more suit to my lord for yourself than ye do, and therefore they do the worse to me for your sake.

Item, as for my coming up to London, so God help me, and (*if*) I may choose I come not there for, argent me faut, without an appeal or an inkyr (*q. inquiry*) of some special matters of yours cause it. Item, I pray you remember Calais, for I am put out of wages in this country.

Item, I pray you send me some tidings how the world goeth *ad confortandum stomachum*.

---

[1] This expression "for wappys" I do not understand.

[2] J. Paston's honour and courage are apparent from his thinking a safeguard shameful.

Item, ye must purvey a new attorney in his country as for me, for our matters and clamour is too great and our purse and wit oo slender; but I will rub on as long as I may both with mine own and other means that will do for me till better peace be. Written this Saturday at Norwich.

JOHN PASTON.

Saturday,
December or January, 1469. 9 E. IV.

LETTER CCXC.—(CI. vol. iv. p. 421.)

As this letter contains a variety of matter I have given it to the reader. The bargain with the archbishop was I suppose relative to the expenses attending the probate of the will, &c. It seems extraordinary that the Norfolk family should speak favourably of J. Paston, and yet pursue the appeal against him for murder. His device to interrupt the keeping of the court at Saxthorp deserves notice, and shows the plain dealing of the times.

To my right worshipful brother, Sir John Paston, Knight, be this delivered.

RIGHT worshipful Sir, I recommend me to you in my best wise. Liketh it you to weet that I have this day delivered your mantle, your ray gown,[1] and your cross-bows with elers and windlass, and your Normandy bill, to Kerby, to bring with him to London.

Item, in any wise and (*if*) ye can, ask the probate of my father's will to be given you with the bargain that ye make with my Lord of Canterbury, and I can think that ye may have it; and as soon as it is proved ye or I may have a letter of administration upon the same, and an acquittance of my lord cardinal even forthwith; and this were one of the best bargains that ye made this two year I assure you; and he may make you acquittance, or get you one of the Bishop of Winchester for Sir John Fastolf's goods also, and in my reason this were light to be brought about with the same bargain; and (*if*) ye purpose to bargain with him ye had need to hie you, for it is told me that my Lord of Norfolk will enter into it hastily, and if he so do it is the worse for you, and it will cause them to proffer the less silver.

Item, I pray you send me some secret tidings of the likelihood of the world by the next messenger that cometh between, that I may be either merrier or else more sorry than I am, and also that I may guide me thereafter.

Item, as for Sir Robert Wingfield, I can get no ten pounds of him, but he saith that

I shall have the fairest harness that I can buy in London for silver, but money can I none get.

I cannot yet make my peace with my Lord of Norfolk nor my lady by no means, yet every man telleth me that my lady saith passingly well of me always; notwithstanding I trow that they will sue the appeal this term, yet there is no man of us indicted, but if (*unless*) it were done afore the coroners ere then we came out of the place; there is now but three men in it, and the bridges always drawn. No more, but God lat you mine her.[2] Written the Tuesday next after Saint Agnes the first.[3]

JOHN PASTON.

Item, yesterday W. Gornay entered into Saxthorp, and there was he keeping of a court, and had the tenants attorned to him; but ere the court was all done I came thither with a man with me and no more, and there, before him and all his fellowship, Gayne, Bomsted, &c. I charged the tenants that they should proceed no further in their court upon pain that might fall of it; and they letted for a season, but they saw that I was not able to make my party good, and so they proceeded

---

[1] This means a gown made of cloth that was never either coloured or dyed.

[2] This sentence I wish to have explained.

[3] The festival of St. Agnes the first (and the most noted of the two), was kept on the 21st of January; her second festival was on the 28th of the same month, which it is to be observed was not the octave of the former, but a distinct feast upon a different occasion, and it is sometimes written "Agnetis Nativitas," but it was on account of a miracle wrought at her tomb that this second feast was instituted

further : I saw that, and sat me down by the steward, and blotted his book with my finger as he wrote, so that all the tenants affirmed that the court was interrupted by me 'as in your right, and I requested them to record that there was no peaceable court kept, and so they said they would.

Tuesday,
23 January, 1469—70. 9 E. IV.

LETTER CCXCI.—(CII. vol. iv. p. 425.)

This letter shows the means that were laboured by the enemies of the Pastons to prosecute this appeal.

To John Paston, Esq., be this delivered.

I GREET you well, and send you God's blessing and mine; letting you weet that the woman that sueth the appeal[1] against your brother and his men is come to London to call thereupon, and when that she should come to London there was delivered her an hundred shillings for to sue with, so that, by that I hear in this country, she will not leave it, but that she shall call thereupon (*at*) such time as shall be to your most rebuke but if (*unless*) ye lay the better watch; she hath evil counsel, and that will see you greatly uttered (*outed or displayed*), and that ye may understand by the money that was taken her (*given her*) when she came up, and ye should find it, I know it well, if they might have you at advantage; therefore for God's sake make diligent search by the advice of your counsel, that there be no negligence in you in this matter nor other for default of labour, and call upon your brother, and tell him that I send him God's blessing and mine, and desire him that he will now awhile, while he hath the lords at his intent, that he seek the means to make an end of his matters, for his enemies are greatly couraged now of late; what is the cause I know not.

Also I pray you speak to Playters that there may be found a mean that the sheriff or the gatherer of the green-wax[2] may be discharged of certain issues that ran up on Fastolf for Maryot's matter, for the bailiff was at him this week, and should have distrained him, but that he promised him that he should within this eight days labour the means that he should be discharged, or else he must content him, &c.

Also I send you by the bearer hereof closed in this letter, five shillings of gold, and pray you to buy me a sugar-loaf, and dates, and almonds, and send it me home, and if ye beware (*lay out*) any more money, when ye come home I shall pay it you again; the Holy Ghost keep you both, and deliver you of your enemies. Written on Saint Agas (*Agatha's*) day in haste.

Item, I pray you speak to Master Roger for my syrup;[3] for I had never more need thereof, and send it me as hastily as ye can.

By
MARGARET PASTON.

Monday,
5th of February, 1469-70. 9 E. IV.

LETTER CCXCII.—(XXIX. vol. ii. p. 27.)

John de Vere, Earl of Oxford, retaining his loyalty to the House of Lancaster, in whose cause his father and elder brother had lost their heads upon the scaffold in 1461-2, and for whose sake he himself had suffered a long imprisonment, seems now privately to be preparing to join the Earl of Warwick in favour of the deposed King Henry. I should suppose this letter to have been written either in July, 1469, at the time

---

1 [Two men were killed of the Duke of Norfolk's party ; and the finding of the coroner's inquest, though asserted to be invalid, was unfavourable to the Pastons. But we hear of no trial preceding the appeals or appeal, for though appeals are talked of, there appears to have been actually but one.]

2 Estreats delivered to the sheriff out of the Exchequer, to be levied in his county under the seal of that court, made in green wax, were from thence called green-wax.

3 [Master Roger was, I suppose, some leech, famous for his syrups, &c.]

that the Earl of Warwick and his adherents were meditating the plan for dethroning Edward, or in 1470, when they had come to a resolution of reinstating Henry on the throne. The order to Sir John Paston, for providing the horse-harness, was to be executed, "*as it were for himself,*" and the referring him to the Countess for money, shows it to be at a time when his finances were very low. The expression "*Yet she must borrow it,*" implies too that his lady had not already the money, but that she had it *still* to procure. Though the Earl desired that his horse-harness might be of the same price with one which Lord Hastings had purchased, yet he wished it not to be like his; the reason seems to be, he did not choose to appear with caparisons similar to those of a Yorkist. The words "I trust to God we shall do right well" refer to some scheme then in agitation; and on the success of which he had placed great confidence.

To Sir John Paston, Knight.

RIGHT worshipful, and my especial true-hearted friend, I commend me unto you, praying you to ordain (*order for*) me three horses' harness as goodly as ye and Genyns can devise as it were for yourself; and that I may have them in all haste order; also Skern saith ye would ordain two standard staves; this I pray you to remember, and my wife shall deliver you silver, and yet she must borrow it. Six or seven pounds I would bestow on a horse-harness; and so Skern told me I might have. The Lord Hastings had for the same price, but I would not mine were like his: and I trust to God we shall do right well, who preserve you. Written at Canterbury in haste, the 18th day of July.

OXYNFORD.

Canterbury,
18th of July, 1469
or 1470. 9 or 10 E.
IV.

LETTER CCXCIII.—(XXX. vol. ii. p. 29.)

This letter was written in February or March 1469, 1470, or 1471, for in these years civil dissentions were on foot. The caution respecting tidings, and the uncertainty of what may befall, shows that this letter was written during some convulsion of the state. By the Earl of Warwick's being supposed to go with the king into Lincolnshire, it appears as if this letter was written during the restoration of Henry VI., and that their going there was to oppose Edward's return.

To John Paston, Esquire, being at Norwich, be this letter delivered.

I COMMEND me to you, letting you weet, &c. (*Here follows an account of bills, and receipts, &c. of no consequence.*)

Item, as for Mistress Katherine Dudley I have many times recommended you to her, and she is nothing displeased with it; she rekkythe not how many gentlemen love her, she is full of love; I have betyn (*enforced*) the matter for you, your unknowledge (*without your knowledge*) as I told her; she answered me that she would (*have*) no one this two years, and I believe her: for I think she hath the life that she can hold her content with. I trow she will be a sore labouring woman this two years for the meed of her soul.

And Mistress Gryseacress is sure to Selenger (*St. Leger*), with my Lady of Exeter, [1] a foul loss.

Item, I pray you speak with Harcourt [2] of the abbey, for a little clock, which I sent him by James Gresham to mend, and that ye would get it of him, and (*if*) it be ready, and send it me; and as for money for his labour, he hath another clock of mine, which Sir Thomas Lyndes, God have his soul! gave me; he may keep that till I pay him; this clock is my lord archbishop's, but let not him weet of it, and that it (*be*) easily carried hither by your advice.

Also as for oranges I shall send you a serteyn by the next carrier, and as for tidings the bearer hereof shall inform you; ye must give credence to him.

---

[1] Anne, daughter of Richard Duke of York, and sister of King Edward IV., married Henry Holland, Duke of Exeter, and in 1462 had possession of his forfeited estates, and remained with her brother, Edward IV. She afterwards married Sir Thomas St. Leger, and died in 1475.

[2] This shows that our curious mechanical arts were practised in the religious houses, and performed there by the monks, &c. for money.

As for my good speed, I hope well, I am offered yet to have Mistress Anne Hawte, and I shall have help enough as some say.

(*Here follows an account of some disputes between Sir William Yelverton, and Sir John Paston, his uncle William, &c., of no consequence.*)

Item, it is so that I am half in purpose to come home within a month hereafter, or about Midlent, or before Easter, under your correction, if so be that ye deem that my mother would help me to my costs, ten marks (6*l.* 13*s.* 4*d.*) or thereabouts. I pray you feel her disposition and send me word.

Item, I cannot tell you what will fall of the world, for the king verily is disposed to go into Lincolnshire, and men wot not what will fall thereof, nor thereafter, they ween my Lord of Norfolk shall bring 10,000 men.

Item, there is come a new little Turk, which is a well-visaged fellow of the age of forty years; and he is lower than Manuel by an handful, and lower than my little Tom by the shoulders, and more little above his pap; and he hath, as he said to the king himself, three or four children, (*sons*) each one of them as high and as likely as the king himself; and he is legged right enough.

Item, I pray you show, or read to my mother, such things as ye think are for her to know after your discretion; and to let her understand of the article of the treaty between Sir William Yelverton and me.

Item, my Lord of Warwick, as it is supposed, shall go with the king into Lincolnshire; some men say that his going shall do good, and some say that it doth harm.

I pray you ever have an eye to Caister, to know the rule there, and send me word, and whether my wise lord and my lady be yet as sotted upon it (*as fond of it*)[1] as they were; and whether my said lord resorteth thither as often as he did or not; and of the disposition of the country.

JOHN PASTON, *knight.*

LETTER CCXCIV.—(XXXI. vol. ii. p. 35.)

This letter, from George Nevile, Archbishop of York, and brother to Richard Earl of Warwick, must have been written either when he was in opposition to Edward in conjunction with his brother the Earl of Warwick, or after his return from his imprisonment abroad not long before his death, when it is probable he found it difficult to raise even a small sum of money. George Nevile was consecrated Bishop of Exeter in 1455, when he was not completely twenty years of age. In 1460 he was appointed Lord Chancellor, and in 1466 advanced to the Archbishopric of York. In 1470 he had the custody of Edward IV. when taken prisoner by the Earl of Warwick, and died in 1476, æt. 41.

To my right trusty and well-beloved Sir John Paston.

Ius.

RIGHT trusty and well beloved, I greet you heartily well, and send you by Thomas your child 20*l.* praying you to spare me as for any more at this time, and to hold you content with the same, as my singular trust is in you; and I shall within brief time ordain and purvey for you such as shall be unto your pleasure with the grace of Almighty God, who have you in his protection and keeping.

Written in the manor of the Moor,[2] the 7th day of May. G. EBORAC.

The Moor, in Hertfordshire,
7th of May. Between 1466 and 1476,
6 and 16 E. IV.

---

[1] [*Besotted* upon or about it.]

[2] In Hertfordshire, a seat of the Archbishop's.

LETTER CCXCV.—(XXXII. vol. ii. p. 37.)

This letter was written a short time after the battle of Stamford, wherein Edward was victorious, having slain and dispersed the forces commanded by Sir Robert Welles, who in this engagement had fought most furiously; being exasperated at the recent death of his father the Lord Welles. We are here acquainted with the movements of the king after his victory, and with some of the executions which took place by his order on those who had opposed him. [After the quarrel of Edward IV. with Warwick his rule became much more severe and sanguinary than it had been. A proof that the previous moderation was owing, as it is usually asserted, to the counsels of Warwick.]

To my cousin, John Paston.

THE king came to Grantham, and there tarried Thursday[1] all day, and there was headed Sir Thomas Delalaunde and one John Neille, a great captain; and upon the Monday[2] next after that at Doncaster, and there was headed Sir Robert Welles and another great captain; and then the king had word that the Duke of Clarence and the Earl of Warwick was at Easterfield,[3] twenty miles from Doncaster; and upon the Tuesday,[4] at nine of the bell, the king took the field, and mustered his people; and it was said, that (*there*) were never seen in England so many goodly men and so well arrayed in a field; and my lord[5] was worshipfully accompanied, no lord there so well; wherefore the king gave my lord a great thank.

And than (*when*) the Duke of Clarence and the Earl of Warwick heard that the king was coming to themward, incontinent (*immediately*) they departed, and went to Manchester in Lancashire, hoping to have had help and succour of the Lord Stanley;[6] but in conclusion there they had little favour, as it was informed the king; and so men say they went westward, and some men deem to London.

And when the king heard they were departed and gone, he went to York, and came thither the Thursday[7] next after, and there came into him all the gentlemen of the shire; and upon our Lady-day[8] (*he*) made Percy Earl of Northumberland, and he that was earl[9] afore Marquis Montague; and so the king is purposed to come southward; God send him good speed.

Written the 27th day of March.

FOR TRUTH.[10]

Tuesday, 27th of March, 1470. 10 E. IV.

LETTER CCXCVI.—(CIII. vol. iv. p. 420.)

I have given this letter as not only containing a case of law, but to show the steps taken by the Duke of Norfolk's counsel to harass and distress Sir John Paston and his party for the death of two men who, I presume, were shot by those in the place during the siege of Caister. It appears from this and some other letters in this collection, that the Townshend therein mentioned was a lawyer. It is therefore most probable that the person was Roger Townshend, of Lincoln's Inn, afterwards a serjeant-at-law, and by Richard III. appointed one of the judges of the Common Pleas, in which important office he was continued by Henry VII. and knighted. His second son John (the issue of the elder being extinct) was ancestor to the present most noble the Marquis Townshend, of Rainham, in Norfolk.

To Sir John Paston, Knight, or to Thomas Stomps, to deliver to the said Sir John.

RIGHT worshipful Sir, and my special good brother, I recommend me to you; and forasmuch as I cannot send you good tidings ye shall have such as I know.

---

[1] 15th March, 1469.
[2] 19th March, 1469.
[3] [Probably Austerfield; but this is not half the distance here stated from Doncaster.]
[4] 20th March, 1469.
[5] John Mowbray, Duke of Norfolk.
[6] Thomas Lord Stanley, afterwards Earl of Derby.
[7] 22nd March, 1469.
[8] 25th March, 1470. N.B. The date changed on the 25th of March, yearly.

[9] John Nevile, brother to the Earl of Warwick; by this advancement in honour we must suppose that the king had no suspicion of the loyalty of the marquis. I have been more particular in ascertaining the dates of the occurrences in this letter, as they differ from some of those in our historians.
[10] The name of the writer is not put to this letter, but at the end, in a hand of the time, though in a different one from that used in the letter, is written "for trowyth."

It is so, that on Wednesday last past ye and I, Pampyng, and Edmund Broom were indicted of felony at the sessions here in Norwich, for shooting off a gun at Caister, in August last past, which gun slew two men, I Pampyng, and Broom as principal, and ye as accessary, notwithstanding Townshend and Lomner hold an opinion that the verdict is void, for there were two of the inquest that would not agree to the indictment, and inasmuch as they two were agreed in other matters and not in that, and that they two were not discharged from the remnant at such time as that verdict of your indictment was given, their opinion is that all the verdict is void, as well of all other matters as of yours, whether their opinion be good or not I cannot determine, nor themselves neither.

I pray you let not this matter be slept, for I can think that my Lord of Norfolk's counsel will cause the widows to take an appeal, and to remove it up into the King's Bench at the beginning of this term; Townshend hath promised me that he shall be at London on Tuesday next coming, and then ye may commune with him in that matter, and take his advice.

Item, Townshend and Lomner think that and (*if*) ye have good counsel, ye may justify the keeping of the place for the peaceable possession that ye have had in it more than three year; but in conclusion, all this is done for nought else but for to enforce you to take a direction with my Lord of Norfolk.

I understood by R. Southwell, for he and I communed in this matter right largely betwixt him and me, insomuch he telleth me that and (*if*) I be at London in the week next after St. Peter, at which time he shall be there himself, he saith that my lady hath promised me her good ladyship, and sent me word by him, inasmuch as he spake for me to her, that she would remember mine old service, and forget the great displeasure, in

such wise that I shall understand that the suit that I have made to my lord, her husband, and her, shall turn to your advantage and mine more than we ween as yet or shall understand till such time as I have spoken with her good grace; and upon this promise I have promised Southwell to meet with him at London that same week next after St. Peter; wherefore I would passingly fain that ye were in London at that season, or nigh about London, so that I might understand at your place where that I might speak with you or them (*before*) [1] I speak with my lady.

I purpose to go to Canterbury [2] on foot this next week with God's grace, and so to come to London from thence.

I pray you see that I be safe for Parker's and Harry Collett's matter.

Southwell [3] told me this, that if so be that ye will yourself, ye shall have both good lordship and ladyship, and money, or lands, or both, and all your matters set clear; what that he meaneth I cannot say.

As for all other matters in this country, I shall do as well as I may for fault (*default*) of money till I speak with you: I have many collars on as I shall tell you when I come.

No more, but God preserve you and yours; written at Norwich, Friday next after Corpus Christi day.

JOHN PASTON.

I did as much as I could to have let (*hindered*) the indictments, but it would not be, as I shall inform you, and Townshend knoweth the same.

Norwich,
Friday, 22nd of June, 1470.
10 E IV.

---

1 [In the original—*or then I spek, &c.*—which is clearly *ere then I speak, &c.*]
2 On pilgrimage to the shrine of St. Thomas Becket, I suppose.
3 Richard Southwell, Esq., of Wood-Rising; he acquired this estate by marrying Amy, daughter and co-heir of Sir Edmund Wichingham, knight.

LETTER CCXCVII.—(CIV. vol. iv. p. 435.)

The former part of this letter gives us the same information as we received from the last, and would not have been inserted, had I not thought the account of the proceedings relative to the levying the fine worthy of notice   The being able to produce the copy of the fine shows the propriety of Margaret Paston's cautions to Sir John, respecting the great care which he ought to take of his deeds and writings.

To Sir John Paston, Knight, or to Thomas Stomps, to deliver to the said Sir John.

As I sent you word, by a letter that John Wymondham brought to London, J. Pampyng is indicted of felony, and Edmund Broom, as principals, and ye as accessary, for shooting off a gun in August last past, which gun killed two men, and I trow that my Lord of Norfolk's counsel will make one of the widows or both to sue an appeal upon the same indictment this term, wherefore I pray you see well to this matter, that when it is certified into the King's Bench, Broom and Pampyng may have warning that they may purvey for themselves if there come any capias out for them ; Townshend can tell you all the matter.

Also, ye must in any wise beware, for my grandam,[1] and mine Lady Anne,[2] and mine uncle William, shall be at London within these eight or ten days; and I wot well it is for nought else but to make mine uncle William sure of her land, notwithstanding she hath reared (*levied*) a fine of it before Goodred,[3] the justice, in my grandfather's days; and my mother telleth me that ye have the copy of the same fine, I would advise you

to have it ready whatsoever betide; I trow they will be the more busy about the same matter, because they think that ye dare not come in London nor at Westminster to let them, but if so be that ye have not the copy of the same fine, look that ye spare for no cost to do (*make*) search for it, for it will stand you on hand I feel by the working.

This day sev'nnight I trust to God to be forward to Canterbury at the farthest, and upon Saturday come sev'nnight I trust to be in London, wherefore I pray you leave word at your place in Fleet-street where I shall find you, for I purpose not to be seen in London till I have spoken with you.

I pray you remember these matters, for all is done to make you to draw to an end with these lords that have your land from you. No more, but I pray God send you your heart's desire in these matters and in all others. Written at Norwich, the Monday next after St. John Baptist.

JOHN PASTON.

Norwich, Monday, 25th of June, 1470   10 E IV.

LETTER CCXCVIII.—(XXXIII. vol. ii. p. 41.)

These letters of King Edward were copied, and the copies appear to have been sent inclosed immediately to the person to whom the letter containing them was directed.   The letters were written by the king in 1470, either immediately before he was taken prisoner by the Earl of Warwick, or soon after his escape and re-assuming the government, when a conference was held at Westminster under a safe conduct, or (which is most probable) they were written at the time that the king had ordered his forces to rendezvous at Nottingham, in order to oppose Warwick , when, on the earl's approach, he retreated, and marched for Lynn, in Norfolk, from whence he embarked for Holland   The date will not coincide with the time as fixed by our historians.   The letters are short and concise, but contain everything the writer intended, and, as royal letters, are certainly curious.   The signature at the top is copied from an autograph of King Edward.

---

[1] Agnes, widow of Sir W. Paston, the judge
[2] Anne, daughter of Edmund Beaufort, Duke of Somerset, married William Paston, the uncle of Sir John Paston.

[3] William Goodrede was created a serjeant-at law in 1425, in 1431 he was appointed king's serjeant,and in 1424 became a justice of the King's Bench.

These three letters underwritten, the king of his own hand wrote unto my Lords of Clarence, Warwick, and Archbishop of York. The credence whereof in substance was, that every of them should in such peaceable wise, as they have be (*been*) accustomed to ride, come unto his highness.

Rex Edwardus, to our brother of Clarence.

BROTHER, we pray you to give faith and credence to our well-beloved Sir Thomas Montgomery[1] and Morice Berkley[2] in that on our behalf they shall declare to you; and we trust ye will dispose you according to our pleasure and commandment; and ye shall be to us right welcome. At Nottingham the 9th day of July.

To our cousin the Earl of Warwick.

COUSIN, we greet you well, and pray you to give faith and credence to Sir Thomas Montgomery and Morice Berkley (in that on our behalf they shall declare to you); and we ne trust (*do not believe*) that ye should be of any such disposition towards us, as the rumour here runneth, considering the trust and affection we bear in you. At Nottingham the 9th day of July. And cousin ne (*do not*) think but ye shall be to us welcome.

To our cousin the Archbishop of York.

COUSIN, we pray you that ye will, according to the promise ye made us, come to us as soon as ye goodly may; and that (*ye*) give credence to Sir Thomas Montgomery and Morice Berkley in that on our behalf they shall say to you; and ye shall be to us welcome. At Nottingham the 9th day of July.

Nottingham,
9th of July, 1470.   10 E. IV.

LETTER CCXCIX.—(XXXIV. vol. ii. p. 43.)

Under the direction of this letter is written in a hand of the time "A° x°," which, I suppose, means the 10 E. IV., and accordingly I have so dated this letter, though, had it not been for this memorandum, I should have placed it after that of Sir John Paston to John Paston, Esq., dated 3d of February, 1472-3, 12 E. IV., and to which I refer the reader, as likewise to the letter dated between 8 and 9 November, 1472, 12 E. IV. No. cccxxxi. and cccxxvi.

To my master, Sir John Paston, Knight, be this delivered.

RIGHT worshipful Sir, I recommend me to you, thanking you most heartily of your great cost which ye did on me at my last being with you at London; which to my power I will recompense you with the best service that lyeth in me to do for your pleasure while my wits be my own.

Sir, as for the matter of Caister,[3] it hath been moved to my lady's good grace by the Bishop of Winchester,[4] as well as he could

---

[1] Sir Thomas Montgomery had a command at the battle of Barnet, and was a Knight of the Garter.

[2] Maurice Berkeley was second son of James Lord Berkeley, and in great favour with King Edward. He succeeded his brother William as Lord Berkeley in 1491, and died in 1506.

[3] The estate and the hall at Caister were part of the possessions of Sir John Fastolf, knight. John Paston, father of Sir John, was one of his executors, by which means the Pastons got into possession of this seat, &c. The right of possessing it was disputed both by the Duke of Norfolk, and by King Edward IV., the former in 1469 laying a regular siege to it, the Pastons had at last quiet possession.

[4] William de Wainfleet, or Patten, was a firm adherent to the House of Lancaster; and notwithstanding that, continued Bishop of Winchester from 1447 to 1486.

imagine to say it considering the little leisure that he had with her; and he told me that he had right an agreeable answer of her; but what his answer was he would not tell me; then I asked him what answer I should send you, inasmuch as ye made me a solicitor to his lordship for that matter ; then he bade me, that, under counsel, I should send you word that her answer was more to your pleasure than to the contrary; which ye shall have more plain knowledge of this next term, at which time both my lord and she shall be at London.

The bishop came to Framlingham on Wednesday at night, and on Thursday by ten of the clock before noon my young lady was christened, and named Anne,[1] the bishop christened it and was godfather both ; and within two hours and less after the christening was do, my Lord of Winchester departed towards Waltham. (*Then follows the sub-*

stance of a conversation between the Lady of Norfolk and Thomas Davers, wherein she promises to be a friend to Sir John Paston concerning Caister, but T. Davers swore J. Paston not to mention her good will to any person except to Sir John.) And I let you plainly weet I am not the man I was; for I was never so rough in my master's conceit as I am now, and that he told me himself before Richard Southwell, Tymperley, Sir W. Brandon, and twenty more, so that they that loved not laughed upon me ; no more but god look (*q good luck*).

Written at Framlingham the Friday next after that I departed from you. This day my lord is towards Walsingham, and commanded me to overtake him to-morrow at the farthest.

J. Paston.

Framlingham,
Friday, 1470. 10 E. IV.

LETTER CCC.—(XXXV. vol. ii. p. 47.)

This letter was written at a time when the nation was in a most unsettled state, the late king's adherents every day expecting the arrival of the Duke of Clarence and the Earl of Warwick, their new friends   Some expressions in this letter seem to insinuate that Sir John Paston wished well to their cause ; and his putting himself, as soon as the revolution in the government happened, under the protection of the Earl of Oxford, shows he did so.

To J. Paston, &c.

BROTHER, I commend me to you, &c. (*Here follows an order about searching for some writings, &c.*) Also tell John Pampyng that the maid at the Bull at Cludey's at Westminster, sent me on a time, by him, to the Moor, a ring of gold to a token, which I had not of him; wherefore I would that he should send it hither, for she must have it again or else 5s. for it was not hers. Item, I pray you be ready, the matter quickeneth both for you and yours, as well as for us and ours.

As for tidings, my lord archbishop[2] is at the Moor, but there is beleft with him diverse of the king's servants; and as I understand he

hath licence to tarry there till he be sent for. There be many folks up in the north, so that Percy[3] is not able to resist them ; and so the king hath sent for his feodmen to come to him, for he will go to put them down ; and some say that the king should come again to London, and that in haste; and as it is said Courtneys[4] be landed in Devonshire, and there rule.

Item, that the Lords Clarence and Warwick[5] will assay to land in England every day as folks fear.

I pray you let not John Mylsent be long from me, with as much as can be gathered ; and also that ye write to me of all things that

---

[1] Anne, daughter and heir of John Mowbray, the last Duke of Norfolk of that name She was married in 1477 (being quite a child) to Richard Duke of York, second son of Edward IV , who on this marriage was created Duke of Norfolk, &c.
[2] This must mean George Nevile, Archbishop of York, and brother to the Earl of Warwick, who

seems to have been suspected by the king, and left at the Moor as a kind of state prisoner
[3] Henry Percy, the lately created Earl of Northumberland
[4] The Courtneys were late Earls of Devonshire.
[5] These noblemen landed about the beginning of the month following.

I have written to you for, so that I may have answer of everything.

Other things Batchelor Walter, bearer hereof, shall inform you. Written at London, the Sunday next before Saint Lawrence's day.[1]

Also my brother Edmund is not yet remembered; he hath not to live with, think on him, &c.

JOHN PASTON, *knight.*

London,
Sunday, 5th of August, 1470.
10 E. IV.

LETTER CCCI.—(CV. vol. iv. p. 439.)

The original, with the king's signature, from which this letter is copied, is placed in a MS folio volume, containing many curious original state-papers, and copies of state-papers of various dates and reigns, formerly belonging to Sir Edward Coke, and is thus endorsed in his own hand "Privye Seale from Ritchard ye thyrd enhabling Mr Swannes Auncetours to leavye Armes" How he came to mistake this signature for that of Richard III. I cannot conceive, it being so evidently R.E. Rex Edwardus, that of Edward IV , neither was there any invasion intended or expected from France, either in September 1483, in the very beginning of the reign of Charles VIII , or in the following year, when that prince desired a safe conduct for the ambassadors which he intended sending to England This volume came into the possession of that great antiquary Sir Andrew Fountaine, knight, and thence into the valuable library of his nephew and heir Brigg Price Fountaine, Esq of Narford, in Norfolk, whence I copied the above letter, 4th July, 1788. This warrant, under the king's signature and privy seal, seems to have been issued in 1470, after the escape of Edward from his confinement at Middleham Castle, and after his having defeated the Lord Wells near Stamford, when the Duke of Clarence and the Earl of Warwick, returning into France, were reconciled to Queen Margaret, and, aided by Lewis XI., meditated an invasion of England in favour of Henry VI This invasion they accomplished, and landed at Dartmouth in September : on their march they daily increased in numbers, when Edward, on their approach towards him and proclaiming Henry VI., was seized with such a panic that, retreating towards the sea-shore on the Norfolk coast, he embarked aboard a small vessel, and after several escapes from corsairs, &c , he landed safely in Holland, when Henry for a few months reascended the throne A William Swan is mentioned in Letter cccCv ; but whether he is the same person here addressed does not appear.

To our well-beloved William Swan, Gentleman.

REX EDWARDUS. BY THE KING.

TRUSTY and well-beloved, we greet you well, and forsomuch as we be credibly ascertained that our ancient enemies of France, and our outward rebels and traitors, be drawn together in accord, and intend hastily to land in our county of Kent or in the parts thereof near adjoining, with great might and power of Frenchmen utterly to destroy us and our true subjects and to subvert the common weal of the same our realm.

. We straitly charge and command you, upon the faith and liegeance that ye bear unto us, that ye arredie (*make ready*) you with all the fellowship ye can make; and as soon as ye may understand that they land in our said county or nearby, that ye draw thither, as we have commanded other our subjects to do, and put you in uttermost devoir, with them to resist the malice of our said enemies and traitors ; and if they and ye be not of power so to do, that then ye draw you to our city of London, by which time we trust to be there in our person or nearby; and if we be not that, that then ye do farther all ye shall be commanded by our council there, upon the pain above said.

Given under our signet, at our city of York, the seventh day of September.

York, Friday,
7th of September, 1470.
10 E. IV.

---

[1] St. Laurence's day is the 10th of August.

LETTER CCCII.—(XXXVI. vol. ii. p 51.)

This letter was written after the flight of Edward, and very soon after the restoration of Henry VI to the throne Sir John Paston, and his brother John Paston, the writer of this letter, had been and still were of the household of the Duke of Norfolk, but were now making their court to the Earl of Oxford , and hoped by his favour to have appointments under this new government, which took place the beginning of October. [This letter is a curious specimen of the rapidity and facility with which changes took place, even among the great political characters of the time, and the subservience of the Duke of Norfolk to the Earl of Oxford is very strikingly marked]

To my right worshipful mother, Margaret Paston, be this delivered.

AFTER humble and most due recommendation, as lowly as I can I beseech you of your blessing. Please it you to weet, that, blessed be God, my brother and I be in good hele (*health*); and I trust that we shall do right well in all our matters hastily; for my Lady of Norfolk[1] hath promised to be ruled by my Lord of Oxford[2] in all such matters as belong to my brother and to me; and as for my Lord of Oxford, he is better lord to me, by my truth, than I can wish him in many matters; for he sent to my Lady of Norfolk by John Bernard only for my matter, and for none other cause, mine on weeting (*forgetting*),[3] or without any prayer of me, for when he sent to her I was at London and he at Colchester, and that is a likelihood he remembered me.

The Duke and the Duchess sue to him as humbly as ever I did to them ; insomuch that my Lord of Oxford shall have the rule of them and theirs, by their own desires and great means.

As for the offices that ye wrote to my brother for and to me, they be for no poor men; but I trust we shall speed of other offices meetly for us For my master the Earl of Oxford biddeth me ask and have. I trow (*think*) my brother Sir John shall have the constableship of Norwich Castle, with 20*l.* of fee: all the lords be agreed to it.

Tidings, the Earl of Worcester[4] is like to die this day, or to-morrow at the farthest; John Pilkington, M. W. at Clyff, and Fowler, are taken, and in the castle of Pomfret, and are like to die hastily without they be dead. Sir Thomas Montgomery and Joudone be taken, what shall fall of them I cannot say.

The Queen[5] that was, and the Duchess of Bedford,[6] be in sanctuary at Westminster; the Bishop of Ely,[7] with other bishops are in Saint Martin s ; when I hear more I shall send you more , I pray God send you all your desires. Written at London on Saint Edward s even.

Your son and humble servant,
J. PASTON.

London, Thursday,
11th of October, 1470,
10 E IV (49 H VI)

Mother, I beseech you that Brome may be spoken to to gather up my silver at Guyton in all haste possible. for I have no money. Also that it like you, that John Milsent may be spoken to, to keep well my grey horse an (*if*) he be alive, and that he spare no meat on him, and that he have cunning leeches to look to him. As for my coming home I know no certainty, for I tarry till my Lady of Norfolk come to go through with the matters, and she shall not be here till Sunday.

1 John Mowbray, Duke of Norfolk, Elizabeth, daughter of John Talbot, first Earl of Shrewsbury, Duchess of Norfolk.
2 John de Vere, a firm friend to the House of Lancaster, and who, during the short exaltation of Henry, was amongst the first statesmen of that party. He died 10th of March, 1412, 4 H VIII.
3 [On weeting is unweeting—without his knowledge]
4 John Tiptoft, Lord Treasurer and Lord Constable, absconded on the departure of his royal master, but was taken in Weybridge Forest, in Huntingdonshire, concealed in a tree, and being brought to the Tower, was there beheaded upon a charge of cruelty, on the 18th of October, 1470.
5 Elizabeth, Queen of Edward IV.
6 Jaqueline, of Luxemburgh, Duchess-dowager of Bedford, and widow of Sir Richard Widville or Woodville, mother to Elizabeth.
7 William Gray, a man of family and great learning, was placed in this see by Pope Nicholas V. in 1454 He was lord treasurer to Edward IV., and died in 1478.

LETTER CCCIII.—(CVI. vol. iv. p. 441.)

We here see the various artifices that had been made use of to bring forward this appeal against the Pastons, and the pains that had been taken by those who seemed to have been their friends to distress them by it. The endeavours used to induce the widow to put herself under the Duke of Norfolk's protection, and to become his vassal under the different titles of waive and widow, are curious, and throw some light upon the feudal system I do not exactly understand the sense in which the word weve or waive is used here, farther than it means to convey the idea of subjection The widow, however, chose to be her own mistress in the second year, and to take another husband.

To his worshipful master, John Paston, Esquire.

RIGHT worshipful Sir, I commend me to your good mastership, &c. Please it you to understand that Redford desired me, on your behalf, that I should go and commune with the woman that was the fuller's wife at South Walsham, which woman is now married to one Thomas Styward, dwelling in the parish of Saint Giles in Norwich; which woman said to me that she sued never the appeal, but that she was by subtle craft brought to the New Inn at Norwich, and there was Master Southwell, and he intreated her to be my lord's wewe (*waive*)[1] by the space of an whole year next following, and thereto he made her to be bound in an obligation; and when that year was past, he desired her to be my lord's widow another year; and then she said that she had lever (*rather*) lose that that she

had done than to lose that and more, and therefore she said plainly that she would no more of that matter, and so she took her an husband, which is the said Thomas Styward; and she saith that it was full sore against her will that ever the matter went so far forth, for she had never none avail thereof but it was sued to her great labour and loss, for she had never of my lord's counsel but barely her costs to London. No more, but God have you in his keeping. Written at Norwich, the Monday next after the feast of Saint Luke.

By your servant,

R. L.

Monday,
22d of October, 1470.
10 E IV

LETTER CCCIV.—(CVII. vol. iv. 445.)

The date of this letter from J. Paston, the younger, to his mother, cannot be certainly ascertained, though I think I may venture to fix it between 1470 and 1474.

To my right worshipful mother, Margaret Paston, at Mawteby.

RIGHT worshipful mother, after all humble recommendations, as lowly as I can I beseech you of your blessing. Please you to weet that late yesternight I came to Norwich, purposing to have been at this day with you at Mawteby, but it is so that I may not hold my purpose, for he that shall pay me my quarter wages[2] for me and my retinue is in

Norwich, and waiteth hourly when his money shall come to him; it is one Edmund Bowen of the Exchequer, a special friend of mine, and he adviseth me to tarry till the money be come, lest that I be unpaid, "for who cometh first to the mill, first must grind."

And as I was writing this bill, one of the grooms of my lord's chamber came to me, and told me that my lady[3] will be here in

---

[1] [The original is *wewe*—may it not be meant for *widow*? If not, *waif* is used in its ordinary sense of a *stray* appertaining to the manorial lord, she having been deprived of her husband and natural protector, and thence, feudally, recurring to her lord.]

[2] We are here informed that those who had engaged in the king's service received their pay out

of the Exchequer quarterly, for themselves and their waged men

[3] Elizabeth, Duchess of Norfolk, wife of John Mowbray the last Duke of Norfolk of that name, was most probably on her way in pilgrimage to the image of our Lady at Walsingham, to offer at her shrine, and to obtain through her intercession an easy pregnancy and happy delivery.

Norwich to-morrow at night towards Walsing-ham, which shall I wot well be another let to me, but I had more need to be otherwise occupied than to await on ladies, for there is as yet I trow no spear that shall go over the sea so evil horsed as I am, but it is told me that Richard Calle hath a good horse to sell, and one John Butcher of Oxborough hath another, and if it might please you to give Sym leave to ride into that country at my cost, and in your name, saying that ye will give one of your sons an horse, desiring him that he will give you a pennyworth for a penny, and he shall, and the price be reasonable, hold him pleased with your payment out of my purse, though he know it not ere his horse depart from his hands. Mother I beseech you, and (if) it may please you to give Sym leave to ride on this message in your name, that he may be here with me to-morrow in the morn-ing betimes, for were I once horsed I trow I were as far forth ready as some of my neigh-bours.

I heard a little word that ye purposed to be here in Norwich the next week, I pray God it be this week.

Mother, I beseech you that I may have an answer to-morrow at the farthest of this mat-ter, and of any other service that it please you to command me, which I will at all seasons (be) ready to accomplish with God's grace, whom I beseech to preserve you and yours.

Written at Norwich, this Wednesday in Easter week,

By your son and servant,

JOHN PASTON.

Norwich, Wednesday, April, between 1470 and 1474. 10 and 14 E IV.

LETTER CCCV.—(CVIII. vol. iv. p. 419.)

The wages due to these men was for their attendance, under the command of the Duke of Suffolk at the battle of Lincoln Field, usually called the battle of Stamford, where the king [Edw. IV], in the beginning of March, 1469-70, obtained a complete victory over the rebel forces, commanded by the son of Lord Welles, who, being there taken prisoner, was a few days after beheaded On the news of this defeat the Duke of Cla-rence and the Earl of Warwick repaired to Exeter, from thence they went to Dartmouth, and there, about May, embarked, for France. We find by this letter that the king's army followed them to Exeter. This letter by the date appears to have been written just about the time of Edward's leaving the kingdom, when Henry VI was re-instated on the throne, unless the payment of the men had been longer delayed; if so it was not written till after Edward's return and re-accession. [They were of course Lancasterians, as Suf-folk himself was; and this letter must have been written during Henry's short restoration They had retreated to Exeter, and had probably had no chance of obtaining payment till this time. The battle was fought, March 12, at Erpingham in Rutlandshire]

To the Bailiffs, Constables, and Chamberlains of our Borough of Eye, and to every of them.

THE DUKE OF SUFFOLK.[1]

FORASMUCH as Edmund Lee and John Barker, which were waged for your town to await upon us in the King's service to Lincoln Field, and from thence to Exeter and (back) again; and for that season, as we be informed, they are not yet fully contented and paid of their wages; wherefore, upon the sight hereof, we will and charge that ye without any longer delay pay them their whole duties accord-ing the covenants that ye made with them, and ye fail not hereof as ye intend our plea-sure. Written at Wingfield, the 22nd day of October.

SUFFOLK.

Wingfield, Monday, 22nd of October, 1740. 10 E. IV.

[1] John de la Pole, Duke of Suffolk, died in 1491.

LETTER CCCVI.—(CIX. vol. iv. p. 451.)

It appears plainly from the contents of this letter, that it was written during the short time that Henry VI. was in possession of the throne. The Earl of Oxford was coming to Norwich to see how the county of Norfolk stood affected to the present change in the government, and most probably to be present at the election of members to be returned for that city, as well as for the county, to serve in the ensuing parliament. It is a most curious letter, and gives us a very particular description both of the parties and of the politics of the times

To John Paston, Esq., in haste.

BROTHER. I commend me to you, praying you that this be your guiding, if other folks will agree to the same, that Master Roos, old Knivet,[1] ye, and the worshipfullest that will do for our sake, as Arblaster, John Jenney, Wodehouse,[2] and all other gentlemen that at the day will be in Norwich, that ye all whole as one body come together, that my Lord of Oxford may understand that some strength resteth thereby, which if it be well handled and prove in the handling, I trow Heydon's party will be but an easy comparison; nevertheless, then must ye beware of one pain, and that is this, Heydon will of craft[3] send among you per case (*probably*) six or more with harness, for to slander your fellowship with saying that they be riotous people and not of substance; require the gentlemen above written that if any men be in Norwich of the country that bear any such harness to do (*make*) them leave it, or any glistering bill (*pole-axe*).

The mayor and citizens of Norwich were wont to have a certayne (*a number*) of men in harness of men of the town to the number of two or three or five hundred, which if they now do in like case, these will owe better will to Master Roos and you than to other folks; and if it be so that they thought not to have none such at this time, I think the mayor will do it at the request of Master Roos and you, if lack of time cause (*prevent*) it not.

Item, be well ware of Clopton, for he hath advised my lord to be altogether ruled by Heydon, insomuch he hath reported that all things and all matters of my lord s and in all the country should (*be*) guided by Heydon; if Clopton or Hygham or Lewis John be busy, press into my lord before them, for they be no

sufficient matters, and tell the railing;[4] praying them not to cause my lord to owe his favour, for their pleasure, to some folks there present; for if my lord favour, or they either, by likelihood my lord and they might lose six times as many friends as he should win by their means.

Also, if ye could find the means, Master Roos and ye, to cause (*the*) mayor in my lord's ear to tell him, though he should bind my lord to conceal (*it*), that the love of the country and city resteth on our side, and that other folks be not beloved nor never were; this would do none harm.

If it be so that all things go olyver[5] current with more, to remember that there is out of that country that be not at Norwich, beside me, that be right worshipful, and as worshipful as few belonging to Norfolk, that will and shall do my lord service the rather for my sake and Master Roos's, and the rather if my lord remit not much thing to Heydon's guiding.

Also the goodly means whereby ye best can entreat my cousin Sir William Calthorpe at the said day wse (*advise*)[6] them to cause him, if it will be, to come ye in his company and he in yours, in chief at your chief show, and Master Roos and he in company, letting my said cousin weet that I told him once that

---

[1] John Knevet, Esq, of Buckenham Castle
[2] Sir Edward Wodehouse, knight, of Kimberley in Norfolk.
[3] This is a curious scheme, and worthy the conductor of a modern election contest.

[4] [In the original " for the be no suff. mat?ys, and tell the rayling" We think the translation should be " for they be no sufficient masters, and tell the real thing," i e the truth]
[5] This appears to be the word in the original, but the meaning of it I shall be glad to have explained. [May it not be *clever*—cleverly *If it be so that all these things, with more, go cleverly current*, that is smoothly, *then to remember*, &c. This appears to us the construction The whole letter is very obscurely worded; we have altered even more of the punctuation here than elsewhere, and a few of the words that appeared wrong translated, and we trust the meaning is now generally to be understood.]
[6] [*Wse* is probably *use*—" the goodly means.... use them to cause him," &c]

I should move him of a thing I trusted should be increasing both to his honour and weal.

I sent you a letter, come to Norwich by likelihood, to you on Monday last past, it came somewhat the later, for I wend (*to*) have died not long before it.

Also, I received one from you by Master Blomvile yester even. Tell my cousin W. Yelverton[1] that he may not appear of a while in no wise, I trow my cousin his father shall send him word of the same; do that ye can secretly that my lord be not heavy lord unto him · it is understood that it is done by the craft of Heydon, he gat him into that office to have to be against me, and now he saith that he hath done all that he can against me, and now may do no more, now he would remove him.

The day is come that he fasted the even for, as an holy young monk fasted more than all the convent, after that for his holiness and fasting hoped to be abbot, which afterward was abbot, then left he his abstinence, saying, "the day was come that he fasted the even for."

Brother, I pray you recommend me to my Lord of Oxford s good lordship; and whereas I told my lord that I should have awaited upon his lordship in Norfolk, I would that I might so have done lever (*rather*) than an hundred pound ; but in good faith these matters that I told my lord (*I*) trowed should let me

were not finished till yesterday, wherefore of that cause, and also since Hallowmass every other day must not hold up mine head, nor yet may, insomuch that since the said day, in Westminster Hall and in other place, I have gone with a staff as a ghost, as men said, more like that I rose out of the earth than out of a fair lady's bed, and yet am in like case, saving I am in good hope to amend, wherefore I beseech his lordship to pardon me, and at another time I shall make double amends, for by my troth a man could not have hired me for five hundred marks (333*l*. 6*s*. 8*d*.) with so good will to have ridden into Norfolk, as to have at this season there to have awaited on his lordship ; and also I would have been glad, for my lord should have known what service that I might have done his lordship in that country.

Item, your gear is sent to you as Thomas Stomps saith, saving Mylsent s gear and the chaffron which I cannot intreat Thomas Stomps to go there for this three or four days, wherefore I knocked him on the crown, &c.

Item, look that ye take heed that the letter were not broken[2] ere that came to your hands, &c Written at London, on Thursday next after Saint Erkenwald's day[3] (*14th November*).

JOHN PASTON, *knight.*

London, Thursday,
15th of November, 1470,
10 E. IV. (49 H VI)

LETTER CCCVII.—(CX. vol. iv. p. 459.)

These facetious verses seem to have been written without any regard to quantity, the rhyming of the lines in each stanza appears to be all that was attended to, they are here produced only as a specimen of the Latin poetry of the age, for other merit of any kind they have none, as they abound in false quantity, false concord, &c &c They were written by the seneschal of the Earl of Oxford, but to whom, unless by the Black Knight we may suppose Sir John Paston to be intended, it is not to be discovered.

Senescallus Comitis Oxoniæ nigro Militi.

Non decet senescallo tam magni comitis
Ut comes Oxoniæ verbis in Anglicis
Scribere epistolas, vel suis in nunciis
Aliquid proponere si non in Latinis.

Igitur ille pauperculus prædicti comitis
Magnus senescallus magni comitatis
Nuncupatur Norff Latinis in verbis
Apud Knapton in curiâ in formâ judicis.

---

[1] William Yelverton had been in the interest of Edward IV. and therefore durst not appear till he had secured a pardon from the present government.

[2] The caution concerning the safe delivery of the letter unopened is worthy of observation

[3] Erkenwald, Bishop of London, founded one monastery at Chertsey, in Surrey, for men, and another at

Barking, in Essex, for women, who before that time were often obliged to retire into France for want of a proper retreat in England He was the son either of Offa or Ina, a king of the East Angles, and died at Barking, in the latter end of the seventh century, when his body was interred in his own cathedral, but was taken up in 1148, and deposited anew with great veneration, on the 14th of November.

Tibi nigro militi salutem, et omnibus
  Notifico, quod Langdon ille homunculus
Nullam pecuniam liberare vult gentibus,
    Quod est magnum impedimentum nostris
      operibus;

Idcirco tibi mando sub pœnâ contemptûs,
    Quod tu indilate propriis manibus
Scribas tuas litteras, quod ille homunculus
    Copiam pecuniæ deliberat gentibus :

Sin autem per litteras has nostras patentes
  Ego and operarii, qui sunt consentientes
Omnes unâ voce promemus suos dentes
  Nisi liberet pecuniam, cum simus egentes.

Teste meipso apud Knapton predicta,
  Est et mihi testis Maria Benedicta,
Quod vicesimo die Julii non inderelicta
  Erat summe solidi, res hæc non est ficta.
  20th of July.

LETTER CCCVIII.—(XXXVII. vil. ii. p. 55.)

Sir Thomas de Vere, knight, was third brother to John de Vere, Earl of Oxford It appears from this letter, that the county of Norfolk was in the interest of Henry VI , and by the orders which it contains, that the Earl had had advice from his brother of the appearance of Edward's fleet on that coast, and of its proceeding from thence to the north. Holinshed informs us that Edward came before Cromer, in Norfolk, on the 12th of March, where he sent on shore Sir Robert Chamberlaine, Sir Gilbert Debenham, and others, to understand how the country stood affected They found the vigilance of the Earl of Oxford, and the great preparations he had made, were such, that it would be unsafe to land, and therefore they steered northwards.

To my right dear and well-beloved Brother, Thomas Vere.

RIGHT dear and well-beloved brother, I commend me heartily unto you; certifying you that I have received your writing, directed now last unto me, by my servant William Cooke, by which I understand the faithful guiding and disposition of the country to my great comfort and pleasure; which I doubt not shall redound to the greatest praising and worship that ever did till (*to*) any country; certifying you farthermore that by Nicheson of your other tidings last sent unto me; also these by Robert Porter. I have disposed me with all the power that I can make in Essex and Suffolk, Cambridgeshire, and other places to be on Monday next coming at Bury, which purpose I intend to observe with God's grace, towards you into Norfolk, to the assistance of you and the country, in case Edward with his company had arrived there, and yet I shall do the same notwithstanding; for if he

arrive northward, like as ye weet by likelihood he should, I cast (*intend*) to follow and pursue him, and where(*as*) ye desire that I should send you word what disposition shall be taken in the country where ye be, I desire you, that ye, by the advice of the Gentlemen which be there, chuse three or four and send them to me at Bury on Monday next; and then I and they, with my council, shall take a direction for the surety of all that country by God's grace; by whom I shall send then to you relation whether ye shall remain still there yourself, or resort to me with all those that be accompanied with you, and Jesu preserve you. At Hithingham (*Heningham*) the 14th day of March.

By your loving brother,
                    OXYNFORD.

Heningham, or Hedingham Castle, in Essex,
  14th of March, 1470, 11 E. IV. (49 H. VI.)

LETTER CCCIX.—(XXXVIII. vol. ii. p. 59.)

This spirited letter was written immediately after notice of the landing of Edward at Ravenspur, in Yorkshire, on the 14th of March; but whether the forces raised in Norfolk, and the neighbouring counties, marched towards Newark does not appear :—if they did, they and those they might meet there, never faced Edward's army, which came forwards to the Earl of Warwick's forces entrenched at Coventry. Edward there made a feint of attacking them, but being joined by his brother the Duke of Clarence, it was determined to omit that, and proceed immediately to London; where he arrived on the 11th of April without opposition, and instantly re-assumed the government of the kingdom.

To my right trusty and well-beloved Henry Spilman, Thomas Seyve, John Seyve, James Radclif, John Brampton the elder, and to each of them.

TRUSTY and well beloved, I commend me to you, letting you weet that I have credible tidings that the king's great enemies and rebels, accompanied with enemies estrangers, be now arrived and landed in the north parts of this his land, to the utter destruction of his royal person, and subversion of all his realm, if they might attain; whom to encounter and resist, the king's highness hath commanded and assigned me, under his seal, sufficient power and authority to call, raise, gather, and assemble, from time to time, all his liege people of the shire of Norfolk, and other places to assist, aid, and strengthen me in the same intent.

Wherefore, in the king's name, and by authority aforesaid, I straitly charge and command you, and in my own behalf heartily desire and pray you that, all excuses laid a-part ye and each of you, in your own persons, defensibly arrayed, with as many men as ye may goodly make, be on Friday next coming at Lynn, and so forth to Newark; where with the leave of God I shall not fail to be at that time; intending from thence to go forth with the help of God, you, and my friends, to the rencounter of the said enemies; and that ye fail not hereof, as ye tender the weal of our said sovereign Lord and all this his realm.

Written at Bury, the 19th day of March.
OXYNFORD.

Bury, 19th of March,
1470, 11 E. IV. (49 H. VI.)

LETTER CCCX.—(XXXIX. vol. ii. p. 61.)

To the right worshipful and special singular master, Sir John Paston, Knight, be this delivered.

AFTER due recommendation had, with all my service, &c. (*Here follow copies of indictments and appeals procured against Sir John Paston, and his servants;—and likewise other law business.*)

As for tidings, here in this country be many tales, and none accord with other; it is told me by the under-sheriff that my Lord of Clarence is gone to his brother late king; inso-much that his men have the gorget on their breasts, and the rose over it. And it is said that the Lord Howard [1] hath proclaimed King E(*dward*) king of England in Suffolk.

Yours, and at your commandment,
JAMES GRESHAM.

Latter end of March,
or beginning of April,
1471, 11 E. IV. (49 H. VI.)

LETTER CCCXI.—(XL. vol. ii. p. 63.)

This curious letter was written by Sir John Paston to his mother, the fourth day after the battle of Barnet, wherein he had personally fought; and which may be said to have settled Edward almost securely on the throne, by depriving him of his implacable enemy the great Earl of Warwick, who here fell, most furiously fighting. His brother, the Marquis of Montagu, shared the same fate; Sir John Paston shows himself a true Lancastrian, and even now entertains great hopes of a change of affairs favourable to Henry;—these, I suppose, were raised by the landing of Queen Margaret and her son, Prince Edward, in Dorsetshire, but they proved of short continuance, for at the fatal battle of Tewkesbury, fought on the 4th of May following, her army was totally routed, and herself and son taken prisoners; when the latter was almost immediately most basely murdered in the presence of Edward; and our historians say that this young prince fell by the swords of the Dukes of Clarence and Gloucester, and of the Lords Dorset and Hastings. He was only eighteen years of age, and was buried, without any funeral pomp, in the church of the Black Friars, in Tewkesbury. It seems somewhat surprising that Sir John should commit to paper his wishes and opinions so fully at a time when he was scarcely at liberty himself, and had reason to fear that, if his sentiments were discovered, his life might be in danger. [Hall is the first historian who mentions Clarence and Gloucester

[1] John Howard, afterwards the first Duke of Norfolk of that name.

as participating in this murder. The monk of Croyland, a contemporary, merely says it was done by " certain persons;" and Fabyan, a boy at the time, that the king " strake him with his gauntlet upon the face; after which stroke so by him received, he was by the king's servants incontinently slain "]

To my Mother.

MOTHER, I recommend me to you, letting you weet, that blessed be God, my brother John (*Paston*) is alive and fareth well, and in no peril of death; nevertheless he is hurt with an arrow on his right arm beneath the elbow; and I have sent him a surgeon, which hath dressed him, and he telleth me that he trusteth that he shall be all whole within right short time.

It is so that John Mylsent is dead, God have mercy on his soul! and William Mylsent is alive, and his other servants all be escaped by all likelihood.

Item, as for me, I am in good case, blessed be God; and in no jeopardy of my life as me list myself; for I am at my liberty if need be.

Item, my lord archbishop [1] is in the Tower; nevertheless I trust to God that he shall do well enough: he hath a safe-guard for him and me both; nevertheless we have been troubled since, but now I understand that he hath a pardon, and so we hope well.

There are killed upon the field, half a mile from Barnet, on Easter day, the Earl of War-wick, the Marquis Montagu,[2] Sir William Tyrell,[3] Sir Lewis Johns, and divers other esquires of our country, Godmerston, and Booth.

And on the King Edward's party the Lord Cromwell,[4] the Lord Say,[5] Sir Humphrey Bourchier[6] of our country, which is a sore moonyd (*moaned*) man here; and other people of both parties to the number of more than a thousand.[7]

As for other tidings, (*it*) is understood here, that the Queen Margaret[8] is verily landed and her son in the west country, and I trow (*believe*) that as to-morrow, or else the next day, the King Edward will depart from hence to her ward to drive her out again.

Item, I beseech you that I may be recommended to my cousin Lomner, and to thank him for his good will to me ward if I had had need, as I understood by the bearer hereof; and I beseech you on my behalf to advise him to be well ware of his dealing or language as yet, for the world I assure you is right queasy (*unsettled*), as ye shall know within this month; the people here feareth it sore.

God hath showed himself marvellously like him that made all, and can undo again when him list; and I can think that by all likelihood shall show himself as marvellous again, and that in short time; and as I suppose oftener than once in cases like.

Item, it is so that my brother is unpurveyed (*unprovided*) of money, I have holpen (*helped*) him to my power and above; wherefore, as it pleaseth you, remember him, for [I] cannot purvey for myself in the same case.

Written at London the Thursday in Easter week.

I hope hastily to see you. All this bill must be secret.[9] Be ye not a doubted (*suspicious*)[10] of the world, I trust all shall be well; if it thus continue I am not all undone, nor none of us; and if otherwise then, &c. &c.

London, Thursday,
18th of April, 1471. 11 E. IV.

[1] George Nevile, Archbishop of York,—it was from the custody of this prelate that Edward escaped, after having been surprised and taken prisoner by the Earl of Warwick in 1470, perhaps the kind treatment of his then prisoner now procured his pardon.

[2] The bodies of these two noblemen were exposed three days to public view in St Paul's Cathedral, and then buried at Bisham Abbey, Berkshire

[3] Sir William Tyrel was cousin to Sir James Tyrel, the afterwards supposed murderer of Edward V. and his brother the Duke of York

[4] Humphrey Bourchier, third son of Henry Earl of Essex, had summons to parliament in 1461, as Lord Cromwell, in right of his wife.

[5] William Fienes, Lord Say.

[6] Son of John Lord Berners.

[7] This number is considerably less than the least

given by any of our historians, who, some of them, made the list of slain to amount to 10,000, others to 4000, and those who speak the most moderately to 1500 men The battle of Barnet began on the morning, and lasted till afternoon on Easter Sunday, the 14th of April, 1471

[8] Queen Margaret, and Prince Edward her son, landed at Weymouth, in Dorsetshire, about the 13th or 14th of April

[9] Sir John had sufficient reason to say, "All this bill must be secret," for if the conclusion of this letter had been seen by the York party, his liberty, if not his life, would have been at stake.

[10] [We rather think *suspected* is meant, i. e. if they do nothing to make them suspected.]

LETTER CCCXII.—(XLI. vol. ii. p. 69.)

This curious and secret letter, without name, date, or direction, was written by some person of consequence in this reign, and I believe by John de Vere, Earl of Oxford, after the unsuccessful battle of Barnet when he retreated with some of his men towards Scotland; but discovering a design to betray him, he privately left them, and went into Wales to join the Earl of Pembroke. The supplies of men and money, &c. herein required to be sent to him were intended to strengthen the queen's army, which was now with the utmost expedition assembling, and which before the Earls of Pembroke and Oxford could join it, was totally routed at Tewkesbury on the 4th of May following.

To the right reverend and worshipful Lady.[1]

RIGHT reverend and worshipful lady, I recommend me to you, letting you weet that I am in great heaviness at the making of this letter; but thanked be God I am escaped myself, and suddenly departed from my men; for I understand my chaplain would have betrayed (*betrayed*) me: and if he come into the country let him be made sure, &c.

Also ye shall give credence to the bringer of this letter, and I beseech you to reward him to his costs; for I was not in power at the making of this letter to give him, but as I was put in trust by favour of strange people, &c.

Also ye shall send me in all haste all the ready money that ye can make; and as many of my men as can come well horsed, and that they come in divers parcels.

Also that my horses be sent with my steel saddles, and bid the yeoman of the horse cover them with leather.

Also ye shall send to my mother,[2] and let her weet of this letter and pray her of her blessing, and bid her send me my casket by this token; *that she hath the key thereof, but it is broken.*

Also ye shall send to the Prior of Thetford,[3] and bid him send me the sum of gold that he said that I should have; also say to him by this token;[4] *that I showed him the first privy seal, &c.*

Also let Paston, Felbrig, and Brews, come to me.

Also ye shall deliver the bringer of this letter an horse, saddle, and bridle.

Also ye shall be of good cheer, and take no thought (*be not melancholy*), for I shall bring my purpose[5] about now by the grace of God who have you in keeping.

Ⓞ . . . . . . 𝔇.[6]

April, 1471. 11 E. IV.

LETTER CCCXIII.—(I. vol. v. p. 3.)

[THIS letter is from J. Paston to his mother, and contains an account from J. Paston himself, of his wounded state, and great want of money, confirmatory of the letter of Sir J. Paston his brother (cccxi.). It was written in London, April 30, 1471; and although he says "now I have neither meat, drink, clothes, leechcraft, nor money, but upon borrowing, and I have essayed my friends so far that they begin to fail now in my greatest need;" yet he is in high spirits, most probably from his knowledge of Queen Margaret's return, and of a large army having assembled in her favour. He appears to have

[1] Margaret, daughter of Richard Nevile, Earl of Salisbury, and sister to the late Earl of Warwick, and wife of John de Vere, Earl of Oxford.
[2] Elizabeth, daughter and heir of Sir John Howard, knight, who was uncle to John Howard, first Duke of Norfolk of that name. She was now the widow of John de Vere, late Earl of Oxford.
[3] John Vescey, Prior of Thetford, from 1441 to 1479.

[4] The precision of the privy tokens shows the caution observed, lest the money, &c. should be fraudulently obtained by making use of his name only.
[5] This shows the expectations formed by this last attempt of the Queen and Prince Edward.
[6] The first character of this signature may be supposed to resemble an O, and the last a D, though this is *only* supposition.

been very sanguine of her success, for he says " it shall not be long to or than (*before*) my wrongs and other men's shall be redressed, for the world was never so like to be ours as it is now;" but a few days after the battle of Tewkesbury was fought, and the queen totally defeated. One of the principal objects of the letter was to procure money. "Mother, I beseech you, and ye may spare any money, that ye will do your alms on me and send me some in as hasty wise as possible." His horses, however, appear to have as much or even more of his attention than his own affairs. His directions are most minute ; one, " if he be not takyn up for the king's hawks," is to have " as much meat as he may eat ;"

" that he have every week three bushels of oats, and every day a pennyworth of bread ;" others are to " be put to some good grass in haste." He writes also for several articles of his wardrobe, and desires his mother most particularly " that nobody look over my writings ;" and he adds, no doubt anticipating the success of his party, " I thank God I am whole of my sickness, and trust to be clean whole of all my hurts within a sev'nnight at the farthest, by which time I trust to have other tidings ; and those tidings once had, I trust not to be long out of Norfolk." The letter is signed John of Gelston, from Geldestone in Norfolk, where he sometimes resided.]

LETTER CCCXIV.—(II. vol. v. p. 7.)

[THE battle of Tewkesbury was fought on May 4, 1471, and in this letter, like the last, from J. Paston to his mother, dated July 17, he tells her, " that this Wednesday Sir Thomas Wingfield sent for me, and let me weet that the king had signed my bill of pardon, which the said Sir Thomas delivered me ; and so, by Friday, at the farthest, I trust to have my pardon ensealed by the chancellor, and soon after, so as I can furnish me, I trust to see you." The sudden turns in political events and in the personal opinions of men are perhaps not more remarkable in these times than our own, but when the weightiest arguments were swords or bullets, it is gratifying to observe how little rancour existed in the middle classes, at least against each other. With the leaders of course the

downfal or ruin of one was necessary to the rise or maintenance of the other ; but among their followers the ties of family, relationship, friendship or acquaintance, though not sufficient to prevent their taking opposite sides in political matters, were seldom ineffectually urged by the defeated towards their conquerors. We have repeated instances in these letters of the interference of friends to procure pardons for their political opponents, and the present is one instance of the facility with which they were granted. J. Paston does not forget his horses in this letter, "he would fain his gray horse were kept in mewe for gnattys," that is, kept in the stable (or mews as is often now used in London) to preserve him from the gnats or flies ; and all are to have as much meat as they will eat.]

LETTER CCCXV.—(XLII. vol. ii p. 73.)

This letter contains no anecdotes of much consequence, yet we may learn from it how little intercourse was kept up between one part of the kingdom and another, no opportunity perhaps having occurred of sending a letter from Norwich to London, unless at the time of the fair ; another thing strikes us, which is, the use that pilgrims were of in conveying intelligence. The advice which Sir John hints to his brother is good, and his anxious concern for the safety of his young brethren gives us a favourable opinion of his kind disposition towards them.

To Mrs. Margaret Paston, or to John Paston, Esquire, her son, in haste.

RIGHT well-beloved brother, I commend me to you, letting you weet that I am in welfare, I thank God, and have been ever since that I spake last with you ; and marvel for that ye sent never writing to me since ye departed; I heard never since that time any word out of Norfolk ; ye might at Bartholomew fair[1] have had messengers enough to London, and if ye had sent to Wykes he should have conveyed it to me. I heard yesterday that a Worsted man of Norfolk, that sold worsteds at Winchester, said that my Lord of Norfolk and my lady were on pilgrimage at our lady[2] on foot, and so they went to Caister; and that at Norwich one should have had large language to you, and called you traitor,[3] and picked many quarrels to you; send me word thereof; it were well done that ye were a little surer of your pardon than ye be; avise you, I deem ye will hereafter else repent you.

I understand that Bastard Fauconbridge[4] is either headed or like to be, and his brother both; some men say he would have deserved it and some say nay.

I purpose to be at London the first day of the term, send me word whether ye shall be there or not.

Item, I would weet whether ye have spoken with my Lady of Norfolk or not, and of her disposition and the household's to me and to you wards, and whether it be a possible (*thing*) to have Caister again and their good wills, or not.

And also I pray you understand what fellowship and guiding is in Caister; and have a spy resorting in and out, so may ye know the secrets amongst them.

There is much ado in the North, as men say; I pray you beware of your guiding, and in chief of your language, so that from henceforth by your language no man perceive that ye favour any person contrary to the king's pleasure.

I understand that the Lord Rivers[5] hath licence of the king to go to Portugal now within this sev'nnight.

I pray you recommend me to my mother, and beseech her of her blessing on my behalf. (*Here follow some directions about payments of money.*)

Item, I pray you send me word if any of our friends or well-willers be dead, for I fear that there is great death in Norwich and in other borough towns in Norfolk; for I ensure you, it is the most universal death that ever I wist in England; for by my truth, I cannot hear by pilgrims that pass the country, nor none other man that rideth or goeth any country, that any borough town in England is free from that sickness; God cease it when it please him.[6]

Wherefore, for God's sake, let my mother take heed to my young brethren that they be not in none place where that sickness is reigning, nor that they disport not with none other young people which resorteth where any sickness is ; and if there be any of that sickness dead or enfect (*infected*) in Norwich, for God's sake let her send them to some friend of hers into the country, and do ye the same by mine advice; let my mother rather remove her household into the country.

Even now Thyrston brought me word from London that it was Doctor Allen that caused your trouble that ye had at Norwich; and that John Pampyng rode for a discharge for you, and that he hath sped well, but how that, wot I not; if ye be clear out of Doctor Allen's danger keep you there, and hereafter ye may scoff as well at his carte (*q. cost*) ; I pray you send me word of all the form of his dealing with you.

I had almost spoken with Mrs. Anne Hawte, but I did not, nevertheless this next term I hope to take one way with her or

---

[1] Bartholomew fair, in Smithfield.

[2] Of Walsingham.

[3] This refers to the part he had taken previous to, and at, the restoration of Henry VI.

[4] Thomas Nevile, the natural son of William Lord Fauconberg, called the Bastard Fauconberg, having adhered to Henry VI was, on his taking the government, appointed vice-admiral of the Channel, which place, on the change of affairs, he lost, and being a man of loose character, first turned pirate, and then, landing, collected a large army, with which he attempted to surprise London, where being repulsed, he retired, and on the king's advancing towards him submitted, when he was not only pardoned but knighted, and again appointed vice admiral. This happened in May, 1471, but was of short continuance, for between the 13th and 29th of September following he was beheaded, though whether for any fresh crime or not is uncertain.

[5] On a pilgrimage.

[6] I do not find this year marked by our historians as a year of sickness.

other; she is agreed to speak with me, and she hopeth to do me ease as she saith.

I pray you send me word how ye do with my Lady Elizabeth Bourchier. ye have a little chafed it but I cannot tell how; send me word whether ye be in better hope or worse.

I hear say that the Earl of Oxford's brethren be gone out of sanctuary.[1] Sir Thomas Fulforth[2] is gone out of sanctuary, and a great fellowship fetched him, a three score, and they say that within five miles of London he was 200 men, and no man weeteth (*knoweth*) where he is become not yet. The Lords Hastings and Howard be in Calais and have it peaceably; and Sir Walter Wrottesly and Sir Jeffrey Gate be coming thence, and will be at London this day as it is said.

Written at Waltham beside Winchester the day next Holyrood day.[3]

JOHN PASTON, *knight*.

13th or 15th of September, 1471. 11 E. IV.

LETTER CCCXVI.—(XLIII. vol. ii. p. 81.)

We may from this letter pick out some curious particulars relative to the church of Bromholm Priory in Norfolk, and likewise form some plan of the embattled mansion of the Pastons at Gresham in Norfolk, buildings which are now both in ruins.

To his well-beloved John Paston, Esquire, at Norwich, or to Mrs. Margaret, his mother.

I COMMEND me to you, letting you weet that, &c. (*Here follows an account that the Duchess of Suffolk[4] and Duke of Norfolk intend again commencing appeals against Sir John Paston and his brother, &c. concerning Caister, &c.*) I would fain have the measure where my father lieth at Bromholm;[5] both the thickness and compass of the pillar at his head, and from that the space to the altar, and the thickness of that altar, and imagery of timber work; and what height the arch is to the ground of the aisle, and how high the ground of the choir is higher than the ground of the aisle.

Item, I pray you let the measure by packthread be taken, or else measured by yard, how much is from the north gate where the brigg was at Gresham[6] to the south wall, and in like form from the east side to the west; also the height of the east wall, and the height of the south-east tower from the ground, if ye may easily. Also what breadth every tower is within the wall, and which tower is more than other within. Also how many foot, or what breadth each tower taketh within each corner of the quadrate overthwart[7] the doors, and how many tailor's yards

---

[1] Till the reign of Henry VIII. all our churches and churchyards were sanctuaries, and protected traitors, murderers, &c. if within forty days they acknowledged their fault, and submitted themselves to banishment;—the most eminent sanctuaries in England were St. John's of Beverley, St. Martin's Le Grand, Ripon in Yorkshire, St. Burien's in Cornwall, and Westminster.

[2] Sir Thomas Fulford was son of Sir Baldwin Fulford, beheaded at Bristol in 1461; he likewise ended his life on the scaffold.

[3] Holyrood day, 14th of September.

[4] Elizabeth, sister of Edward IV.

[5] John Paston was most sumptuously buried in the priory church of Bromholm in 1466; these measures, I suppose, were required in order to adopt a plan for his monument.

[6] This mansion, built by the Stutevilles, was, by licence from Edward II., embattled by the Bacons; Sir William Paston, the judge, purchased this estate.

[7] The drawing, here given in the original letter, is intended, by Sir John Paston, for a plan of the quadrangle at Gresham, and if we suppose that the projection in the side represents the bridge, then that must be the north side, and so we have a complete ichnography of the whole.

is from the mote side, where the brigg was, to the highway, or to the hedge all along the entry, and what breadth the entry is between the dikes.

I pray you, if ye have a leisure in any wise, see this done yourself if ye may, or else if Pampyng do it, or who that ye think can do it; I would spend 20*d.*, or as ye seem [*more if you think proper*], to have the certain of everything herein.

And as for my father's tomb I charge you see it yourself, and when I speak with you I will tell you the causes why that I desire this to be done.

As for tidings, the king and the queen and much other people are ridden and gone to Canterbury, never so much people seen in pilgrimage heretofore at once as men say

Also it is said that the Earl of Pembroke[1] is taken unto Bretagne; and men say that the king shall have delivery of him hastily; and some say that the king of France will see him safe, and shall set him at liberty again.

Item, Thomas Fauconbridge his head was yesterday set upon London Bridge looking into Kent ward; and men say that his brother was sore hurt, and escaped to sanctuary to Beverley.

Sir Thomas Fulforth escaped out of Westminster with 100 spears[2] as men say, and is unto Devonshire, and there he hath stricken off Sir John Crokker's head and killed another knight of the Courtenays as men say: I would ye had your very (*absolute*) pardon at once; wherefore I pray you fail not to be at London within four days after Saint Faith's;[3] ye shall do good in many things, and I pray you send me word hereof by the next messenger; and if it come to Mrs. Elizabeth Higgens, at the Black Swan, she shall convey it to me, for I will not fail to be there at London again within this six days.

Mrs. Elizabeth hath a son, and was delivered within two days after Saint Bartholomew;[4] and her daughter A. H. was, the next day after, delivered of another son, as she saith eleven weeks ere her time; it was christened John,[5] and is dead, God save all, no more till I speak with you.

Written at London on Michaelmas even.

JOHN PASTON, *knight.*

Item, I pray you let some witty fellow, or else yourself, go to the towns there as (*where*) these two women dwell, and inquire whether they be married since and again or not, for I hold the hoorys (*whores*) wedded, and if they be, then the appeals were abated thereby. I remember not their names, ye know them better than I. Also in the sheriff's books there may ye find of them.

London,
Saturday, 28th of September, 1471. 11 E IV.

LETTER CCCXVII.—(III vol. v. p. 11.)

[THIS letter is from M. Paston to her son J. Paston, dated November 5, 1471, complaining of his brother, Sir J. Paston, neglecting to forward her money which she had borrowed for him, and for which she was security. She very ingeniously shows how his neglect will ultimately occasion him greater loss. The sum required is one hundred dred marks (66*l.* 13*s.* 4*d.*), and she says ·— "I know not how to do therefore by my troth, for I have it not, nor I cannot make shift therefore and (*if*) I should go to prison; therefore commune with your brother hereof, and send me word how that he will make shift

---

[1] Jasper Tudor de Hatfield, Earl of Pembroke, half brother to Henry VI He went into Brittany, to his nephew Henry Earl of Richmond, whom he attended at Bosworth Field, and was by him created Duke of Bedford, he died in 1495
[2] Spearmen,—men armed with spears.
[3] 5th of October.
[4] 24th of August.

[5] The conclusion of this letter seems to refer to some private amours of Sir John, and if A. H. stand for Anne Hawte, she appears to be a mistress of his; but this is not certain, yet it is probable by the next letter but one that she was his mistress, as he there says "he will tempt God no more so" [If so, it appears strange that the letter should be directed to his brother, even though only as an alternative]

therefore in haste; I must else need sell all my woods, and that shall disavail him better than a cc. marks and I die; and if I should sell them now there will no man give so much for them by near an c. marks as they be worth, because there be so many wood sales in Norfolk at this time." She proceeds to recount how much she has given and paid for Sir John, and makes some threats as to what may take place on her death. The rest of the letter is of country news, deaths, sickness, &c., but she adds, " I send you half a rial (5s.) for to buy with sugar, figs, and dates, for me; I pray ye do as well as ye can, and send it me as hastily as ye may; and send me word what price a pound of pepper, cloves, mace, ginger, cinnamon, almonds, rice, galangal, saffron, raisins of Corinth (*currants*), greynes (*probably grains of Paradise*), and comfits, of each of these send me the price of a pound, and if it be better cheap at London than it is here, I shall send you money to buy with such as I will have."]

LETTER CCCXVIII.—(XLIV. vol. ii. p. 87.)

Margaret queen of Henry VI. was taken after the battle of Tewkesbury, and continued a prisoner till 1475, when she was ransomed by her father, for 50,000 crowns, which he borrowed of Lewis XI. king of France.

To my most honourable and tender mother, Margaret Paston, be this letter delivered.

MOST worshipful and kind mother, I commend me to you, and beseech you of your daily blessing and remembrance. Please if you to weet that I have my pardon,[1] as the bearer hereof can inform you, for comfort whereof I have been the merrier this Christmas; and have been part thereof with Sir George Browne,[2] and with my lady mine aunt his wife; and before Twelfth[3] I came to my lord archbishop,[4] where I have had as great cheer, and been as welcome as I could devise; and if I had been in surety that Caister were had again I would have come homeward this day.

(*Here follow directions about Caister, and a hope that it might be had again by the latter end of the term, when he would come home, and put his lands and houses into order.*) And I beseech you to remember my brother to do his devyr (*endeavour*) that I may have again my stuff[5] my books, and vestments, and my

bedding howsoever he do, though I should give 20 scutas by his advice to my Lady Brandon or some other good fellow.

As for any tidings there be none here, save that the king hath kept a royal Christmas; and now they say that hastily he will north, and some say that he will into Wales, and some say that he will unto the west country. As for Queen Margaret, I understand that she is removed from Windsor to Wallingford, nigh to Ewelm, my Lady of Suffolk's place in Oxfordshire.

And men say that the Lord Rivers shipped on Christmas even into (*unto*) Portugal ward; I am not certain.

Also there shall be a convocation of the clergy in all haste, which men deem will avail the king a dyme (*tenth*) and an half some say. I beseech God send you good health and greater joy in one year than ye have had these seven. Written at the Moor, the 8th day of January, in the 11th of Edward IV.

By your son,

JOHN PASTON, *knight.*

Tuesday,
8th of January, 1471-2. 11 E IV.

---

[1] For joining the friends of Henry VI in order to his restoration
[2] Sir George Browne, knight, of Beechworth Castle, in Surry
[3] Twelfth day, 6th of January.
[4] George Nevile, Archbishop of York
[5] These were what had been taken at Caister, I suppose.

LETTER CCCXIX.—(XLV. vol. ii. p. 91.)

We have in this letter a clue to conduct us towards a discovery of the reason for the Duke of Gloucester's dislike to his brother the Duke of Clarence, and if this account be true it had a reasonable foundation. The Duke of Gloucester was desirous of marrying Anne (now the widow of Prince Edward, so cruelly murdered at Tewkesbury), daughter and co-heir of the great Earl of Warwick, and sister to Isabel Duchess of Clarence. This alliance we here find was opposed by the Duke of Clarence; not from any point of delicacy respecting the murder of this lady's late husband, (for according to our historians he was equally concerned in that horrid act with his brother,) but because he did not relish the thought of parting with her share of the possessions now vested in him, by his wife Isabel, the eldest daughter and co-heir of Richard Nevile, Earl of Warwick; his apparent design being to deprive the younger daughter of her moiety of her paternal inheritance, and retain it all himself. This was the part not only of a covetous but of an unjust man, and very probably produced that spirit of revenge which afterwards ended in his destruction.

To John Paston, Esq., be this letter delivered.

BROTHER, I commend me to you, and pray you to look up my Temple of Glass, [1] and send it me by the bearer hereof.

Item, as for tidings, I have spoken with Mrs. Anne Hawte at a pretty leisure, and blessed be God we be as far forth as we were tofore, and so I hope we shall continue; and I promised her, that at the next leisure that I could find thereto, that I would come again and see her; which will take a leisure as (*I*) deem now, since this observance is over done; I purpose not to tempt God no more so.

Yesterday the king, the queen, my Lords of Clarence and Gloucester, went to Shene to pardon; men say not all in charity; what will fall men cannot say.

The king entreateth my Lord of Clarence for my Lord of Gloucester; and as it is said he answereth that he may well have my lady his sister-in-law, but they shall part no livelihood as he saith, so what will fall can I not say.

This day I purpose to see my Lady of Norfolk [2] again, in good hour be it.

There is proffered me merchants for Sporle wood, God send me good sale when I begin; that poor wood is sorely managed and treated.

Yet wot I not whether I come home before Easter or not, I shall send you word; no more, &c.

Written the first Tuesday of Lent.

JOHN PASTON, *knight.*

Tuesday, 17th of February, 1471-2. 11. E. IV.

LETTER CCCXX.—(XLVI. vol. ii. p. 93.)

The proportioning of the money left, amongst the creditors, to pay the debts, seems to be fair, but how Sir John's part should be justly worth three the best I do not understand. [The letter is a favourable specimen of the epistolary style of the age. The subjects are various though not important, and are all touched upon with a lightness and ease that make the whole interesting. His praise of the Earl of Arran, however, seems somewhat extravagant, though extremely well said.]

To my right worshipful brother, Sir John Paston, Knight.

RIGHT worshipful Sir, I recommend me to you. (*Here follows an account of some money transactions, &c.*) Item, Master John Smythe telleth me that Sir T. Lyney's goods are not able to pay a quarter of his debts that be asked him, wherefore such money as is beleft, it must be divided to every man a part after the quantity, which division is not yet made, but when it is made he hath promised me that your part shall be worth three the best, &c.

Item, as for one of Berney's horse, whoso hath least need to him, he shall cost him 20 marks (13*l.* 6*s.* 8*d.*) not a penny less.

---

[1] A poem, written by Stephen Hawes, who flourished in the 15th century.

[2] Elizabeth Duchess of Norfolk, was the daughter of John Talbot the first Earl of Shrewsbury.

Ye sent me word of the marriage of my
Lady June; one marriage for another one,
Norse and Bedford were asked[1] in the
church on Sunday last past.

As for my sister Anne, my mother will
not remove from W. Yelverton for Bedyngfeld, for she hath communed farther in that
matter since ye were in this country, as it
appeareth in her letter that she sendeth you
by Thyrston.

Tidings here, my Lady of Norfolk is with
child she weneth (*thinketh*) herself, and so
do all the women about her, insomuch she
waits the quickening within these six weeks
at the farthest. Also W. Gurney weneth
that Heydon is sure of Saxthorpe, and that
Lady Boleyn of Guyton.

John Osbern adviseth you to take breath
for the wood sale at Sporle, for he hath cast
it that it is worth as good as nine score pounds.
Beware of Montayn, for he may not pay you
so much money with his ease.

I pray you recommend me to Sir John
Parre with all my service, and tell him by
my troth I longed never sorer to see my
lady than I do to see his mastership; and I
pray God that he arise never a morning from
my lady his wife, without it be against her
will, till such time as he bring her to our
Lady of Walsingham.

Also I pray you to recommend me in my
most humble wise unto the good lordship of
the most courteous, gentlest, wisest, kindest,
most companionable, freest, largest, and
most bounteous knight, my lord the Earl of
Arran,[2] which hath married the king's sister
of Scotland. Hereto he is one the lightest,
delynerst (*nimblest*), best spoken, fairest archer;
devoutest, most perfect, and truest to his
lady of all the knights that ever I was
acquainted with; so would God, my lady
liked me as well as I do his person and most
knightly conditions, with whom I pray you
to be acquainted as (*to*) you seemeth best;
he is lodged at the George in Lombard-
street. He hath a book of my sister Anne's
of the Siege of Thebes, when he hath done
with it he promised to deliver it you. I
pray you let Portland bring the book home
with him. Portland is lodged at the George
in Lombard-street also.

And this I promise you, ye shall not be so
long again without a bill from me, as ye
have been, though I should write how oft the
wind changeth, for I see by your writing ye
crosse it
can be wrath and ye will for little.[3]

Written the 5th day of June.

                          JOHN PASTON.

5th of June, 1472, 12 E. IV.
(Or perhaps it may be 5th of June,
1470, 10 E. IV. See Letter ccxcix.)

LETTER CCCXXI.—(IV. vol. v. p. 17.)

[JOHN Paston in this letter proceeds with the
affairs of Sir J. Lyney's (or Lynes), whose
effects he says, in this country draweth but
5l.; he recommends his brother to send an
inventory of Sir J. Lyney's goods, &c., in
London, "which inventory if once had, ye
shall have as cometh to your part and more
also;" but that "his debts draw 30l. 18s. 6d.
He states also that there is some objections to
Sir J. Paston's bill for the funeral, in which
twenty shillings is charged for wax (lights, we
suppose) "which to Master John Smith's

imagination, and to all other officers of the
court, should not draw past twenty pence."
The rest of the letter is chiefly about his
mother intending to settle her property by
will, and of his own disagreement with Sir
J. Gloys. "Many quarrels are picked to get
my brother Edmund and me out of her (his
mother's) house; we go not to bed unchidden

---

[1] Banns of marriage we here find were published
at this time in the church.

[2] Thomas Boyd, Earl of Arran, in 1466, married
Mary, daughter of James II. and sister of James
III., kings of Scotland. He was appointed regent,
but becoming unpopular, was banished, and died in
exile before 1474.

[3] These two words are crossed as here represented.
and over them is written, " crosse it

lightly; all that we do is ill-done, and all that Sir James and Peacock doth is well-done. Sir James and I be twain: we fell out before my mother, with 'thou proud priest,' and 'thou proud squire,' my mother taking his part, so I have almost beshut the bolt (*barred myself out*) as for my mother's house." This is a curious picture of the discontent and un-happiness arising from the improper predominance of a domestic (Sir James Gloys was priest and confessor to his mother) in a family. Sir James, however, died in 1173, when administration of his effects was granted to Margaret Paston. The letter is dated Wednesday, July 8, 1472.]

LETTER CCCXXII.—(XLVII. vol. ii. p. 99.)

This letter exhibits to us almost a picture of modern manners, in the terms and address used in recommending a member of parliament to the corporation of Maldon. The agent of the great lady writes to the bailiff of the borough, and to the tenants, &c., to use their influence with the electors in favour of Sir John Paston, a friend of the lady's, in the good graces of the king, and in the interest of the council and the lord chamberlain. It appears too, that a seat in parliament was then an object of pursuit, and not a burden laid upon the representative as we are informed by some of our historians; and although we are apt to suppose that there is now more interest made and more bribery used in obtaining a seat in the House of Commons than there was three hundred years ago; the desire of parliamentary interest, we here see, was much the same.—Engines were set at work, the patronage of the great was held out, and promises were made even as at this day; and though the friends of a candidate would not now come from divers parts of the country to Norwich, (see the next letter) break their fasts, and return home again at the expense of the candidate, for a bill amounting to nine shillings and one penny halfpenny, yet the motive is still the same, the manners, customs, and expenses of the times forming the only difference. [The postscript contains also a gently insinuated threat, that he is coming for the rents.]

To my right trusty friend John Carenton, bailiff of Maldon.

RIGHT trusty friend, I commend me to you, praying you to call to your mind, that like as ye and I communed of, it were necessary for my lady and you all, her servants and tenants, to have this parliament as for one of the burgesses of the town of Maldon, such a man of worship and of wit as were towards my said lady; and also such one as is in favour of the king, and of the lords of his council nigh about his person: certifying you, that my said lady for her part and such as be of her council, be most agreeable that both ye and all such as be her farmers and tenants and well-willers, should give your voice to a worshipful knight, and one of my lady's council, Sir John Paston; which stands greatly in favour with my lord chamberlain; and what my said lord chamberlain may do with the king and with all the lords of England, I trow it be not unknown to you most of any one man alive. Wherefore, by the means of the said Sir John Paston to my said lord chamberlain, both my lady and ye of the town could not have a meeter (*properer*) man to be for you in the parliament to have your needs sped (*interests forwarded*) at all seasons. Wherefore I pray you labour all such as be my lady's servants, tenants, and well-willers, to give their voices to the said Sir John Paston, and that ye fail not to speed my lady's intent in this matter as ye intend to do her as great a pleasure as if ye gave her an 100*l.* And God have you in his keeping. Written at Fishly, the 20th day of September.

JAMES ARBLASTER. [1]

I pray you be ready with all the accounts belonging to my lady, at the farthest within eight days next after Pardon Sunday, for then I shall be with you with God's grace, who have you in keeping.

Fishly,
Sunday, 20th of September,
1472. 12 E. IV.

---

[1] James Arblaster, Esq., a gentleman of fortune in the county of Norfolk.

LETTER CCCXXIII.—(XLVIII. vol. ii. p. 103.)

We have here a curious description of the council of a great man, and find it composed of gentlemen of family and fortune. Matters respecting the property of their lord come before them, they debate upon the subject and deliver their opinion; but if that opinion differed from that of the great man, we find he took the liberty of adopting his own.

To my right worshipful brother, Sir John Paston, Knight.

RIGHT worshipful Sir, I recommend me to you; letting you weet that your desire, as for the knights of the shire,[1] was an impossible (*thing*) to be brought about; for my Lord of Norfolk[2] and my Lord of Suffolk[3] were agreed more than a fortnight ago to have Sir Robert Wyngfield and Sir Richard Harcourt, and that knew I not till it was Friday last past. I had sent ere I rode to Framlingham to warn as many of your friends to be at Norwich, as this Monday, to serve your intent as I could; but when I came to Framlingham, and knew the appointment that was taken for the two knights, I sent warning again to as many as I might, to tarry at home; and yet there came to Norwich this day as many as their costs drew to 9s. 11½d. paid and reckoned by Peacock and R. Capron; and yet they did but break their fast and departed; and I thanked them in your name, and told them that ye would have no voice as this day, for we supposed not to be in England when the parliament should be; and so they came not at the Shire-house, for if they had it was thought, by such as be your friends here, that your adversaries would have reported that ye had made labour to have been one, and that ye could not bring your purpose about.

I sent to Yarmouth, and they have promised also to Doctor Aleyn and John Russe to be (*burgesses*) more than three weeks ago.

James Arblaster hath written a letter to the bailiff of Maldon in Essex to have you a burgess there; how Jude shall speed let him tell you when ye speak together.

Sir, I have been twice at Framlingham since your departing; but now the last time the council was there, I saw your letter which was better than well endited. R. C. was not at Framlingham when the council was there,

but I took my own advice, and delivered it to the council with a proposition therewith, as well as I could speak it; and my words were well taken, but your letter a thousand fold better; when they had read it they showed it to my lady;[4] after that my lady had seen it I spoke with my lady, offering to my lord and her your service, and besides that, ye to do my lord a pleasure[5] and her a better, so as ye might depart without any sum specified; she would not tell in that matter, but remitted me again to the council, for she said and she spoke in it till my lord and the council were agreed, they would lay the weight of all the matter on her, which should be reported to her shame; but this she promised, to be helping so it were first moved by the council; then I went to the council and offered before them your service to my lord, and to do him a pleasure, for the having again of your place and lands in Caister 40l., not speaking of your stuff nor thing else; so they answered me your offer was more than reasonable, and if the matter were theirs, they said, they wist (*knew*) what conscience would drive them to, they said they would move my lord with it, and so they did; but then the tempest arose, and he gave them such an answer that none of them all would tell it me; but when I asked an answer of them they said; "And (*if*) some lords or greater men moved my lord with it, the matter were yours;" (keep counsel.) And with this answer I departed, but Sir W. Brandon, Southwell, Tymperley, Harry Wentworth, W. Gurney, and all other of council understand that ye have wrong; insomuch that they moved me that ye should take a recompense of other land to the value, but they would not avow the offer; for I answered them, if they had right they would have offered no recompense; discover not this, but in my reason and (*if*) my lord chamber-

[1] For the county of Norfolk.
[2] John Mowbray
[3] John de la Pole
[4] Elizabeth Duchess of Norfolk.
[5] Make him a present.

lain[1] would send my lady a letter with some privy token between them, and also to move my Lord of Norfolk when he cometh to the parliament, certainly Caister is yours.

If ye miss to be burgess of Maldon, and my lord chamberlain will, ye may be in another place; there be a dozen towns in England that choose no burgess which ought to do it, ye may be set in for one of those towns and (*if*) ye be friended. Also in no wise forget not in all haste to get some goodly ring (*at the*) price of 20s., or some pretty flower of the same price, and not under, to give to Jane Rodon; for she hath been the most special labourer in your matter, and hath promised her good will forth (*in future*); and she doth all with her mistress. And (*if*) my lord chamberlain will he may cause my Lord of Norfolk to come up sooner to the parliament than he should do, and then he may appoint with him for you ere the farm[2] corn be gathered. I proffered but 40l., and if my lord chamberlain proffer my lady the remanent I can think it shall be taken, my lady must have somewhat to buy her a coverchief[3] besides my lord.

A supper that I paid for, where all the council was at Framlingham, 2s. 3d. and my costs at Framlingham twice lying there by eight days, with 9s. 1½d. for costs of the country at Norwich draweth about 20s. I trow more. By our Lady if it be less stand to your harms, and sic remanet 5l 13s. 4d.

I ask no more good of you for all the service that I shall do you while the world standeth, but a goss hawk,[4] if any of my lord chamberlain's men or yours go to Calais, or if any be to get in London; that is a mewed hawk, for she may make you sport when ye come into England a dozen years hence; and to call upon you hourly, nightly, daily, dinner, supper, for this hawk, I pray no more but my brother (*Edmund*), J. Pampyng, Thyrston, J. Myryel, W. Pitt, T. Platting, Jude, Little Jack, Master Botoner and W. Wood to boot, to which persons I pray you to commend me, and if all these list (*be disposed*) to speak to you of this matter when Sir George Browne, W. Knyvet, R Hyde, or any folk of worship and of my acquaintance be in your company, so that they may help forth, (for all is little enough, and ye be not very well willing) I shall so purvey for them, and ever ye come to Norwich, and they with you, that they shall have as dainty victuals and as great plenty thereof for 1d. as they shall have of the treasurer of Calais for 15d.,[5] and ye peradventure a pye of Wymondham to boot, now think on me good lord, for if I have not an hawk I shall wax fat for default of labour, and dead for default of company by my troth. No more, but I pray God send you all your desires, and me my mewed goss hawk in haste, or rather than fail a soar hawk there is a grocer dwelling right over against the Well with two Buckets, a little from Saint Helen s, hath ever hawks to sell.

Written at Norwich the 21st day of September, in the 12th year of Edward IV.

JOHN PASTON.

Rather than fail, a tarssel proved will occupy the time till I come to Calais.

Norwich,
Monday, 21st of September,
1472 12 E IV.

---

[1] William Lord Hastings
[2] Corn paid in part of rent.
[3] A head dress, or handkerchief
[4] From the anxiety here expressed for an hawk, we may judge of the attention which was paid to the diversion of hawking. Latham, in his book of Falconry, says, that a goshawk is the first and most esteemed kind of hawk, that a sore hawk is from the first taking of her from the eiry till she hath mewed her feathers. The tassel, or tiercel, is the male of the goshawk, so called because it is a tierce or third less than the female it appears here that a "grosser," or dealer in foreign fruits, &c, sold hawks.
[5] The attendance on the wars in France, and in our garrisons there, must have been very expensive by this account of the difference in the price of provisions at Calais and at Norwich.

LETTER CCCXXIV.—(V. vol v. p. 25.)

[This letter is from J. Paston to his brother
Sir John, and is little more than a repetition
of his last two letters, complaints of Sir James
Gloys, the want of money, some legal matters,
and his great desire for a hawk.   On this last
topic he writes with an earnestness that may
well raise a smile.   " As for a goshawk, or a
tercel, I weened to have had one of yours in
keeping ere this time, but ' far from eye, far

from heart;' by my troth I die for default of
labour; and it may be by any mean possible
for God's sake let one be sent me in all haste,
for if it be not had by Hallowmas the season
shall pass anon ; memento mei, and in faith
ye shall not lose on it, nor yet much win on
it, by God, who preserve you." Dated Norwich, Sept. 29, 1172.]

LETTER CCCXXV.—(XLIX. vol. ii. p. 113.)

This letter is given as containing a specimen of the free and easy conversation of the time, and shows the
very intimate acquaintance that subsisted between Sir] Paston and the Duchess of Norfolk   Sir William
Brandon, knight, was standard-bearer to the Earl of Richmond, and was slain in Bosworth Field by
Richard III   He was father to Charles Brandon, Duke of Suffolk [who married Mary, sister of Henry VIII.,
and Dowager Queen of France   The conversation seems to have been indeed very " free and easy" on the
part of Sir John.   He seems to have spoken of her as he would of a horse; but it also seems that such
language was not well received   His concluding sneer at his brother's passion for the hawk is well expressed.]

To John Paston, Esq., be this delivered.

Worshipful and well-beloved brother, I
recommend me to you; letting you weet that
I sent you a letter and ring with a diamond ;
in which letter ye might well conceive what
I would ye should do with the same ring,
with many other tidings and things which I
prayed you to have done for me ; which letter
Botoner [1] had the bearing of; it is so now
that I understand that he is either dead or
else hard escaped ; whereof I am right heavy ;
and am not certain whether the said letter
and ring came to your hands or not.

I would not that letter were seen with some
folks, wherefore I pray you take good heed
how that letter cometh to your hands whole
or broken, and in especial I pray you get it
if ye have it not.

Also I pray you feel my Lady of Norfolk's
disposition to me wards, and whether she
took any displeasure at my language, or
mocked or disdained my words which I had
to her at Yarmouth, between the place where
I first met with her and her lodging ; for my
Lady Brandon and Sir William also asked
me what words I had had to her at that time;
they said that my lady said I gave her
thereof,[2] and that I should have said that my

lady was worthy to bear a lord's son,[3] for she
could cherish it and deal warily with it.

In truth either the same, or words much
like, I had to her, which words I meant as I
said ; they say too that I said she took her
ease. Also (*that*) I should have said that
my lady was of stature good, and had sides
long and large, so that I was in good hope she
should bear a fair child ; he was not laced,
nor braced in, to his pain, but that she left
him room to play him in ; they say that I
said my lady was large and great, and that it
should have room enough ;[3] and thus whether
my lady mock me, or they, I wot not; I
meant well by my troth to her and to that
she is with, as any he that oweth her best will
in England ; if ye can by any mean weet
whether my lady take it to displeasure or not,
or whether she think I mocked her, or if she
weet it but lewdness of myself, I pray you
send me word, for I wot not whether I may
trust this Lady Brandon or not.

As for tidings now, here be but few, save
that, as I understand, ambassadors of Brittany
shall come to London to-morrow ; and men
say that the Lord [4] Rivers and Scales shall
hastily come home, and men say that there

---

1 William Botoner, otherwise Worcester.
2 I paid her off, or treated her with unceremonious
language
3 [The words of the original in both passages are
somewhat coarser]

4 Anthony Woodville, Earl Rivers, &c went to
endeavour to obtain possession of the Earls of
Pembroke and Richmond, who were detained as
prisoners by the Duke of Brittany.

s many of the soldiers that went to him into
Brittany been dead of the flux and other
·pidemy, that the remanent should come
1ome with the Lord Scales; and some say that
these ambassadors come for more men , and
his day runneth a tale that the Duke of ¹
Brittany should be dead, I believe it not.

I sent you word of a hawk , I heard not
rom you since; I do and shall do that is
)ossible in such a need.

Also I cannot understand that my Lord of
Norfolk shall come here this time, wherefore
am in a great agony how is best for me to
ue to him for rehaving of my place; that

good lord weeteth full little how much harm
he doth me, and how little good or worship it
doth him. I pray you send me your advice.
No more to you at this time, but God have
you in his keeping.

Written at London, the 4th day of
November, in the 12th year of Edward IV.

I fear me that idleness leadeth your rem;
I pray you rather remember Sir Hugh Laver-
noy's till your hawk come

JOHN PASTON, knight.

London, Wednesday,
4th of November, 1472,
12 E VI

LETTER CCCXXVI.—(L. vol. ii. p. 119.)

should have thought this child was Anne, if it had not been for the memorandum of "Aº. xº." (10 E IV)
on the back of a letter (ccxcix) from John Paston to Sir John Paston, knight, to which I refer the reader
The child here expected therefore, whether boy or girl, died soon after its birth , and whether Sir John's
good wishes, as to the sex of the child, were successful or not, must remain undetermined

To John Paston Esq , be this given.

BROTHER, I commend me to you, letting you
reet, &c. *(The first part of this letter treats
f some money transactions of no consequence,
rc.)*

As for the deliverance of the ring to Mistress Jane Rotton, I doubt not but it shall
be done in the best wise, so that ye shall get
ne a thank more than the ring and I are
worth or deserve.

And whereas ye go to my Lady of Norfolk,
nd will be there at the taking of her chamber,
pray God speed you, and our Lady her, to
er pleasure with as easy labour to overcome
hat she is about, as ever had any lady or

gentlewoman save our Lady herself, and so
I hope she shall to her great joy and all ours ;
and I pray God it may be like her in worship, wit, gentleness, and everything except
the sex.

No more to you at this time, but I will
sleep an hour the longer to-morrow because
I wrote so long and late to-night.

Written between the 8th and the 9th day
of November, in the 12th year of Edward
IV.

JOHN PASTON, knight.

Between the 8th and 9th of November,
1472 12 E. IV.

LETTER CCCXXVII.—(VI. vol. v. p. 29.)

THE beginning of this letter chiefly relates to
he steps taken by Sir J. Paston for the recovery
f Caister, and he writes to his mother, brother,
r Roos to assist him in his efforts. He has
,ot, he writes, the king's letter of recom-
nendation, to an agreement, we suppose, for

he adds "the king hath specially done for
me in this case, and hath put me, and
so have the lords, in right great comfort
that if this fail that I shall have unde-
layed justice." He trusts the duchess will
be his very good lady, but as she is confined,
fears his messenger will not be admitted to
her, nor his brother, to move her in his behalf. In that case, he says, " my mother, if

¹ Francis II., the last Duke of Brittany, was born
u 1435, and died in 1488.

she were at Norwich she might speak with her, for that she is a woman and of worship." In order further "to move" the duchess, he says, "where [whereas] that heretofore I would have departed with an hundred marks (66l. 13s. 4d.) to have had her good help, and to be restored to my place, which, not accepted, I told my said lady that I feared my power should not be hereafter to give so large a pleasure; for at that time I was in hope that the Bishop of Winchester should have paid it, though it had drawn an hundred pound : yet forasmuch as men may not lure none hawks with empty hands, I would yet agree to give my lady 20l. for a horse and a saddle, so that I be restored to my place." One other passage is remarkable for the independent and somewhat chivalrous spirit shown in it. He tells his brother, " ye may largely say on my behalf for such service as I should

to my lord and lady hereafter, which by my troth, I think to do; nevertheless to say that I will be his sworn man, I was never yet lord's sworn man, yet have I done good service, and not left any at his most need for fear; but as, God help me, I think my lady shall have my service above any lady earthly, which she should well have known had I been in such case as I had not been always the worse welcome for that one of my errands always was understood that it was for Caister, which was not acceptable, and I the worse welcome." He also informs his brother that "I am concluded with my lord for you that ye shall be at Calais if ye list, and have three men in wages under you ;" so that Sir John had by this time become an influential courtier under the subverter of his former sovereign. This letter is dated Sunday, Nov. 22, 1472.]

LETTER CCCXXVIII.—(VII. vol. v. p. 37.)

[This letter is only curious as containing a further account of John Paston's hawk. Though he writes to his brother Sir John about it with some humour, yet his vehemence about it, and about the other bird, the pie or magpie, approaches very near to anger. He begins his letter " Right worshipful Sir, I recommend me to you, thanking you most heartily of your diligence and cost which ye had in getting of the hawk which ye sent me, for well I wot that your labour and trouble in that matter was as much as though she had been the best of the world, but so God help me as far forth as the most cunning estragers[1] can imagine, she shall never serve but to lay eggs, for she is both a muer de haye, and also she hath been so bruised with carnage of fowl that she is good as lame in both her legs, as any man may see at eye; wherefore all such folk as have seen her advise me to cast her into some wood, whereas I will have her to eyer [build or rather breed]; but I will do

therein as ye will, whether ye will I send her you again, or cast her into Thorp Wood, and a tercel with her, for I weet where one is; but now I dare no more put you to the cost of a hawk; but for God's sake, and there be any tercel or good cheap goshawk that might be gotten, that the bearer hereof may have her to bring me, and I ensure you by my troth, ye shall have Dolly's and Brown's bond to pay you at Candlemas the price of the hawk. Now and ye have as many ladies as ye were wont to have, I require you, for her sake that ye best love of them all, once trouble yourself for me in this matter, and be out of my clamour." He then presses him to urge on his business matters, tells him of having given a ring sent by Sir John to one of the Duchess of Norfolk's chamber women, who " promised to be more at your commandment than at any knight's in England, my lord's reserved ;" and concludes with the following curious postscript : "I saw the pie, and heard it speak, and by God it is not worth a crow; it is far worse than ye weened ; by God it were shame to keep it in a cage." Dated Framlingham, Tuesday, Nov. 24, 1472.]

---

[1] [Estragers are falconers. Shakspere introduces A gentle Astringer' as one of the characters in All's Well that ends Well.]

LETTER CCCXXIX.—(VIII. vol. v. p. 41.)

[From John Paston to Sir J. Paston is very unimportant. He thanks his brother for a hat which he understands is coming "by John, the Abbot of St. Bennet's man;" and he says " my mother prays you to get a new licence of my Lord of Norwich that she may have the sacrament in her chapel: I got a licence of him for a year, and it is nigh worn out; ye may get it for the bishop's life, an ye will." The remainder of the letter contains nothing but advice as to the furthering of the suit for Caister. Dated Nov. 1472.]

NUMBER CCCXXX.—(IX. vol. v. p. 45.)

[Is a petition from John Paston the younger on behalf of his brother Sir John, to the Duke of Norfolk for the restoration of Caister, "at the reverence of God and by way of charity;" although it asserts somewhat gently that the Duke's servants had taken possession of the same wrongfully, " and have taken the issues and profits in the name of your said highness by the space of three years and more, to the great hurt of my said brother and me your said servant and orator." This last passage fixes the date about the end of 1472, as the Duke had had possession from September, 1469.]

LETTER CCCXXXI.—(LI. vol. ii. p. 121.)

These extracts are given from the original letter chiefly to show the easy and familiar style used by Sir John Paston, in his humorous address to his brother, when telling him of Rabekin's inquiries after him.

To John Paston, Esq., or to Mrs. Margaret Paston, his mother, be this letter delivered.

WELL BELOVED brother, (*Here follows an account of letters sent to him from Calais—of farm barley in Flegg hundred, and of old stuff at Norwich, &c.*)

As for tidings here there be but few, save that the Duke of Burgundy and my lady [1] his wife fareth well; I was with them on Thursday last past at Ghent. Peter Metteney fareth well and Mrs. Gretkin both, and Rabekyn recommend her to you, she hath been very sick, but it hath done her good, for she is fairer and slenderer than she was; and she could make me no cheer but alway my sauce was, "How fareth Master John your brother?" wherewith I was wrath, and spake a jealous word or two, disdaining that she should care so much for you when I was present.

Send me word to Hoxon's in writing, what good the bishop did for me at Framlingham, and how my lord, my lady, and all the court are disposed to me wards.

I hear also say that my lady and yours, Dame Margaret Vere [2] is dead, God have her soul! if I were not sorry for her I trow ye have been.

No more to you at this time, but Almighty God have you in keeping.

Written at Calais, the 3rd day of February, in the 12th year of the reign of Edward IV.

JOHN PASTON, knight.

Calais,
Wednesday, 3rd of February,
1473. 12 E IV.

[1] Charles the Bold, and Margaret, sister to Edward IV

[2] Daughter and heir of Sir William Stafford, and wife to Sir George Vere, their son, John Vere, was afterwards Earl of Oxford.

LETTER CCCXXXII.—(X. vol. v. p. 47.)

[JOHN PASTON requests his brother to use his influence to procure the discharge of his cousin John Blennerhasset from the appointment of collector of the "task" or subsidy, on the ground that he has not a foot of land within the shire. Taxes and tax collecting seem to have been as irksome then as now, and the collecting probably was not sweetened by a salary, or a gentleman would not have been appointed against his will. He wishes to know, if possible, who had caused the appointment, says the Heydons are suspected, and "if they were the causers it lieth in my cousin Harsset's [*Blennerhasset's*] power to quyt [*requite*] them." He then just mentions the committal of a fortune-teller or prophet to Norwich jail; and concludes thus:— "No more, but I pray God send you the Holy Ghost amongst you in the Parliament House, and rather the devil, we say, than ye should grant any more tasks." The letter is dated Friday, March 26, 1473.]

LETTER CCCXXXIII.—(LII. vol. ii. p. 123.)

he business referred to in the beginning of this letter is not mentioned; what is said of Blennerhasset seems to be meant as a pun upon the name, as written *Blunder hare set;* or perhaps it may only refer to its being a sounding name. [The business is clearly the release of Blennerhasset from the appointment of collector. We think Fenn's explanation of starting the hare very unsatisfactory, as also of "beware that 1ᵈ. purse;" but we have no better to offer; unless the latter may be Persey or Percy, whose name has already occurred. The original has "ware that jᵈ perse."]

To his dear and well-beloved brother, John Paston, Esq.

WELL-BELOVED brother I recommend me to you; letting you weet that, at the request of Mrs. Jane Hassett [*Blennerhasset*] and you, I have laboured both the knights of the shire of Norfolk and the knights of the shire of Suffolk; I understand there had been made labour that such a thing should have been as ye wrote to me of, but now it is safe.

Ralph Blaunderhasset were a name to start an hare, I warrant there shall come no such name in our books nor in our house; it might per case start twenty hares at once. Beware that penny purse.[1] I read there in the bill of Norfolk of one John Tendall, Esquire, but I suppose it be not meant by our Tendall; and if it be, he shall not rest there if I may help it.

As for tidings, the worst that I heard was, that my mother will not do so much for me as she put me in comfort of.

Other tidings, I heard say for certain that the Lady Fitzwalter is dead, and that Master Fitzwalter shall have 400 marks (266*l*. 13*s*. 4*d*.) a year more than he had: I am not sorry therefore.

As for the world I wot not what it meaneth, men say here, as well as Hogan,[2] that we shall have ado in haste; I know no likelihood, but that such a rumour there is. Men say the queen with the prince shall come out of Wales, and keep this Easter with the king at Leicester; and some say neither of them shall come there.

Item, of beyond the sea, it is said that the French king's host hath killed the Earl of Armagnac and all his merry men; some say under appointment, and some say they were besieged and gotten by plain assault.

Farthermore, men say that the French king is with his host upon the water of Somme, a sixty miles from Calais; I leave them where I found them.

I made your answer to the friends of Mrs. Jane Godnoston according to your instructions; as for me, I am not certain whether I shall to Calais, to Leicester, or come home into Norfolk, but I shall hastily send you word, &c.

Written the 2nd day of April, the 13th of Edward IV.

Friday, 2nd of April, 1473.
            13 E. IV.

---

[1] It seems to mean—Beware of that covetous man, or of that poor man, which I know not.

[2] Hogan is the conjuror mentioned in the previous letter.

LETTER CCCXXXIV.—(XI. vol. v. p. 51.)

[CONTAINS nothing of consequence. Sir J. Paston tells his brother that "every man saith we shall have ado ere May pass: Hogan the prophet is in the Tower, he would fain speak with the king, but the king saith he shall not avaunt (*boast*) that ever he spake with him." This proves that the public affairs were somewhat troubled, and that tumults were feared, though they did not take place The severe rule of Edward IV. and the known dissensions in the family gave probable cause for apprehension. The remainder of the letter is on his private affairs, and he appears to be much displeased with his mother because she would not lend him money, and expresses himself in terms of harshness in extreme contrast with the usual humility of children to their parents at that period. He says, "My mother doth me more harm than [*the*] good I weened she would have done for me. Playters wrote to me that she would have laid out for me 100*l.*, and received it again in five years off the manor of Sporle, whereto I trusted; if she had performed I had not been in no jeopardy of the manor of Sporle, nevertheless I shall do what I can yet. I pray you call upon her for the same, remember her of that promise." Also, "remember her of my father's tomb at Bromholm, she doth right nought; I am afraid of her that she shall not do well." Dated London, Monday, April 12, 1473.]

LETTER CCCXXXV.—(LIII. vol. ii. p. 127.)

The first part of this curious letter informs us of the unsettled state of the nation, and that the Duke of Clarence, pretending only to be getting his party together to oppose the Duke of Gloucester, was supposed to be meditating some treason against the state These royal brothers had been for some time at variance, and most probably their disputes were heightened at this time, by the late marriage of the latter with Anne, the widow of Prince Edward, Henry VI's son, daughter and co-heir of the Earl of Warwick, and sister to the Duchess of Clarence, whose possessions the Duke was unwilling to divide with her sister, now his brother's wife.

To John Paston, Esq., at Norwich, be this delivered.

WORSHIPFUL and well-beloved brother, I commend me to you; letting you weet that the world seemeth queasy (*unsettled*) here; for the most part that be about the king have sent hither for their harness, and it (*is*) said for certain that the Duke of Clarence maketh him big in that he can, showing as he would but (*only*) deal with the Duke of Gloucester; but the king intendeth, in eschewing all inconvenience, to be as big as they both, and to be a stiffler atween them; and some men think that under this there should be some other thing intended, and some treason conspired; so what shall fall can I not say.

Item, it is said that yesterday two passagers (*passage boats*) of Dover were taken, I fear that if Juddy had no hasty passage, so that if he passed not on Sunday or Monday, that he is taken, and some gear of mine that I would not for 20*l.*

I hope and purpose to go to Calais ward on Sunday or Monday or nigh by, for I came not accompanied to do any service here; wherefore it were better for me to be out of sight.

(*Here follow some money transactions relative to a Doctor Pykenham, his mother, and others.*)

Item, Spring, that waited on my father [1] when he was in Gaol House, whom my father at his dying beset (*bequeathed*) 40s. he cryeth ever on me for it, and in way of alms, and he would be eased though it were but xxs. or xs., wherefore he hath written to my mother, and must have an answer again; I would that my mother send him as though she lend him somewhat, and he will be pleased, and (*cr*) else he can say as shrewdly as any man in England.

---

[1] John Paston, Esq was imprisoned by Edward IV in 1466.

Item, the king hath sent for his great seal; some say we shall have a new chancellor,[1] but some think that the king doth as he did at the last fields, he will have the seal with him, but this day Doctor Morton, Master of the Rolls,[2] rideth to the king and beareth the sease (*seals*) with him.

Item, I had never more need of money than now, wherefore Fastolf's five marks

(3*l.* 6*s.* 8*d.*), and the money of Master John Smythe, would make me whole, &c.

Written on St. Leonard's day, in the 13th year of the reign of Edward IV.

Item, send me my vestment, according to the letter I sent you by Symond Dam, in all haste.

JOHN PASTON, *knight.*

Thursday, 15th of April,
1473. 13 E. IV.

LETTER CCCXXXVI.—(LIV. vol. ii. p. 131.)

The historic facts mentioned in this letter contradict [the dates of them as given by our historians, and place in the year 1473 those which they have given as happening in the year preceding.

To John Paston, Esq., in Norfolk.

WORSHIPFUL and right heartily-beloved brother, I recommend me unto you; letting you weet that on Wednesday last past I wrote you a letter, whereof John Carbalde had the bearing, promitting (*promising*) me that ye should have it at Norwich this day, or else to-morrow in the morning; wherein I pray you to take a labour according after the tenure of the same, and that I may have an answer at London to Hoxon, if any messenger come, as e'en I may do for you.

As for tidings, there was a truce taken at Brussels about the 26th day of March last past between the Duke of Burgundy and the French king's ambassadors, and Mr. William at Clyff for the king here; which is a peace by land and water till the first day of April[3] now next coming between France and England, and also the duke's land; God hold it for ever and (*if*) grace be!

Item, the Earl of Oxford[4] was on Saturday at Dieppe, and is purposed into Scotland with a twelve ships; I mistrust that work.

Item, there be in London many flying tales, saying that there should be a work and yet they wot not how.

Item, my Lord Chamberlain[5] sendeth now at this time to Calais the young Lord Zouch[6] and Sir Thomas Hungerford's daughter and heir,[7] and some say the young Lady Harrington, these be three great jewels; Calais is a merry town, they shall dwell there I wot not whylghe (*how long*).

No more, but I have been and am troubled with mine over large and courteous dealing with my servants, and now with their unkindness; Platting, your man, would this day bid me farewell, to to-morrow at Dover, notwithstanding Thryston, your other man, is from me, and John Myryel, and W. Woode which promised you and Daubeney, God have his soul, at Caister, that if ye would take him in to be again with me that then he would never go from me; and thereupon I have kept him this three years to play Saint

---

1 Robert Stillington, Bishop of Bath and Wells, was the then chancellor.

2 Dr. Morton was a man of great learning and strict loyalty: he was elected Bishop of Ely in 1478; and in the same year appointed Lord Chancellor;—in 1484 he was advanced to the archiepiscopal see of Canterbury, and died in 1500. [Morton's "strict loyalty" is more than doubtful. He had been a Lancastrian, he was now a Yorkist; he conspired against Richard III. in favour of Henry VII., for which he was deprived of his bishopric, and was only restored on the accession of Henry, to whom he became chief adviser and confidant.]

3 From 26th of March, 1473, to 1st of April, 1474.

4 Our historians assert that the Earl of Oxford was taken in St. Michael's Mount, in Cornwall, in 1472, and thence conveyed to the castle of Hammes near Calais, where he was imprisoned during twelve years; this could not be as he was now at Dieppe, concerting an expedition into Scotland.

5 William Lord Hastings.

6 John Lord Zouch of Harringworth; he was attainted in the first year of Henry VII.

7 Mary, daughter and heir of Sir Thomas Hungerford; she afterwards married Edward, son and heir to William Lord Hastings, who in her right became Lord Hungerford, her uncle's attainder being reversed.

George, and Robin Hood, and the sheriff of Nottingham,[1] and now when I would have good horse, he is gone into Bernysdale, and I without a keeper.

Written at Canterbury, to Calais ward on Tuesday, and (*if*) hap be upon Good Friday, he 16th day of April, in the 13th year of Edward IV.[2] Your

JOHN PASTON, *knight*.

Item, the most part of the soldiers that went over with Sir Robert Green have leave, and be coming home; the highway full, my carriage was behind me two hours longer than I looked after, but I wis I wend that I might have eaten my part on Good Friday, all my garees (*finery*) and pride had been gone, but all was safe.[3]

I pray you if W. Mylsent go from you that he might come to me to Calais, I will have him.

Canterbury, Good Friday, 16th of April, 1473. 13 E. IV.

LETTER CCCXXXVII.—(LV. vol. ii. p. 137.)

This letter shows us the unsettled state of the nation, and the apprehensions of the king concerning the coming of the Earl of Oxford.—The man's confession seems to be founded on good authority, as the earl arrived in England soon after.

To John Paston, Esq., in Norwich.

RIGHT worshipful brother, I recommend me to you, &c. (*Then follow some orders concerning servants, debts, securities, &c.*)

As for tidings, the Earl of Wiltshire[4] and the Lord Sudley[5] be dead, and it was said, that Sir W. Stanley was dead, but now it is said nay, &c.

Item, as for your going to Saint James's, I believe[6] it but atween two, &c.

I heard say that a man was this day examined, and he confessed that he knew great treasure was sent to the Earl of Oxford, whereof a 1000*l*. should be conveyed by a monk of Westminster, and some say by a monk of Charterhouse.

Item, that the same man should accuse an hundred gentlemen in Norfolk and Suffolk that have agreed to assist the said earl at his coming thither, which, as it is said, should be within eight days after St. Dunstan,[7] if wind and weather serve him; flying tales.

No more at this time, but God have you in keeping. Written at London on St. Dunstan's day, the 18th day of May, in the 13th year of Edward IV.

JOHN PASTON, *knight*.

London,
St. Dunstan's day,
Tuesday, 18th of May, 1473.
13 E. IV.

---

[1] Meaning, I presume, either that he had kindly kept him when he did not want him; and now that he did want him that he had left him; or that he had kept him to be an actor in such interludes. [There appears to us to be no difficulty in the meaning. On his "promise never to go from me," he says he had kept W. Woode there three years to play St. George. &c., i.e. merely employed him in amusements, and now when he wanted good horsemen, he had left him.]

[2] This is the first letter so fully dated, by which the exact time of King Edward's reign can be precisely ascertained. By the tables to find Easter, it appears that in 1473, the prime being 11, and the Dominical letter C, Easter Sunday was on the 18th of April.

Edward the IVth's reign began the 4th of March. The 16th of April, 1473, was therefore the 13th of Edward IV., and consequently he began his reign on the 4th of March, 1460.—N.B. The date of the new year commenced on the 25th of March.

[3] The sense of this latter part is not clear; perhaps he meant to say that he was so sure that his finery was lost, that he might have ventured to promise to eat his part of it on Good Friday without breaking his fast.

[4] John Stafford was created Earl of Wiltshire in 1470. He was brother to Henry Duke of Buckingham.

[5] . . . . . Butler Lord Sudley.

[6] This seems to signify, *I do not believe it*.

[7] In the next letter he is said to have landed in Essex on the 28th of May.

LETTER CCCXXXVIII.—(LVI. vol. ii. p. 139.)

The former part of this letter is of little consequence, except to show us the attendants necessary for a person of Sir John Paston's rank ; the latter hints to us the unsettled state of the government ; and that the king and the Duke of Clarence were not on amicable terms.

To John Paston, Esq., be this delivered.

RIGHT worshipful brother, 1 recommend me to you; letting you weet that this day I was in very purpose to Calais ward all ready to have gone to the barge: save I tarried for a young man that I thought to have had with me thither, one that was with Rows which is in the country; and because I could not get him, and that I have no more here with me but Pampyng, Edward, and Jack, therefore Pampyng remembered me that at Calais he told me that he purposed to be with the Duchess of Norfolk, my lady and yours; and Edward is sick and seemeth not abiding, he would see what shall fall of this world, and so I am as he that saith ; " come hither, John, my man;" and as hap was yesterday Juddy went afore to Calais ward, wherefore I am now ill purveyed; which for aught that I know yet is like to keep me here this Whitsuntide,[1] wherefore if ye know any likely men, and fair conditioned, and good archers, send them to me though it be four, and I will have them, and they shall have four marks (2*l.* 13*s.* 4*d.*) by the year and my livery.

He may come to me hither to the Goat, or yet (*else*) to Calais with a rial,[2] if he be wise, which if need be I would that Barker took (*gave*) him to come up with, if it be such one as ye trust.

Item, I suppose both Pytte and Kothye Plattyng shall go from me in haste : I will never cherish knaves so as I have done for their sakes.

Item, I pray you send me a new vestment of white damask for a deacon, which is amongst mine other gear at Norwich, for he shall thereto as ye wot of; I will make an arming doublet of it, though I should another time give a long gown of velvet for another vestment; and send it in all haste to Hoxon to send me.

I hoped to have been very merry at Calais this Whitsuntide, and am well apparelled and appointed save that these folks fail me so, and I have matter there to make of right excellent. Some man would have hasted him to Calais, though he had had no better errand, and some men think it wisdom and profit to be there now well out of the way.

Item, as for the bishop[3] and I, we be nearer to a point than we were, so that my part is now all the lands in Flegg wholly, the manor of Heylesdon, Tolthorpe, and tenements in Norwich and Earlham, except Fairchild's; but farewell Drayton, the devil do it them (*do them good of it*).

Item, large and fair communication hath been between Sir John Fagge and Richard Hawte for their sister and me, before Doctor Wyntborne and elsewhere, so that I am in better hope than I was by St. Lawrence[4] that I shall have a deliverance.

Item, as for tidings here, I trow ye have heard your part, how that the Earl of Oxford landed by St. Osyth's in Essex, the 28th day of May, save he tarried not long; for if he had the Earl of Essex[5] rode to him wards, and the Lords Denham and Duras (*Galliard de Durefort*), and other more, which by likelihood should have distressed him ; but yet his coming saved Hogan his head, and his prophecy is the more believed; for he said that this trouble should begin in May, and that the king should northwards, and that the Scots should make us work and him battle.

Men look after they wot not what, but men buy harness fast ; the king's menial men, and the Duke of Clarence's, are many in this town; the Lord Rivers[6] came to day, men say to purvey in like wise.

---

[1] Whitsunday, 6th of June, 1473.
[2] A rial a gold coin of 10*s.* value.

[3] James Goldwell, Bishop of Norwich, 1472.
[4] 10th of August.
[5] Henry Bourchier, Earl of Essex, lord treasurer.
[6] Anthony Wideville, Earl Rivers, beheaded at Pontefract, 1483.

Item, how that the Countess of Warwick[1] s now out of Beverley sanctuary, and Sir [J]ames Tyrell conveyeth her northwards men [s]ay by the king's assent, whereto some men [s]ay that the Duke of Clarence is not agreed.

Item, men say that the Earl of Oxford is [a]bout the Isle of Thanet, hovering, some say [w]ith great company, and some say with few.

No more, but God keep you. Written at London the 3rd day of June, in the 13th year of Edward IV.

JOHN PASTON, *knight.*

London.
Thursday, 3rd of June,
1473. 13 E. IV.

LETTER CCCXXXIX.—(LVII. vol. ii. p. 147.)

Though this letter from Sir John Paston contains nothing very material, it informs us of an engagement at sea between some ships of this country, and those of the Easterlings or inhabitants of the eastern part of Germany It likewise acquaints us with some private anecdotes of Sir John Paston as a man of gallantry.

To Edmund Paston, Esq., at Calais, be this delivered.

BROTHER EDMUND, I greet you well; letting you weet that about this day sev'nnight I sent you a letter by Nicholas Bardesley, a soldier, which is wont to be at border[2] (*query. brother*) Perauntys; and also an hosecloth[3] of black for you; I wend that ye should have had it within two days, but I am afraid that he deceived me.

Item, I let you weet that Plattyng is coming hither, and he saith that ye gave him leave to fetch his gear and Pytt's; and that is his errand hither and none other, nor he thought never to go from me, nor he will not go from me, as he saith; wherefore I pray you send me word of his conditions, and why ye think that he should never do me worship.

He saith also, that he and Pytt were at the taking of the Esterlings, and that he was in he Packer, and Pytt in the Cristopher; I pray you send me word how both he and Pytt quit them by the report of some indif-ferent true man that was there; if they quit ('*acquitted*) them well I would love them the better; wherefore the next day after the sight of this letter I pray you write again, and send it by the next passage.

Item, I send a little pretty box herewith, which I would that Juddy should deliver to the woman that he weeteth of, and pray her to take it to the man that she weeteth of; that is to say as much as ye know all well enough, but ye may not make you wise in no wise. (*You must by no means seem to know anything of the business in hand.*)

Item, I pray you send me word as ye were wont to do of her welfare, and whether I were out and other in or not; and whether she shall forsake Calais as soon as ye sent me word of or not

By God I would be with you as fain as yourself, and shall be in haste, with God's grace.

Item, as for my brother John, I hope within this month to see him in Calais; for by likelihood to-morrow, or else the next day, he taketh ship at Yarmouth, and goeth to St. James[4] ward; and he hath written to me that he will come homeward by Calais.

Item, I suppose that James Songer shall come with me to Calais the rather for your sake.

Item, Mistress Elizabeth fareth well, but as yet Songer knoweth not so perfectly all that ye would weet, that he will not write to you of these two days, till he know more: but if she had been bold, and durst have

---

[1] Anne, widow of Richard Nevile, the great Earl of Warwick, sister and heir to Henry Beauchamp, Duke of Warwick, and mother of Isabel, the wife of George, Duke of Clarence.

[2] May not this sentence be thus read? Is wont to be at border paravant this, i e is accustomed to each the border, march or edge, of Calais much sooner,—before this,—before so much time was lapsed.

[3] Cloth for hosen.

VOL. II.

[4] On a pilgrimage, I suppose, to St James of Compostella, in the province of Gallicia, in Spain. [Not very likely, we think He could scarcely have made this journey, and been at Calais "within this month," it being then the 5th.]

G

abiden still at her gate, and spoken with me, so God help me, she had had this same (*bar*) that I send now where ye wot of, which ye shall see worn hereafter; it is a pretty ribbon with pretty aglets[1] and goodly.

Make you not wise to Juddy, neither not [*note*] that ye would weet anything, for I may say to you at his coming over he brought goodly gear reasonably.

Item, as for my bill[2] that is gilt, I would it were taken heed to; there is one in the town that can glaze (*polish*) well enough as I heard say; also there is one cometh every market day from St. Omer's to Calais, and he bringeth daggers and fetcheth also, he may have it with him, and bring it again the next market day, for 12*d*. or 16*d*. at the most; and (*or*) else let it be well oiled and kept till I come.

No more. Written at London the 5th day of July, in the 13th year of Edward IV.

JOHN PASTON, *knight.*

London,
Monday, 5th of July,
1473. 13 E. IV.

LETTER CCCXL.—(LVIII. Vol. ii. p. 153.)

This and the Letter cccxciv. are perhaps the only letters extant of this nobleman, who, though he disliked King Edward's Queen, was a true and loyal subject to the king; and continued faithful to his young Prince Edward V., for which he lost his head in 1483. If we may judge from his expressions in these letters, he was a polite gentleman and a kind master. His remembering "his fellows, the soldiers," in an age when his noble rank placed him so high above the plebeians, characterises him as a commander attentive to the concerns of those under him.

To my right heartily-beloved friends and fellows, Sir John of Middleton, and Sir John Paston, Knights.

AFTER hearty recommendation, I thank you of the good attendance that ye gave unto the king's counsel at Calais; and the good and effectual devoirs that ye put you in to assist my deputy Sir John Scot, in all such things as might concern the safeguard of my charge there. Letting you weet that if there be anything that I can and may do for you, I shall with right good will perform it to my power. And I pray you to recommend me to my Lady Howard,[3] my Lady Bourgchier,[4] and all other ladies and gentlewomen of the said town. And in likewise to the mayor, lieutenant, and fellowship of the staple; my fellows the soldiers, and all other such as (*to*) you shall seem good. And our Lord send you your desires. Written at Nottingham, the 16th day of September.

Sir John Paston[5] I pray you to give credence to such things as my deputy shall show you from me, and conform you to the same.

Your fellow, HASTINGS.

Nottingham,
16th of September,
1473. 13 E. IV.

---

[1] Pendent ornaments of metal, like tags or points, &c.

[2] A warlike instrument of offence.

[3] Margaret, wife of Sir John Howard, Lord Howard, and afterwards Duke of Norfolk. She was daughter of Sir John Chedworth, knight, and died in 1490, 5 H. VII.

[4] Lady Bourchier was probably the wife of a son of Sir John Bourchier, Lord Berners.

[5] This last paragraph is written by Lord Hastings himself, the former part to "the xvj day of September," by his secretary.

LETTER CCCXLI.—(XII. vol. v. p. 55.)

[This letter, from Sir John Paston to his brother John, touches on many curious matters illustrative of the period. He commences by acknowledging the receipt of a letter from him of the 6th of October, "letting me weet of the decease of Sir James (*Glois*), and that my mother is in purpose to be at Norwich, and I am right glad that she will now do somewhat by your advice, wherefore, beware from henceforth that no such fellow creep in between her and you." He goes on, "ye send me word also that she in no wise will purvey the 100*l.* for the redeeming of Sporle; let it go: as touching that matter, John Osbern told me that he communed with you at Sporle of that matter; further, he devised that Cocket, or such another man, should, to have it the better cheap, lay out the value of six year for to have it seven year, whereto I would agree; and for God's sake, if that may be brought about, let it be done: as ye wot of, it is let for 22*l.* a year, yet the farmer grant but 21*l.*; but to Cocket it would be worth 25*l.*, yea, and better; nevertheless if Cocket will deliver six score pounds, I would he had it for seven years, with this, that my mother be agreeable to the same, because of the interest that she hath for my brother William, which shall not be of age this seven year; nevertheless, as ye know my old intent, I purpose to purvey for him in another place better than there; of which grant of my mother I pray be my solicitor, in which, an it be brought about, Sporle shall be in as good case as ever it was. John Osbern willed me to make you a sufficient warrant to sell and fell wood at Sporle, which I remember ye have in as ample form as may be ; nevertheless, if this mean above written, of letting to farm, may be had, it shall I hope not need to sell or fell much ; but I remit that gear to your discretion : but if ye have such comfort I pray you send me word. I may say to you John Osbern flattered me, for he would have borrowed money of me. Item, in retailing of wood there it were hard to trust him; he is needy. If Cocket, or whosoever had that manor to farm for seven year, and paid therefor but six score pounds, he should, to let it again, win 36*l.*, which be much ; wherefore, if it might be, it were more reasonable six score and seven pounds were received, and yet is there lost 29*l.* ; or else, if ye take less money and fewer years, so it be after the rate, so that there be paid 100*l.* at the least, send word." This is curious, as showing the nature of letting farms, and also would go to show a much lower rate of interest than was generally in use at that time, for 36*l.* as the interest of 120*l.* for seven years is but small, considering the risk of the tenant's rent, &c. &c. The mysterious affair with Mrs. Ann Hawte is again alluded to : " I have answer again from Rome that there is the well of grace, and salve sufficient for such a sore, and that I may be dispensed with : nevertheless, my proctor there asketh a thousand ducats as he deemeth;" but he adds, " another Rome-runner here " has told him he means but a hundred ducats, or two hundred at the most. The rest of the letter contains unimportant directions as to his clothes and other matters, except that he says, "as for other tidings I trust to God that the two Dukes of Clarence and Gloucester shall be set at one by the award of the king." Dated London, Monday, Nov. 22, 1473.]

LETTER CCCXLII.—(XIII. vol. v. p. 63.)

[This letter contains chiefly instructions from Sir John Paston to his brother John and his mother, as to empowering him, Sir John, to administer to his father's will. His father died in 1466, and it appears a long time to elapse without this having been done, but the date of the letter is fixed (London, Thursday, Nov. 25, 1473) by its reference to the Earl of Oxford being besieged in St. Michael's Mount in Cornwall, which happened in 1473, where he was captured, and afterwards imprisoned for several years in the castle of

Hammes near Calais, from whence he escaped, and accompanied Henry VII. in his unsuccessful attempt on England, dying in 1512; and to his anticipated immediate possession of Caister. With reference to this place he says, "send me word if I have Caister again, whether she (his mother) will dwell there or not, and I will find her a priest towards at my charge, and give her the dove-house and other commodities there; and if any horse-keeper of mine lie there, I will pay for his board also, as well as for the priest's. Item, if my mother should have a new priest, I think that my brother Sir J. Goos were a meetly man to be there; he would also do as ye would have him." This is very cunning advice for his own good, and the advantages he offers to his mother of the dove-house and other commodities must have been then thought very seductive.]

LETTER CCCXLIII.—(LIX.—(vol. ii. p. 155.)

[In the previous letter we have a notice of John de Vere, Earl of Oxford, who is here again particularly mentioned. We may add, however, that, as it is here said, all his estates were confiscated, but were restored soon after the accession of Henry VII.]

Mrs. Margaret Paston, at Norwich.

RIGHT honourable and most tender good mother, I recommend me to you, beseeching you to have, as my trust is that I have, your daily blessing; and thank you of your good motherhood, kindness, cheer, charge, and costs, which I had and put you to at my last being with you, which God give me grace hereafter to deserve!

Please it you to weet, that I think long that I hear not from you, or from Peacock your servant, for the knowledge how he hath done in the sale of my farm hurley, nor what is made thereof; wherefore I beseech you, if it be not answered by that time that this bill cometh to you, to haste him and it hitherward; for if that had not tarried me I deem I had been at Calais by this day; for it is so, as men say, that the French king with a great host is at Amiens, but threescore miles from Calais; and if he or his rode before Calais, and I not there, I would be sorry.

Item, men say that the Earl of Oxford hath been constrained to sue for his pardon only of his life; and his body, goods, lands, with all the remanent, at the king's will, and so should in all haste now come in to the king; and some men say that he is gone out of the Mount, men wot not to what place, and yet left a great garrison there, well furnished in victual and all other thing.

Item, as for the having again of Caister, I trust to have good tidings thereof hastily.

Item, my brother John fareth well, and hath done right diligently in my cousin Elizabeth Berney's matter, whereof hastily I trust he shall send her tidings that shall please her; and as to-morrow he purposeth to take his journey to Wales ward to the Lord Rivers.

No more at this time, but Jesu have you in his keeping.

Written at London the 20th day of February, in the 13th year of Edward IV.

Your son,

J. PASTON, knight.

London,
Sunday, 20th of February,
1473. 13 E. IV.

LETTER CCCXLIV.—(LX. vol. ii. p. 159.)

We have in this letter a pleasing account of the intended excursion of the king into divers counties in 1474; the motive of which most probably was to raise, more easily by his presence and cheerful address, benevolences upon his subjects towards the expenses of his war with France. We are here informed likewise that the county of Norfolk had been highly spoken of to the king, not only for the riches and hospitality of its inhabitants, but for the beauty and agreeable behaviour of its women, a reason sufficient for so long a stay amongst them, as seemed intended to be made, by an amorous and handsome monarch.

To his brother Sir John Paston, Knight, be this letter delivered.

Sir, I recommend me unto you, letting you weet that, (*Here follows some account relative to a grant from the crown, &c.*)

As for my lord treasurer[1] he was not with the king of all the council time,[2] the which was ended on the 3d day of March. And thither came my Lord of Northumberland,[3] the first day of March, and departed the even afore the making of this letter; and hath indented with the king for the keeping out of the Scots, and warring on them, and shall have large money, I cannot tell the sum for certain.

Also there is a rover taken at Bristol, one Cowper, as I ween, and he is like to be hanged, and he confesseth more of his fellows. Also Edward Heestowe of Dover is appeached of treason of many strange points; and his accuser and he were both afore the king, and then they were taken apart, and he himself confessed it that his accuser accused him of, and many other things more than he was accused of. And he had many lords and gentlemen to answer for his truth and his demeaning afore time, for as I heard say, both the king in a manner, nor none of the other lords nor gentlemen, believed not his accuser till that he confessed it himself, and so he is in the Tower, and like to be dead.[4]

As for the king's coming into the country; on Monday come fortnight he will lie at the abbey of Stratford, and so to Chelmsford; then to Sir Thomas Montgomery's; then to Heveningham; then to Colchester; then to Ipswich; then to Bury; then to Dame Anne Wingfield's, and so to Norwich; and there will he be on Palm Sunday even,[5] and so tarry there all Easter,[6] and then to Walsingham;[7] wherefore ye had need to warn William Gogney and his fellows to purvey them of wine enough, for every man beareth me in hand that the town shall be drank dry as York was when the king was there.

Sir, Master Sampson recommend him unto you, and he hath sent you a ring by Edmond Dorman; and besides that, he required me to write unto you that it were best for you to purvey you of some gentlemany (*gentlemanlike*) things against the king's coming, for sure he will bring you guests enough, and therefore purvey you thereafter. Also, he sendeth you word that it is my lord's mind that my sister, with all other goodly folks thereabout, should accompany with Dame Elizabeth Calthorp,[8] because there is no great lady thereabout, against the king's coming; for my lord hath made great boast of the fair and good gentlewomen of the country; and so the king said he would see them sure.

Sir, my lord hath sent unto the most part of the gentlemen of Essex to wait upon him at Chelmsford, whereas he intendeth to meet with the king, and that they be well appointed, that the Lancashire men may see that there be gentlemen of so great substance that they be able to buy all Lancashire. Men think that ye among you will do the same.

Your country is greatly boasted of, also the inhabitors of the same. I beseech you to remember my horse that you promised me. God keep you.

Written at Sheen, in haste, the 7th day of March, with the hand of your brother,

WILLIAM PASTON.

Sheen, Monday, 7th of March, 1473. 14 E IV.

---

[1] William Grey, Bishop of Ely.
[2] The sitting of parliament
[3] Henry Percy, Earl of Northumberland, this contract was entered into by him most probably as Warden of the Marches, a place of trust, honour, and profit This nobleman was cruelly murdered by a mob, in Yorkshire, when he was there levying a public tax in 1489.
[4] This expression seems to insinuate that he would be executed privately in the Tower. [We see no reason for this supposition We think it is merely meant that he was not likely to be pardoned.]

[5] 3rd of April, 1474.
[6] 10th of April, 1474. [It will be borne in mind that the year commenced on March 25]
[7] I suppose to pay his devotions to the image of Our Lady there
[8] Widow of Sir John Calthorp, and daughter of Roger Wentworth, Esq.

LETTER CCCXLV.—(XIV. vol. v. p. 67.)

[In this letter John Paston writes to his brother Sir John on the subject of his wooing. He appears a thoroughly careful and wary suitor, as he has two if not three ladies in view, although his "fantazy" inclines him to Mistress Elizabeth Eberton, even if "Eberton wold not geve so moche w⁴ Maistress Elyzabet his dowghter as I myght have w⁴ the other." But we will let him speak for himself. He requests his brother, "ere that ye depart out of London to speak with Harry Eberton's wife, draper, and to inform her that I am proffered a marriage in London which is worth six hundred marks (400*l*.) and better, with whom I prayed you to commune, inasmuch as I might not tarry in London myself; always reserving, that if so be that Mrs. Eberton will deal with me, that ye should not conclude in the other place, though so were that Eberton would not give so much with Mrs. Elizabeth his daughter as I might have with the other, for such fantasy as I have in the said Mrs. Elizabeth Eberton; and that it like you to say to Eberton's wife that such as I spake to her of shall be bettered rather than empeyred [*impaired*] as for my part." If the proffered marriage was not a mere *ruse*, it may or may not refer to the following extracts, which, however, would not justify the assertion of a "proffered marriage" worth six hundred marks. Before giving the passages we may observe that the word "thing," which he applies to her was at that time, and afterward, frequently used as a term of endearment and not of contempt.

"I pray you that ye will, as I desired you, commune with John Lee, or his wife, or both, and to understand how the matter at the Black Friars doth, and that ye will see and speak with the thing yourself, and with her father and mother, ere ye depart. . . . . . Also that it like you to speak to your apothecary, which was sometime the Earl of Warwick's apothecary, and to weet of him what the widow of the Black Friars is worth, and what her husband's name was; he can tell all, for he is executor to the widow's husband." Here he seems to think his own consent to be all that is necessary. We give another passage to show the nature of a gentleman's wardrobe at that time. "I pray you that Pitt may truss in a mail [*trunk*], which I left in your chamber at London, my tawny gown furred with black, and the doublet of purple satin and the doublet of black satin, and my writing-box of cypress, and my 'Book of the Meeting of the Duke and of the Emperor,'" (probably Charles Duke of Burgundy and the Emperor Frederic III.) The writing-desk of cypress-wood could not have been a common article at this period, and, together with the book, show he had a literary taste. The rest of the letter is uninteresting, except perhaps the statement that his mother will labour "that the two hundred marks (133*l*. 6*s*. 8*d*.) may be had for the wood, so that it seems he could not borrow for his brother, but was forced, like many others since, to "fell and sell." Dated Norwich, Monday, July 25, 1475.]

LETTER CCCXLVI.—(XV. vol. v. p. 73.)

[Sir John Paston here writes to his mother about the means of raising money, but the details are uninteresting. He had been on a visit to his mother, and had been ill, but says he had quite recovered, thanks to her care. He mentions that Courby the carrier hath had "40*d*. to pay for the third hired horse, and he bringeth the three horses with him, and is content for the labour and the meat largely;" this seems a small sum for a journey from Norwich to London and back; the more so as in the previous letter his brother sends him ten shillings for the conveyance of the trunk with his clothes and writing-desk. He concludes the letter in a style that does credit to his taste, and displays some humour. "As for the books that were Sir James's (Gloys, the priest's), if it lıke you that I may have them, I am not able to buy them, but somewhat would I giv e, and the remanent, with a good devout heart by my troth, I will pray for his soul; wherefore, if it like you, by the next messenger or carrier to send them in a day, I shall have them dressyd [*re-bound*, or perhaps *addressed*] here, and if any of them are claimed hereafter in faith I will restore it." The last promise shows it waz so common to borrow books, then both scarce and valuable, that it was likely upon a scholar's death that some of them might be reclaimed. Dated Saturday, before November, 1474.]

LETTER CCCXLVII.—(XVI. vol. v. p. 79.)

[Tнıs letter is again about money from Sir John to his mother. His uncle William had lent him money, which enabled him to redeem the manor of Sporle, but only on sufficient security, for he says, "I am as much afraid of this land that is in his hand as I was of that that was in Townshend's (his former creditor) hand." He again reverts to the books. "As for the books that were Sir James's, God have his soul! which it liketh you that I shall have them, I beseech you that I might have them hither by the next messenger; and if I be gone, yet that they be delivered to mine hostess at the George at Paul's Wharf, which will keep them safe; and that it like you to write to me what the pain or payment shall be for them." Dated London, Sunday, Nov. 29, 1471.]

LETTER CCCXLVIII.—(LXI. vol. ii. p. 165.)

I have given the former part of this letter as a specimen of the free and easy epistolary style of an age which we are too apt to consider as almost entirely illiterate; on a similar subject a modern gentleman could scarcely have expressed himself in easier terms, or with more propriety, though in one instance perhaps with more politeness.

To John Paston, Esq. at Norwich, or to Roose, dwelling afore Mrs. Paston s gate in Norwich.

Rıgнt worshipful and well-beloved brother, I recommend me to you; letting you weet that I have communed with your friend Danson, and have received your ring of him, and he hath by mine advice spoken with her two times;[1] he telleth me of her dealing and answers, which if they were according to his saying, a fainter lover than ye would, and well ought to, take therein great comfort, so that (*even though*) he might haply sleep the worse three nights after.

And such dealing in part as was between my Lady W. and your friend Danson he wrote me a bill thereof, which I send you herewith, and that that longeth to me to do therein it shall not fail to leave all other business apart; nevertheless within three days I hope so to deal herein that I suppose to set you in certainty how that ye shall find her for ever hereafter.

It is so, as I understand, that ye be as busy on your side for your friend Danson whereas [*where*][2] ye be; I pray God send you both good speed in these works, which, if they be brought about, each of you is much beholden to other; yet were it pity that such crafty

---

[1] I do not know to whom this refers: it relates to some lady to whom he then paid his addresses, (the Lady W. after-mentioned I suppose,) and who by the next letter appears to be Lady Walgrave, widow of Sir Richard Walgrave, knight [He appears to have been a very general but unsuccessful wooer]

[2] [Fenn translates *whereas* here by *if* We have already noticed the indiscriminate use of *where* and *whereas*; by attending to this, and altering Fenn's punctuation, the sentence is perfectly clear, and justifies his own praise of the style]

wooers as ye be both should speed well, but if (*unless*) ye love truly.[1]

Item, as for Stocton's daughter, she shall be wedded in haste to Skeerne, as she told herself to my silkmaid,[2] which maketh part of such as she shall wear, to whom she broke (*opened*) her heart, and told her that she should have had Master Paston, and my maid weird (*thought*) it had been I that she spoke of; and with more (*moreover*) that the same Master Paston come where she was with twenty men, and would have taken her away; I told my maid that she lied of me, and that I never spoke with her in my life, nor that I would not wed her to have with her three thousand marks (2000*l.*)

Item, as for Eberton's daughter, my brother Edmond saith that he heard never more speech thereof since your departing, and that ye would that he should not break nor do nothing therein but if (*unless*) it came of their beginning.

Item, I had answer from my lord[3] that he is my special good lord, and that by writing; and as for Berney he set him in his own wages for my sake, and that whensoever I come to Calais I shall find all thing there as I would have it, and rather better than it was heretofore.

Item, the king came to this town on Wednesday; as for the French embassade[4] (*embassy*) that is here, they come not in the king's presence by likelihood, for men say that the chief of them is he that poisoned both the Duke of Berry and the Duke of Calabria.

Item, there was never more likelihood that the king should go over sea this next year than was now.

I pray you remember that I may have the pewter vessel hither by the next carrier by the latter end of this week.

Item, I pray you remember so that I may have the books by the same time, which my mother said she would send me by the next carrier.

Written at London, the Sunday the 20th of November, in the 14th year of Edward IV.

JOHN PASTON, *knight.*

London, Sunday,
20th of November, 1474.
14 E. IV.

LETTER CCCXLIX.—(LXII. vol. ii. p. 171.)

We are in this letter brought acquainted with the manners of the time. The lady shows herself a woman of honour, and above giving hope when she meant not to encourage the addresses of J. Paston. She was the widow of Sir Richard Walgrave, knight, a Yorkist, who was with the Earl of Kent at the taking of the town of Coquet and the isle of Rhée; he died young, and was succeeded by his brother Sir Thomas Walgrave. [Another unsuccessful attempt by poor John Paston.]

To John Paston, Esq.

BROTHER, I recommend me to you; letting you weet that I have, like as I promised you, I have done my devoir to know my Lady Walgrave's stomach (*resolution*), which, as God help me, and to be plain to you, I find in her no matter nor cause that I might take comfort of.

1 [This is a very pleasant and good-humoured bit of sarcasm. Sir John seems always to have a pretty correct conception of the characters of those he addresses.]

2 A person who made gowns of silk, &c. for both men and women, as appears from the manner in which she is here mentioned.

3 I am not certain whether the Duke of Norfolk is here meant, or Lord Hastings the then governor of Calais.

4 For the better understanding of this curious anecdote, which reflects honour on King Edward both as a sovereign prince and a man, it will be necessary to inform the reader that, in 1472, Lewis XI., king of France, finding himself drawn into a war with the Duke of Burgundy in order to bring about a marriage between his brother Charles, Duke of Berry and Guienne, and Mary the daughter and heir of that duke, employed proper persons to destroy his brother, and by that means to extricate him from these troubles. The death of the Duke of Berry was effected by a slow poison, of which he died in May, 1472, aged about 26 years. Mary, the richest heiress of her time, was born in 1457, and by her father, the Duke of Burgundy, was promised in marriage to various potentates, and amongst the rest, to Nicholas of Anjou, Duke of Calabria and Lorrain. This prince died in August, 1473, aged about 25, here said by poison administered by the same hand that took off the Duke of Berry.

She will in no wise receive nor keep your ring with her, and yet I told her that she should not be anything bound thereby; but that I knew by your heart of old that I wist well ye would be glad to forbear the levest (*dearest*) thing that ye had in the world, which might be daily in her presence, that should cause her once on a day to remember you; but it would not be, she would not thereby, as she said, put you nor keep you in any comfort thereby.

And moreover she prayed me that I should never take labour more herein, for she would hold her to such answer as she had given you tofore; wherewith she thought both ye and I would have held us content, had (*it*) not been (*for*) the words of her sister Genevieve.

When I understood all this, and that over night she bade her that went between her and me bid me bring with me her muskball[1] which, &c., then I after all this asked if she were displeased with me for it, and she said, nay.

Then I told her that I had not sent it you, for sin of my soul; and so I told her all, how I had written to you why that I would not send it you, because I wist well ye should have sleeped the worse; but now, I told her, as God help me, that I would send it you,

and give you mine advice not to hope over much on her, which is over hard an hearted lady for a young man to trust unto; which I thought that for all my words ye could not nor would not do for all mine advice.

Yet againwards she is not displeased, nor forbid me not but that ye should have the keeping of her muskball; wherefore do ye with it as ye like; I would it had done well by good, I spake for you so that in faith I trow I could not say so well again; wherefore I send you herewith your ring and the unhappy muskball; also make ye matter of it hereafter as ye can, I am not happy to woo neither for myself nor none other.

I told her all the process of the Lord Howard[2] and of your grounds as I could, all helps not.

(*Here follows some displeasure at his uncle William's proceedings in matters between them, &c. of no consequence.*)

I hear no word of my vessel nor of my books; I marvel. No more. Written at London, the 11th day of December, in the 14th year of Edward IV.

JOHN PASTON, *knight.*

London,
Sunday, 11th of December,
1474. 14 E. IV.

LETTER CCCL.—(LXIII. vol. ii. p. 175.)

Though this letter has no signature, yet it is written by Sir John Paston, knight. The business mentioned in the first part of this letter, on which Sir John was so anxious to attend the Duke and Duchess of Norfolk, was relative to Caister, &c.; and his journey into Flanders, to purchase horse and harness, was in consequence of the treaty entered into between Edward and the Duke of Burgundy, which would be productive of a war with France.

To the right worshipful John Paston, Esq., at Norwich, or to his mother, Margaret Paston, in his absence, in haste.

I RECOMMEND me to you, praying you heartily, that I may have weeting (*knowledge*) when that my Lord and Lady of Norfolk shall be at London, and how long they shall tarry there, and in especial my Lord of Norfolk; for upon their coming to London were it for me to be guided; nevertheless I would be sorry to come there but if (*unless*)

I needs must. I think it would be to you over irksome a labour to solicit the matters atween them and me, but if (*unless*) I were there myself; wherefore, if ye think it be convenient that I come thither, I pray you send me word as hastily as ye may, and by what time ye think most convenient that I should be there; and of all such comfort as ye find or hear of the towardness thereof, and when also that ye shall be there yourself; for

---

[1] This muskball, or ball of perfume, seems to have been taken from Lady Walgrave by Sir John Paston in a jesting manner, to send to his brother as a present from her.

[2] He was afterwards Duke of Norfolk.

it is so that as to-morrow I purpose to ride into Flanders to purvey me of horse and harness; percase (*perchance*) I shall see the siege of Nuys [1] ere I come again if I have time; wherefore, if I so do, by likelihood it will be a fourteen days ere I be here again; and after, as I hear from you and others thereupon, that at the next passage, and God will, I purpose to come to London ward: God send me good speed; in chief for the matter above written; and secondly, for to appoint with the king and my lord for such retinue as I should have now in these wars into France; wherefore I pray you in Norfolk and other places, commune with such as ye think likely for you and me that are disposed to take wages in gentlemen's houses and elsewhere, so that we may be the more ready when that need is; nevertheless at this hour I would be glad to have with me daily three or four more than I have, such as were likely; for I lack of my retinue that I have near so many.

I pray you send me some tidings, such as ye hear, and how that my brother Edmund doth; for as for tidings here there be but few, save that the siege lasteth still by the Duke of Burgundy afore Nuys, and the emperor[2] hath besieged also, not far from thence, a castle and another town in like wise, wherein the duke's men be.

And also the French king, men say, is coming nigh to the water of Somme with 4000 spears, and some men trow (*think*) that he will, at the day of breaking of truce,[3] or else before, set upon the duke's countries here.

When I hear more I shall send you more tidings.

The king's ambassadors Sir Thomas Montgomery and the Master of the Rolls[4] be coming homeward from Nuys,[5] and as for me I think that I should be sick but if (*unless*) I see it.

Sir John of Parre and William Berkeley came this way to Flanders ward to buy them horse and harness, and (*I*) made Sir J. Parre (*as*) good cheer as I could for your sake; and he told me that ye made him haulte (*high*) cheer, &c. at Norwich. No more. Written at Calais, the 17th day of January, in the 14th year of Edward IV.

Calais, Tuesday, 17th of January,
1474. 14 E. IV.

LETTER CCCLI.—(XVII. vol. v. p. 83.)

[MARGARET PASTON writes to her son John again about money, complaining that Robert Clere had not been paid 20l. lent by him and his mother to Sir John; she supposes that William Paston ought to have paid it, " for he hath a surety for all that and more," but he had refused unless on the delivery of some pledges of Margaret Paston's then in the hands of Clere. Margaret Paston requests her son to ascertain " in haste," and let her " understand how it is," " for I were loath to lose my pledges; I wot it well your good uncle would be in possession with good will, but I would not so." She next alludes to other matters of family discontent. Agnes Paston had been for some time living in London, and Margaret says " Remember me to your grandam; I would she were here in Norfolk, as well at ease as ever I saw her, and as little ruled by her son as ever she was, and then I would hope that we all should fare the better for her." This son was no doubt the " uncle William" so often alluded to, of whom the rest of the family seem to have been very willing to borrow money, and very much surprised at being expected to pay; whether or not he was aware of this

[1] [Nuys is a town in Germany, in the government circle of Cologne, in Rhenish Prussia, on the west side of the Rhine.]

[2] Frederick III. of Austria, emperor of Germany.
[3] This truce between Lewis XI., king of France, and the Duke of Burgundy, was to be at an end in the beginning of the summer in 1475.
[4] Dr. John Morton, afterwards Bishop of Ely, Lord Chancellor, Archbishop of Canterbury, and Cardinal.
[5] The duke persisted in this siege, though the emperor with a large force was in the neighbourhood, much to his own disadvantage, as it prevented his meeting the King of England; and at last the siege was raised on certain conditions.

amily defect, he seems to have been by no neans wanting in a due regard to his own dvantage in all these bargains, and to have onsidered all that was legal as just and ight. From money-lending Margaret Paston asses to religious matters, and one of her easons for desiring a license for her chapel ppears to point to the evil of non-residence ven in those days. She says, "I would ye hould speak with my Lord of Norwich, and ssay to get a license of him that I may have ne sacrament here in the chapel, because it , far to the church, and I am sickly, and the arson is often out." She was then residing t Mawteby, whence this letter is dated,

Saturday, Jan. 29, 1474. In a sort of post-script she mentions a curious circumstance connected with the currency. Fenn considers it to allude to the alloy oxydising, but this could hardly be the case to an extent sufficient to prevent the money from passing. At least we have never seen specimens of any such coin. She says:—"My cousin Robert told me that there was more than 7*l*. of the money that was paid him that was right on [*thoroughly*] rusty, and he could not have it changed: he was ungoodly [*not well*] served therein." We rather think it means coin of an early date, not at that time commonly current.]

LETTER CCCLII.—(XVIII. vol. v. p. 87.)

This letter is written from Norwich on the ame day as the last, by Margaret Paston to er other son, Sir John, and contains nearly a epetition of the money affairs mentioned in ne previous letter. Edward IV. had been ecently exacting a benevolence, as it was ermed (a task or tax, as the writers of these etters call it), in the city and county, and he withdrawal of such large sums of money re stated to have had a *most depressing* ffect upon prices. She says:—"As for porle wood, before the king's coming into lorfolk I might have had chapmen to have ought it a gret (*in the gross*) for twelve core marks (160*l*.), and now there will no nan buy it a gret, because of the great ood (*large sums*) that the people is laid to assessed] for the king; wherefore we are bout to retail it as well as we may * * * * is for your barley in this country, it cannot e sold above 10*d*. or 11*d*. that is the greatest rice of barley here, and but it be at a better rice I purpose for to do it malt (*malt it*) * * * Ialt is sold here but for 13*d*., and wheat s. or 26*d*. at this time, and oats 12*d*. There

is none outload suffered to go out of this country as yet; the king hath commanded that there should none go out of this land. I fear me we shall have right a strange world; God amend it, when his will is." The quantity worth the above-named prices was no doubt the comb, equal to two bushels, a term still frequently used in reckoning in the eastern counties. The low price is confirmed by the list of prices, in Eden's 'State of the Poor;' in Appendix, page xi. he gives the price of oats in 1475 as 1*s*. 10*d*. per quarter. The attempt to regulate prices by preventing traffic seems to have been constant, and always to have been attended with suffering. She concludes with an account of the books so earnestly desired by Sir John. " As for the books that ye desired to have of Sir James's, the best of all and the fairest is claimed; nor it is not in his inventory. I shall assay to get it for you an I may; the price of these other books, besides that, is 20*s*. 6*d*. the which I send ye a bill of. If ye like by the price of them, and ye will have them, send me word."]

LETTER CCCLIII.—(XIX. vol. v. p. 93.)

Sir J. Paston writes from Calais, Sunday, 'eb. 5, 1474-5, to "his brother John Paston, r to his uncle William Paston in Warwick ane, or to Edmund Paston at the George at 'aul's Wharf," explaining that he is pre-

vented from leaving Calais to urge his suit respecting Caister, and entreating of all or any of them to do all for him that they possibly can The details are wholly uninteresting.]

LETTER CCCLIV.—(XX. vol. v. p. 97.)

[IN this letter Sir John Paston answers his mother's letter (ccclii.) Having now got a price fixed on the books, he seems indifferent about them; he probably wished his offer as to paying in prayers to have been accepted. " As for the books that were Sir James's, God have his soul! [he continues to pray] I think best that they be still with you, till that I speak with you myself. My mind is not now most upon books." The rest of the letter consists of details as to his money transactions. It is dated Calais, Feb. 22, 1474-5.]

LETTER CCCLV.—(LXIV. vol. ii. p. 179.)

[This letter is written on the back of Letter cccl., from J. Paston, and is a curious instance of the uncertainty of the transmission of correspondence. If it is meant that she had received no letter since St. Matthew's even, she had not yet had that of Nov. 20 (Letter cccxlvii.), a period of nearly four months. But she may mean that she had written this letter on St. Matthias' even, but could not send it, as she adds, "if I might have had a messenger ere this time, I had sent it you." She could scarcely have thought it long not to have *received* a letter since Matthias' even, a period of only ten days. We are inclined to think she alludes to her own writing.]

Mrs. Margaret Paston, to her son John Paston.

JOHN PASTON, I send you God's blessing and mine; letting you weet, that I had none ere this letter than on Saint Matthew's even;[1] if I might have had a messenger ere this time I had sent it you; I con you thank for the letter that ye sent to my cousin Calthorp and me of the tidings; I would ye should do so more. As ye may remember that I spake to you for the 20l. for my cousin Clere, speak to your uncle thereof, and send me an answer thereof in haste.

And for the licence[2] that I spake to you, for to have the sacrament in my chapel, if ye cannot get it of the Bishop of Norwich, get it of the Bishop of Canterbury, for that is most sure for all places.

God keep you. Written on Midlent Sunday.

Midlent Sunday,
5th of March, 1474.
15 E. IV.

LETTER CCCLVI.—(XXI. vol. v. p. 103.)

[A NEGOTIATION for a marriage. Fenn says that the gentleman was John Berney, of Reedham, Esq., and that the negotiation was successful, as he married Alice, daughter of Richard Southwell, Esq. of Wood-rising in Norfolk, the writer of this letter to John Paston, Esq. We give all but the complimentary part of the letter. " And, cousin, in the matter that it liked you to remember me in, both to my worship and pleasure, I fear me that neither my poor daughter nor poor purse can nor may be to his pleasure; would God either might; and I should take me right near to his pleasure, saving myself, I ensure you by my troth; and how to understand his disposition and pleasure therein, I see no mean as thus advised, but if it might please you by your wisdom to attempt it farther, as ye seem most convenient, and thereupon to be guided by your good advice, as the case shall require, wherein ye shall bind me hereafter to do that may be your pleasure to my power, and yet with no better will than I have had, so God help me, who have you ever in his keeping, and send you your heart's desire to his pleasure; and if it please you to remember farther in the premises, I trust ye shall lose no labour on my poor part; howbeit I fear me sore, as I began, both of my poor daughter and purse." Dated Wood-rising, March 26, about 1475.]

---

[1] [St. Matthew's anniversary is September 21. St. Matthias's (in original " Sent Matheus") is Feb. 23.]

[2] We are here informed that the archbishop's licence was preferable to that of the diocesan, and seems to have had greater privileges annexed to it.

LETTER CCCLVII.—(XXII. vol. v. p. 105.)

MARGARET Paston again writes to Sir John, chiefly details about money matters; money, he says, is very scarce; "the king goeth so near us in this country, both to poor and rich, that I wot not how we shall live, but if the world amend: God amend it, when his will is. I can neither sell corn nor cattle to no good preve (*profit*.) Malt is here but at 10*d*. comb; wheat, a comb, 28*d*.; oats, a comb, 10*d*.; and thereof is but little to get here at this time." She says Peacock, apparently his steward, hath paid for him two tasks (*subsidies*) at this time. Her ideas of soldiership are remarkably clear for a female, and her recommendation to Sir John, who had served, good. "If your brethren go over the sea, advise them as ye think best for their safe-guard, for some of them be but young soldiers, and wot full little what it is to be as a soldier, nor for to endure to do as a soldier should do." The letter is dated Mawteby, Tuesday, May 23, 1475.]

LETTER CCCLVIII.—(XXIII. vol. v. p. 111.)

SIR John Paston writes to his brother Edmund, that a vacancy has occurred at Calais, and that he may "come and live like a gentleman,' if he can manage to obtain the appointment, "else," he adds, "if ye dispose you to abide in England, since it is so that the Bishop of Lincoln is chancellor, his service is the meeter for you, he is next neighbour to Norfolk of any estate : God send you some good ward of his." Place-hunting, from a place under the government to one under a private nobleman, seems to have been the general pursuit, and by no means incompatible with the character of a gentleman. The letter is dated Calais, Tuesday, June 13th, 1475.]

LETTER CCCLIX.—(LXV. vol. ii. p. 181.)

The abbey of St Bennet at Holm was situated in the parish of Horning in Norfolk, in the midst of a now dreary and solitary marsh, not likely to be chosen for the wholesomeness of the air The remains of this once grand and mitred abbey are now very small, standing in the midst of a level marsh, intersected by a great number of almost stagnant ditches I am, however, informed by a most respectable gentleman, whose seat is in the neighbourhood, that many of the towns surrounding this spot are remarkable for the longevity of their inhabitants. If such is the effect of this air now, perhaps in the flourishing state of the abbey it might be still more salubrious. [1787 It is now much improved.]

To the right worshipful Sir John Paston, Knight, in haste.

RIGHT well-beloved son, &c. (*The chief part of this letter relates to Sir John Paston's private affairs, his rents and lands, and it informs him that William Jenney had entered into Holmhall, in Filby, in the right and title of his daughter-in-law, which was Boys' daughter, &c.*)

As for tidings here in this country, we have none but that the country is barren of money; and that my Lady of York[1] and all her household is here at Saint Bennet s, and purposed to abide there still till the king come from beyond the sea,[2] and longer if she like the air there, as it is said.

I think right long till I hear some tidings for you[3] and from your brethren. I pray God send you, and all your company good speed in your journeys, to his pleasure and to your worships and profits.

Written at Mawteby, on Saint Laurence's even, the 15th year of the reign of King Edward the IV.

By your MOTHER.

Mawteby, Thursday,
10th of August, 1475.
15 E IV.

---

[1] Cecily, Duchess of York, daughter of Ralph Nevile, Earl of Westmoreland, was the widow of Richard Plantagenet, Duke of York, and mother of King Edward IV &c She died in 1495, and was buried near her husband in the college of Fotheringay.

[2] He was at this time in France.
[3] Quære, from ?

LETTER CCCLX.—(XXIV. vol. v. p. 113.)

[Sir John Paston writes to his mother from Calais, and announces the conclusion of the journey to France of Edward IV. He had raised large sums in England to carry on a war against the French in alliance with the Duke of Burgundy, but the latter failing him, and, it is said, his ministers being bribed by the French king, a peace for seven years was concluded, after a personal interview between the two monarchs at Pecquigni, where they met on a bridge across the Somme. It contains no other matter of interest, and to this there is a mere allusion. Dated Monday, Sept. 11, 1475.]

LETTER CCCLXI.—(XXV. vol. v. p. 117.)

[John Paston writes to his brother Sir John of the further progress towards the recovery of Caister. He says the king has promised there shall be no delay beyond the 3rd Nov. of the present year; that the Duke of Norfolk's council acknowledge his right; and that "my lady sweareth, and so doth Barnard on her behalf, that she would as fain ye had it as any body; notwithstanding she said not so to me since I came home, for I spake not to her but once since I saw you last." He complains of illness occasioned by taking cold, both at Calais and since his return home; and says "but I was never so well armed for the war, as I have now armed me for cold; wherefore I advise you take example by me if it happen you to be sick, as ye were when I was at Calais, in any wise keep you warm. I ween Harry Wodehouse nor James Arblaster wear never at once so many coats, hose and boots as I do, or else by God we had gone therefore; what we shall yet I cannot say, but I bear me bold on two days amending." Rather a short time to recommend his experience so confidently. Dated Norwich, Tuesday, Oct. 10, 1475.]

LETTER CCCLXII.—(LXVI. vol. ii. p. 183.)

This letter records a most curious conversation between the king, the Duke of Norfolk, and Sir William Brandon, relative to Caister. Sir William Brandon was father of Charles Brandon, afterwards created Duke of Suffolk.

To Sir John Paston, Knight, lodged at the George, by Paul's Wharf, in London.

After all duties of recommendation, please it you to understand that I have spoken with my lady since I wrote to you last; and she told me that the king had no such words to my lord for Caister as ye told me; but she saith that the king asked my lord at his departing from Calais how he would deal with Caister, and my lord answered never a word. Sir W. Brandon stood by, and the king asked him what my lord would do in that matter; saying that he had commanded him before time to move my lord with that matter, and Sir W. Brandon gave the king to answer that he had done so; then the king asked Sir W. B. what my lord's answer was to him, and Sir W. B. told the king that my lord's answer was that the king should as soon have his life as that place; and then the king asked my lord whether he said so or not, and my lord said, yea. And the king said not one word again, but turned his back, and went his way; but my lady told me and (*if*) the king had spoken any word in the world after that to my lord, my lord would not have said him nay.

And I have given my lady warning that I will do my lord no more service; but ere we parted she made me to make her (*a*) promise, that I should let her have knowledge ere I stened myself in any other service; and so I eparted, and see her not since, nor nought urpose to do till I speak with you.

I pray you bring home some hats with you, r and (*if*) ye come not hastily send me one, c. and I shall pay you for it a comb (*of*) ats[1] when ye come home.

My mother would fain have you at Mawte-y; she rode thither, out of Norwich on aturday last past to purvey your lodging ?ady against your coming.

I have been right sick again since I wrote) you last,[2] and this same day have I been passing sick; it will not out of my stomach by no mean, I am undone, I may not eat half enough when I have most hunger, I am so well dieted, and yet it will not be. God send you heele (*health*), for (*I*) have none three days together, do the best I can.

Written at Norwich, the Monday next before Saint Simon and Jude,[3] in the 15th year of Edward IV.

JOHN PASTON.

Norwich,
Monday, 23rd of October,
1475. 15 E IV.

LETTER CCCLXIII.—(LXVII. vol. ii. p. 187.)

[This letter contains an account of the death of the Duke of Norfolk, and of his funeral] John Mowbray, Duke of Norfolk, &c , was retained by Edward IV. to serve him in his wars in France in 1473, he married Elizabeth, daughter of John Talbot, first Earl of Shrewsbury, and died suddenly at his castle of Framlingham on the 17th of January, 1475, 15 E IV., and was buried in the abbey church of Thetford in Norfolk He left an only daughter and heir, Anne, married in her early age to Richard Plantagenet, Duke of York, who dying without issue, the great possessions and honours of this noble family came to Sir John Howard, knight, Lord Howard, whose mother was a sister and co-heir of Thomas Mowbray, Duke of Norfolk [Though Sir John says the Duke's death occurred " not in the most happy season" for him, he instantly took possession of Caister, and succeeded in retaining it.]

This letter has no direction, but it is written either to John Paston, Esq , or Margaret Paston.

.ike it you to weet, that, not in the most appy season for me, it is so fortuned that, hereas my Lord of Norfolk, yesterday being) good health, this night died about mid-ight, wherefore it is for all that loved him) do and help now that that may be to his onour and weal to his soul; and it is so 1at this country is not well purveyed of cloth f gold for the covering for his body and erse; wherefore every man helping to his owel, I put the council of my lord in com-)it that I hoped to get one for that day, if it ?ere so that it be not broken or put to other se; wherefore please it you to send me word if t be so that ye have, or can come by, the cloth f tissue that I bought for our father's tomb, and I undertake it shall be saved again for you unhurt at my peril; I deem hereby to get great thanks and great assistance in time to come; and that either Sym or Mother Brown may deliver it to me to-morrow by seven of the clock.

Item, as for other means I have sent my servant Richard Toring to London, which I hope shall bring me good tidings again, and within four days I hope to see you.

Written on Wednesday, the 17th day of January, in the 15th year of Edward IV.

JOHN PASTON, *knight.*

Framlingham,
Wednesday, 17th of January, 1475.
15 E IV

LETTER CCCLXIV.—(XXVI. vol. v. p. 121.)

JOHN PASTON writes to his brother that his ntering so quickly upon Caister has been very ill taken, "insomuch that some say that ye tendered little my lord's death, inasmuch

---

[1] In 1475, a comb of oats sold for 11*d*, we have herefore the value of a hat in this reign [The price f " hattes of wolle" in 1480, varied from xiid to iiid each; while bonnets, in the same entry, are et down at lis. vid. and iiis. each. See Sir N H

Nicolas's ' Wardrobe Expenses of Edward IV ' p. 119]

[2] [The extra clothing appears to have been not so efficacious as he had anticipated]

[3] 28th of October.

as ye would so soon enter upon him after his decease, without advice and assent of my lord's council; wherefore it is thought here by such as be your friends in my lord's house, that if my lady have once the grant of the wardship of the child,[1] that she will occupy Caister with other lands, and lay the default on your unkind hastiness of entry without her assent; wherefore in any wise get you a patent of the king ensealed before her's, an ye may by any mean possible." We shall see that this advice was successfully followed. The rest of the letter is about raising of money for John Paston, who it appears was going again to Calais, as he requests his brother to get him excused from keeping a horse there because hay was so dear. Dated Norwich, Tuesday, Jan. 23, 1475.]

LETTER CCCLXV.—(LXVIII. vol. ii. p. 191.)

I have given the whole of this letter as conveying to us some information relative to the ordinary transactions of the times. The anecdote of the Duke of York's marrying Anne, the daughter of the deceased Duke of Norfolk, depending on the duchess (who appears to have been left with child at the duke's decease) not having a son, is I believe both new and curious, and shows us that alliances as well in those days as at present, were estimated according to the possessions and pecuniary advantages they brought with them.

To John Paston, Esq., at Norwich, be this delivered.

I RECOMMEND me to you, letting you weet that I was informed by Richard Radle that one Scarlett, that was under-sheriff to Hastings,[2] would sue to me on your behalf, for that ye were displeased with a return of nichil[3] upon you in the said Hastings' time; wherefore Richard Radle thought that the said Scarlett would be glad to give a noble (6s. 8d.) or a rial (10s.) for a saddle to amends, so that ye would cease and stop the bill which ye intend to put into the court against his master Hastings. Wherefore the said Scarlett came to me, and prayed me to help in the same, and so I have done my devoir to feel of him the most he can find in his stomach to depart with to please you, and in conclusion I trow he shall give you a doublet cloth of silk, price 20s. or thereabout; which, upon such answer as I hear from you, I deem that Bishop the attorney shall, if I conclude with him on your behalf, pay in money or otherwise to whom that ye will assign here.

I shall by the means of Radle weet at whose suit it was taken out; I deem it something done by craft, by the means of them that have entresse (*interest*) in your land to the intent to noise it theirs, or to make you past shame of the selling thereof.

Item, I have received a letter from you writen on Tuesday last.

Item, where that (*whereas*) some towards my Lady of Norfolk noise that I did unkindly to send so hastily to Caister as I did, there is no discreet person that so thinketh; for if my lord had been as kind to me as he might have been, and according to such heart and service as my grandfather, my father, yourself, and I, have ought and done to my Lords of Norfolk that dead been, and yet (*even*) if I had wedded his daughter yet must I have done as I did; and moreover, if I had had any deeming of my lord's death four hours ere he died, I must needs but if (*unless*) I would be known a fool have entered it the hour before his decease; but in effect they that in that matter have always meant unkindly to me, they feign that rumour against me; but there is none that meant truly to him that dead is that would be sorry that I had it, and in especial such as love his soul.

Item, where(*as*) it is deemed that my lady would hereafter be the rather mine heavy (*unkind*) lady for that dealing, I think that she

---

[1] [The duchess had just been delivered of a daughter, the Lady Anne, mentioned in the preceding letter.]
[2] John Hastings was sheriff of Norfolk the preceding year.
[3] Nihils, or Nichils, are issues which the sheriff that is apposed in the Exchequer says are *nothing worth* and illeviable through the insufficiency of the parties from whom due.

is too reasonable so to be, for I did it not un-wist (*unknown*) to her council; there was no man thought that I should do otherwise, and as to say that I might have had my lady's advice and leave, I might have tarried yet ere I could have spoken with her, or yet have had any body to have moved her there on my behalf, as ye wot I did what I could; moreover I tarried by the advice of Sir Robert Wingfield three days there, for that he put me in comfort that the Lord Howard,[1] and his brother Sir John, should have come to Norwich, at whose coming he doubted not but that I should have a good direction taken for me in that matter; they lay to me unkindness for overkindness.

Item, as for my matter here, it was this day before all the lords of the council, and among them all it was not thought that in my sending of Wheatley thither, immediately after the decease of the duke, that I dealt unkindly or unfittingly, but that I was more unreasonably dealt with; wherefore let men deem what they will, greatest clerks are not always wisest men; but I hope hastily to have one way in it or other.

Item, I wend to have found a gown of mine here, but it come home the same day that I come out, brought by Harry Berker, loader (*carrier*). I would in all haste possible have that same gown of puke[2] furred with white lamb.

Item, I would have my long russet gown of the French russet in all haste, for I have no gown to go in here.

Item, I pray you recommend me to my mother, and let us all pray God send my Lady of Norfolk a son, for upon that resteth much matter; for if the king's son[3] marry my lord's daughter, the king would that his son should have a fair place in Norfolk though he should give me two times the value in other land as I am done to weet (*informed*). I pray you send me word of my lady's speed as soon as ye can.

Item, as for Bowen I shall feel him (*sound his inclination*), and should have done though ye had not sent.

Item, there is offered me a good marriage for my sister Anne, Skipwith's son and heir of Lincolnshire, a man (*of*) 500 or 600 marks (*between 300l. and 400l.*) by the year.

No more. Written at London the 27th day of January, in the 15th year of Edward IV.

Item, my Lady of Exeter[4] is dead, and it was said, that both the old Duchess of Norfolk,[5] and the Countess of Oxford,[6] were dead, but it is not so yet.

Item, I shall remember Calais both for horse and all, &c.

London, Saturday,
27th of January, 1475. 15 E. IV.

LETTER CCCLXVI.—(XXVII. vol. v. p. 125.)

[JOHN PASTON writes to Lord Hastings in this letter, recommending to him a person "meet to be clerk of your kitchen." The description of him is minute, and the qualifications curious enough for one filling such an office. " This man is mean of [*of middle*] stature, young enough, well witted, well mannered; a goodly young man on horse and foot; he is well

[1] Afterwards Duke of Norfolk.
[2] Puke or pouk is an old Gothic word signifying the devil, see Pierce Plowman, Spencer, &c. Hence puke became synonymous to black, or dark gray, and consequently might be used for mourning. In Barrett's Alveare, 1580, it is explained as a colour between russet and black, and is rendered in Latin by *pullus*. On Good Friday the lord mayor and aldermen always wore their *pewke gowens*.
[3] Richard Plantagenet, Duke of York, second son of King Edward IV. in January, 1477, married Anne, sole daughter and heir of John Mowbray, late Duke of Norfolk.
[4] Anne, daughter of Richard Duke of York, sister
of Edward IV., and widow of Henry Holland, the last Duke of Exeter, her first husband; she died 14th of January, 1475, and lies buried with Sir Thomas St. Leger, knight, her second husband, in a private chapel at Windsor.
[5] Ellenor, only daughter of William Bourchier, Earl of Ewe, in Normandy, and widow of John Mowbray, Duke of Norfolk.
[6] Margaret, daughter of Richard Nevile, Earl of Salisbury, and wife of John de Vere, Earl of Oxford, now a prisoner in the castle of Hammes, in Picardy: or it may refer to Elizabeth, widow of the late Earl of Oxford, and daughter and heir of Sir John Howard, knight.

H

spoken in English, meetly well in French, and very perfect in Flemish; he can write and read; his name is Richard Stratton, his mother is Mistress Grame of Calais; and when I had showed him mine intent, he was agreeable and very glad if that it might please your lordship to accept him into your service." He also mentions having procured two other persons for his lordship's service, but these seem to be intended to serve in a military capacity. The letter is dated Norwich, Saturday, March 2, 1475-6.]

LETTER CCCLXVII.—(XXVIII. vol. v. p. 131.)

[Sir John Paston in this letter announces to his brother or mother his having crossed the sea to Calais, and being safe and well at Guisnes. He had gone with the governor of Calais, Lord Hastings, and informs his brother that a Master Fitzwalter intended to return to England in order to settle at Attleborough, and how extremely well-disposed the said Fitzwalter was toward him. This Fitzwalter was son of John Ratcliffe, Lord Fitzwalter in right of his wife, and who was killed at Ferrybridge in 1460. Master Fitzwalter was himself summoned to parliament as Lord Fitzwalter in 1485, but joining in the rebellion of Perkin Warbeck, he was taken prisoner, and confined in Calais; he attempted to escape from thence, but was retaken and beheaded. The letter is dated Tuesday, March 12, 1475-6.]

LETTER CCCLXVIII.—(XXIX. vol. v. p. 133.)

[The first part of this letter, which is from John Paston in Norwich to his mother, dated Tuesday, March, 1475-6, informs her that "my lady," probably the Duchess of Norfolk, had been inquiring whether she would be present at her accouchement, and recommends that she should accede to her wishes as it might be advantageous. In the latter part two curious subjects are noticed. He says:—" Here was here with me yesterday, a man from the prior of Bromholm, to let me have knowledge of the ill speech which is in the country now of new that the tomb [of his father] is not made, and also he saith that the cloth that lieth over the grave is all torn and rotten, and is not worth twopence, and he saith he hath patched it once or twice, wherefore the prior hath sent to you at the least to send thither a new cloth before Easter." The other subject—the inability to procure tiles in a town like Norwich,—is a remarkable instance of the want of progress in manufactures. He writes, " Master Stoley prayeth you, for God's sake, and ye will do no alms of tile, that he might borrow some of you till he may buy some and pay you again; for one, the fairest chamber of the fryars, standeth half uncovered for default of tile, for here is none to get for no money." Dated Tuesday, March, 1475-6.]

LETTER CCCLXIX.—(LXIX. vol. ii. p. 199.)

This letter furnishes us with a curious anecdote relative to Earl Rivers, who, we may suppose, had been on a pilgrimage to Rome; for Caxton tells us, that he was " sometime full vertuously occupied in goyng of pilgrimagis :" he likewise procured " greet and large indulgance and grace from our holy fader the pope." But it is plain he had not procured a papal protection from robbers.

To Mrs. Margaret Paston, at Norwich, or her son John Paston, Esq., and to each of them.

I recommend me to you; like it you to weet, that I am not certain yet whether my lord and I shall come into England the week before Easter, or else the week after Easter;

wherefore, mother, I beseech you to take no displeasure with me for my long tarrying, for I must do none otherwise for (*fear of*) displeasing of my lord.

I was nothing glad of this journey if I might goodly have chosen; nevertheless, saving that ye have cause to he displeased with me for the matter of Koketts, I am else right glad, for I hope that I am far more in favour with my lord than I was tofore.

Item, I send you, brother John, a letter herewith, which was brought hither to Calais from the George at Paul's Wharf; I deem it cometh from my brother Walter.

Item, if ye intend hitherwards, it were well done that ye hygthed (*hied*) you, for I suppose that my lord will take the view of all his retinue here, now before his departing; and I think that he would be better content with your coming now than another time; do as ye think best, and as ye may.

Item, where(*as*) Master Fitzwalter made me to write to you to advise you to tarry, I remit that to your discretion.

As for tidings here we hear from all the world; first, the Lord Rivers was at Rome right well and honourably, and other lords of England, as the Lord Hurmonde, [1] the Lord Scrope,[2] and at their departing, twelve miles on this half Rome, the Lord Rivers was robbed of all his jewels and plate, which was worth 1000 marks[3] (666*l.* 13*s.* 4*d.*) or better, and is returned to Rome for a remedy.

Item, the Duke of Burgundy[4] hath conquered Lorrain, and Queen Margaret[5] shall not now by likelihood have it; wherefore the French king cherisheth her but easily[6] (*slightly, little*); but after this conquest of Lorrain, the duke took great courage to go upon the land of the Swiss to conquer them, but they berded (*confronted*) him at an unset (*unlooked for*) place, and hath distressed him, and hath slain the most part of his vanward, and won all his ordnance and artillery, and moreover all stuff that he had in his host, except men and horse, that fled not; but they rode that night twenty miles; and so the rich salets,[7] helmets, garters, nowches[8] gelt (*gold*), and all is gone, with tents, pavilions, and all, and so men deem his pride is abated; men told him that they were froward carles, but he would not believe it, and yet men say that he will to them again; God speed them both.

Item, Sir John Myddleton took leave of the duke to sport him, but he is set in prison at Brussels.

I pray you send me some word, if ye think likely that I may enter Caister when I will, by the next messenger.

Written at Calais, in reasonable health of body and soul, I thank God, the 21st day of March, in the sixteenth year of Edward IV.

JOHN PASTON, *knight.*

Calais, Thursday,
21st of March, 1475. 16 E. IV.

LETTER CCCLXX.—(XXX. vol. v. p. 139.)

[JOHN PASTON writes from Norwich to his mother of his brother, Sir John, having suddenly departed for London to the king " for the surety of the manor of Caister." The cloth of gold, presented to the Duchess of Norfolk by Margaret Paston, it appears had

---

[1] Quære, Lord Ormond?

[2] John Lord Scroop, of Bolton.

[3] Allowing for the difference of weight, and value of money between this and the present time, he lost to the amount of nearly 4000*l.*

[4] During the preceding autumn the Duke of Burgundy, having subdued the whole duchy of Lorrain, he now attacked the Swiss, and took a town called Grauson just as a body of troops were arriving to its relief; these he went to meet as they came down the narrow passes of the mountains; when his army, being seized with a panic, fled, and

left his baggage to be plundered by the enemy. Within a short time after this he besieged Morat, a small town near Bern, when a battle ensued in which he was totally routed.

[5] This queen had been lately delivered from her imprisonment in the Tower, to the French king, on his engaging to pay 50,000 crowns for her ransom.

[6] So in Letter xv., vol. i., p. 9, " I have but easy stuff of money," that is, *little store* of money.

[7] Light head-pieces.

[8] Embossed ornaments—chains—buckles, &c.

been returned; and Sir John says: "Sir Robert Wingfield offered me yesterday twenty marks (13*l.* 6*s.* 8*d.*) for it; but I wot well ye shall have more for it, if ye will sell it." It will be seen from a subsequent letter that it was to be sold in order to purchase a cloth for her husband's tomb, which we have already seen had been much neglected. The latter part of the letter alludes to some domestic matter, implying that the "hostess at Fritton," who had been rebuking "our chyldyr" for "playing wanton," "hath gotten her such a thing to play with, that our other chyldyr shall have leave to sport them. God send her joy of it." The letter is dated Sunday, May or June, 1476.]

LETTER CCCLXXI.—(XXXI. vol. v. p. 141.)

[In this letter, dated Norwich, May 6, 1476, J. Paston writes to his brother Sir John again on the old subject of marriage. He says: "I understand that Mistress Fitzwalter hath a sister, a maid, to marry; I trow, an ye entreated him, she might come into Christian men's hands. I pray you speak with Master Fitzwalter of that matter; and ye may tell him that since he will have my service, it were as good, an such a bargain might be made, that both she and I awaited on him and my mistress his wife, at our own costs, as I alone to await on him at his cost, for then he should be sure that I should not be flitting an I had such a quarrel (*quarry*) to keep me at home; an I have his good will, it is none impossible to bring about." He had evidently not seen the lady, but he is constant to his old idea of *bargaining* his marriage.]

LETTER CCCLXXII.—(XXXII. vol. v. p. 145.)

[Sir John Paston writes from London to his mother or brother of his good success in having at length procured a decree for the restitution of the manor of Caister, which "now lacketh nothing but the privy seals, and writing to Master Colvill to avoid." He says, however, "that it shall cost me great money and hath cost me much labour; it is so that the king must have an hundred marks (66*l.* 13*s.* 4*d.*), and other costs will draw forty marks (26*l.* 13*s.* 4*d.*)." He adds that he shall "have much pain to get so much money," but hopes to accomplish it with the assistance of his uncle William, the resource in all straits. He lets us into an approximation of the real value of Caister with great naïveté, for he states that "the king would have bought it, but he was informed of the truth, and that it was not for a prince, and of the great price that I would sell it at, for that I might not forbear [*do without*] it, for [*though*] he should have paid two thousand marks (1333*l.* 6*s.* 8*d.*), or more if he had had it. Sir John seems to have been greatly excited by his success, for he addresses his brother as John Paston, knight, and he dates his letter on Monday the 26th of May, 1476, Monday being in fact the 29th.]

LETTER CCCLXXIII.—(XXXIII. vol. v. p. 149.)

[This letter contains a very curious notice of the *bargaining* in marriage. It is from Sir John in answer to one from that general wooer John Paston, who seems at length to have come to *terms* with some lady. Sir John objects to the proposed terms as improvident: "To be bound in five hundred marks (333*l.* 6*s.* 8*d.*) I think it is too much; whereas I felt [*understood*] by you ye should have with the gentlewoman but four hundred marks (266*l.* 13*s.* 4*d.*); nevertheless I agree; but ye shall understand that I will not be bound for you that ye shall make her jointure past 20*l.* by year, within a certain day limited, be it one year or two, that is the largest that ye may perform; for as for the manor of Sparham, my mother and ye accord not in your sayings; she will nought grant you therein while she liveth, save, as she saith to me, she hath granted you ten marks (6*l.* 13*s.* 4*d.*) by year till 40*l.* be paid, that is but six years; and after her death she will agree with good will, so that it may your proferment [*preferment—advantage*], that ye should have that manor in jointure with your wife to the longer liver of you both, paying ten marks (6*l.* 13*s.* 4*d.*) by year, so [imperfect in M.S.] or as she will that it shall be; therefore as for fifty marks (33*l.* 6*s.* 8*d.*) jointure, I pray you bind me in no such clause; but if it be for 20*l.* by a reasonable day, and twenty marks (13*l.* 6*s.* 8*d.*) after the decease of my mother." He then goes on to say, " ye make

you surer than I deem you be, for I deem that her friends will not be content with Bedingfield's surety, nor yours; I deem this matter will occupy longer leisure than ye deem for. Item, I remember that this money that she should have is not ready, but in the hands of merchants of the staple, which at a proof ye shall find per case so slack payers that ye might be deceived thereby; I know divers have lost money ere they could get their dues out of the staple." This is very curious, as the merchants of the staple have been generally considered as so opulent, that their security would have been undeniable. If the lady here in question was Mistress Fitzwalter's sister, the negotiation was fruitless, as the marriage was not effected. Sir John then reminds his brother of "the gown cloth of old camblet, I would have it home for my sister Ann, ye forgot it; I pray you send it home by the next messenger." He concludes his letter by saying, "Blessed be God, I have Caister at my will; God hold it better than it (*has*) done heretofore." Dated Sunday, June 30, 1476.]

LETTER CCCLXXIV.—(XXXIV. vol. v. p. 153.)

[MARGARET Paston being absent from home, though it is not said where, writes to her steward or some trusty domestic, about various matters, in all of which he has given her much satisfaction. The principal matter is of her son Walter. We must premise that she says some letters had miscarried that should have been brought by Thomas Holler's son. She then proceeds—" Wherefore I pray you heartily, if it be no disease to you, that ye will take the labour to bring Walter where he should be, and to purvey for him that he may be set in good and sad [*sober*] rule, for I were loath to lose him, for I trust to have more joy of him than I have of them that be older; though it be more cost to me to send you forth with him, I hold me pleased, for I wot well ye shall best purvey for him, and for such things as is necessary for him, than another should do, after mine intent. As for any horse to lead his gear, methink it were best that ye purvey at Cambridge, less than

(*unless*) ye can get any carrier from thence to Oxford more hastily, and I marvel that the letters come not to me, and whether I may lay the default to the father or to the son thereof. And I will Walter should be coupled with a better than Holler's son is there, as he shall be; howbeit I would not that he should make never the less of him, by cause he is his countryman and neighbour; and also I pray you write a letter in my name to Walter, after that ye have known mine intent before this to him ward; so that he do well, learn well, and be of good rule and disposition, there shall nothing fail him that I may help with so that it be necessary to him; and bid him that he be not too hasty of taking of orders that should bind him, till that he be of twenty-four years of age or more, though he be counselled the contrary, for often rape (*haste*) rueth. I will love him better to be a good secular man than a lewd (*ignorant*) priest." The whole of this is said in good sound sense and in most excellent feeling, and is alike honourable to her head and her heart, and creditable to her epistolary powers. The object of this good counsel and maternal care was her fourth son; he took his degree at Oxford in 1479, and died soon afterwards. The rest of her letter relates to the illness of her cousin Berneys, and here her good and right feelings are again displayed. She says, "And I pray you gif my white wine, or any of my waters, or any other thing that I have that is in your award, may do him comfort, let him have it, for I would be right sorry if anything should come to him but good; and for God's sake advise him to do make his will if it be not done, and to do well to my cousin his wife, and else it were pity." She afterwards remembers "that water of mint or water of millefoil (*yarrow—Achillæ'a millefólium*) were good for my cousin Berney to drink for to make him to brouke; and if they send to Dame Elizabeth Calthorpe, there ye shall not fail of one or both, she hath other waters to make folks to brouke." We do not know exactly the meaning of "brouke;" in Percy's Reliques the word "brok" is used in the sense of enjoy or please, but it will not bear that meaning. It may be from the German *brechen*, to be sick, but mint-water can hardly be an emetic. She speaks very favourably of the place where she is staying: "Me liketh mine abiding and the country here right well, and I trust when summer cometh and fair weather I shall like it better, for I am cherished here but too well." This interesting letter is dated Monday, Jan. about 1476 or 1477.]

LETTER CCCLXXV.—(XXXV. vol. v. p. 159.)

[This letter is from Dame Elizabeth Brews, the wife of Sir Thomas Brews, of Stinton Hall in Salle, and of Topcroft, to John Paston, and is chiefly interesting as being the commencement of a new treaty for a wife, that at length proved successful. Dame Brews seems from the first to have been decidedly favourable to him, and this letter contains an urgent invitation to come to Topcroft and meet some of her influential relations, she promising in the mean time that she will "go as well and as rightfully and as consciensly (*conscientiously*) as I can for both the parties." It is dated Jan. or Feb. of either 1476 or 1477.]

LETTER CCCLXXVI.—(XXXVI. vol. v. p. 161.)

[Another letter, evidently quickly following the preceding, from Dame Elizabeth Brews to John Paston. She gives the following account of the progress she has already made. "I sent mine husband a bill of the matter that ye know of, and he wrote another bill to me again touching the same matter, and he would that ye should go unto my mistress your mother, and assay if ye might get the whole 20*l.* into your hands, and then he would be more glad to marry with you, and will give you an 100*l.*; and, cousin, that day that she is married my father [Sir Giles Debenham] will give her fifty marks (33*l.* 6*s.* 8*d.*). But an we accord I shall give you a great treasure, that is, a witty gentlewoman, and, if I say it, both good and virtuous; for if I should take money for her I would not give her for a 1000*l.*; but, cousin, I trust you so much, that I would think her well beset on you an she[1] were worth much more." Parental fondness is here very pleasingly exhibited, but the sums mentioned on each side are much smaller than any that John Paston had been bargaining for previously, and we may, therefore, hope that he properly estimated her goodness and virtue. The letter concludes with another invitation to Topcroft. It is dated in Jan. or Feb. about 1476-7.

[1] [Erroneously printed *ge* in Fenn.]

LETTER CCCLXXVII.—(LXX. vol. ii. p. 205.)

The politicians of these times, we here see, looked upon the death of Charles the Bold, Duke of Burgundy, as an event of great importance to all Europe. He was dismounted from his horse, and slain in a battle fought on the 5th of January, 1476, before Nancy, the capital city of Lorrain, between his forces and those of Renate, Duke of Lorrain.

To John Paston, Esq., at Norwich, in haste.

I RECOMMEND me to you; letting you weet that yesterday began the great council, to which all the estates of the land shall come to, but if (*unless*) it be for great and reasonable excuses; and I suppose the chief cause of this assembly is to commune what is best to do now upon the great change by the death of the Duke of Burgundy, and for the keeping of Calais and the Marches, and for the preservation of the amities taken lately, as well with France as now with the members of Flanders; whereto I doubt not there shall be in all haste both the Dukes of Clarence and Gloucester, whereof I would that my brother Edmund wist.

Item, I feel but little effect in the labour of W. Alyngton, nevertheless I deem it is not for you, she shall not pass 200 marks as far as I can understand apart.

Item, I will not forget you otherwise.

Item, it is so that this day I hear great likelihood that my Lord Hastings shall hastily go to Calais with great company; if I think it be for you (*for your advantage*) to be one, I shall not forget you.

Item, this day the matter between Mrs.

Anne Hawte and me hath been soor (*in a sure manner*) broken both to the cardinal,[1] to my lord chamberlain,[2] and to myself, and I am in good hope; when I hear and know more, I shall send you word.

It seemeth that the world is all quavering, it will reboil somewhere, so that I deem young men shall be cherished, take your heart to you; I fear that I cannot be excused, but that I shall forth with my Lord Hastings over the sea, but I shall send you word in haste, and if I go I hope not to tarry long.

Item, to my brother Edmund. I am like to speak with Mistress Dixon in haste, and some deem that there shall be condescended that if E. P. (*Edmund Paston*) come to London that his costs shall be paid for.

I shall hastily send you word of more things.

Written at London, the 14th day of February, in the 16th year of Edward IV., the Friday afore Fastingong (*Fasting-going*, i. e. *Lent*). JOHN PASTON, *knight*.

London, Friday, 14th of February, 1476. 16 E. IV.

LETTER CCCLXXVIII.—(LXXI. vol. ii. p. 209.)

This is another curious letter from Lady Brews. We here see that the custom of choosing valentines was a sport practised in the houses of the gentry at this time.

To my worshipful cousin, John Paston[3] be this bill delivered, &c.

COUSIN, I recommend me unto you, thanking you heartily for the great cheer ye made me and all my folks the last time that I was at Norwich; and ye promised me that ye would never break the matter to Margery[4] unto

such time as ye and I were at a point. But ye have made her such (*an*) advocate for you, that I may never have rest night nor day for calling and crying upon to bring the said matter to effect, &c.

---

[1] Thomas Bourchier, Archbishop of Canterbury.
[2] William, Lord Hastings. Though this important business between Sir John Paston and Mrs. Anne Hawte has been so often mentioned, it has never been so clearly stated as to be exactly ascertained.

[3] John Paston was the next brother to Sir John Paston, knight, and his heir in 1479. He was high-sheriff of Norfolk, &c., in 1485, created a knight banneret in 1487, and died in 1503.
[4] Margery, daughter of Sir Thomas and Elizabeth Brews, of Stinton Hall, in Salle.

And, cousin, upon Friday is Saint Valentine's Day, and every bird chuseth him a make (*mate*); and if it like you to come on Thursday at night, and so purvey you that ye may abide there till Monday, I trust to God that ye shall so speak to mine husband; and I shall pray that we shall bring the matter to a conclusion, &c.

> For, cousin. "it is but a simple oak,
> That's cut down at the first stroke,"

for ye will be reasonable I trust to God,

which have you ever in his merciful keeping, &c.
                    By your cousin,
            DAME ELIZABETH BREWS,
        Otherwise shall be called by God's grace.[1]

Between the 8th and 14th
of February, 1476-7. 16 E. IV.

[1] [That is, not *cousin*, but *cn.*]

LETTER CCCLXXIX.—(LXXII. vol. ii. p. 211.)

Some parts of the letter seem intended for verse, as the lines, though unequal, rhyme. I have written them, in the modernised letter, so that the rhymes end the lines, though perhaps I am wrong. The lady appears conscious that she has opened her heart in the letter, and with a becoming modesty conjures J. Paston, that it may "be seyn of non' erthely creatur safe only himself." [This is certainly an interesting specimen of the love-letters of a young lady of the fifteenth century, and goes far to justify John Paston's final choice, though from the tenour of her letter he does not seem perfectly satisfied with her fortune, and to have been endeavouring to get it increased; the lady indeed fears that it may break off the match; as from the next letter appears to have been nearly the case; her own sentiments are much more honourable and disinterested. We have great doubts as to the intended versification, but we have let it stand.]

Unto my right well-beloved valentine, John Paston, Esq., be this bill delivered, &c.

RIGHT reverend and worshipful, and my right well-beloved Valentine, I recommend me unto you, full heartily desiring to hear of your welfare, which I beseech Almighty God long for to preserve unto his pleasure and your heart's desire.

And if it please you to hear of my welfare, I am not in good heele (*health*) of body nor of heart, nor shall be till I hear from you;

> For there wottys (*knows*) no creature what pain
>   that I endure,
> And for to be dead (*for my life*), I dare it not
>   dyscur' (*discover*).

And my lady my mother hath laboured the matter to my father full diligently, but she can no more get than ye know of, for the which God knoweth I am full sorry. But if that ye love me, as I trust verily that ye do, ye will not leave me therefore; for if that ye had not half the livelihood that ye have, for to do the greatest labour that any woman alive might, I would not forsake you.

And if ye command me to keep me true wherever
  I go,
I wis I will do all my might you to love, and
  never no mo.
And if my friends say that I do amiss,
  They shall not me let so for to do,
Mine heart me bids evermore to love you
  Truly over all earthly thing,
And if they be never so wrath,
I trust it shall be better in time coming.

No more to you at this time, but the Holy Trinity have you in keeping; and I beseech you that this bill be not seen of none earthly creature save only yourself, &c.

And this letter was endited at Topcroft, with full heavy heart, &c.

                    By your own
                    MARGERY BREWS.

Topcroft,
February, 1476-7. 16 E. IV.

LETTER CCCLXXX.—(LXXIII. vol. ii. p. 215.)

. Paston seems by this letter to have answered the last, but not to her satisfaction, respecting his being content to take her with the fortune her father proposed to give on her marriage She acknowledges the pleasure it would give her to find that he would marry her with the fortune her father had fixed, and with great sensibility requests him, if he cannot acquiesce, not to come to Topcroft, but to let matters remain as they were. The letter, at the same time that it acknowledges her regard for J. Paston, shows that she had a proper attention to her own consequence and her father's determination [It is indeed a most frank, kind-hearted, and right minded letter. It makes one thoroughly ashamed of the brokering spirit of her Valentine, and fearful that her anticipation of being "the merriest maiden on ground" could in any case hardly be realised]

To my right well-beloved cousin, John Paston, Esq., be this letter delivered, &c.

RIGHT worshipful and well-beloved Valentine, in my most humble wise I recommend me unto you, &c. And heartily I thank you for the letter which that ye send me by John Beckerton, whereby I understand and know that ye be purposed to come to Topcroft in short time, and without any errand or matter but only to have a conclusion of the matter betwixt my father and you; I would be most glad of any creature alive so that the matter might grow to effect. And thereas (*whereas*) ye say, and (*if*) ye come and find the matter no more towards you than ye did aforetime, ye would no more put my father and my lady my mother to no cost nor business for that cause a good while after, which causeth mine heart to be full heavy; and if that ye come, and the matter take to none effect, then should I be much more sorry and full of heaviness.

And as for myself I have done and understand[1] in the matter that I can or may, as

God knoweth; and I let you plainly understand that my father will no more money part withal in that behalf, but an 100*l.* and 50 marks (33*l.* 6*s.* 8*d.*), which is right far from the accomplishment of your desire.

Wherefore, if that ye could be content with that good and my poor person I would be the merriest maiden on ground; and if ye think not yourself so satisfied, or that ye might have much more good, as I have understood by you afore; good, true, and loving Valentine, that ye take no such labour upon you as to come more for that matter, but let (*what*) is, pass, and never more to be spoken of, as I may be your true lover and beadwoman during my life.

No more unto you at this time, but Almighty Jesu preserve you both body and soul, &c.

By your Valentine,
MARGERY BREWS.

Topcroft, 1476-7.

LETTER CCCLXXXI.—(LXXIV. vol. ii. p. 217.)

This letter seems written by a common friend of both the parties, who appears solicitous for the marriage taking effect. He informs J Paston that in addition to the fortune intended to be given by Sir Thomas Brews, the furniture of her chamber and her apparel should amount to the sum of 100 marks, or 66*l.* 13*s.* 4*d.* And he hints, as from Lady Brews, that they should be entertained at her table for three years after their marriage. [This is a striking instance of the want of currency. Here, as in many other instances, we see that persons possessing a superfluity of the products of their landed property, had great difficulty in converting it into money. The entertainment for three years of the married couple was thought less of than any the slightest increase of the dowry money.]

Unto my right worshipful master, John Paston, Esq., be this bill delivered, &c.

RIGHT worshipful Sir, I recommend me unto you; letting you know, as for the young gentlewoman, she oweth you her good heart and love; as I know by the communication that I have had with her for the same.

And, Sir, ye know what my master and

my lady hath proffered with her, 200 marks (133*l.* 6*s.* 8*d.*), and I dare say, that her chamber and arrayment (*apparel*) shall be worth 100 marks (66*l.* 13*s.* 4*d.*), and I heard my lady say that and (*if*) the case required, both ye and she should have your board with my lady three years after.

And I understand by my lady that she

---

[1] [Probably *understood—supported—acted in*]

would that ye should labour the matter to my master, for it should be the better.

And I heard my lady say,

"That it was a feeble oak,
That was cut down at the first stroke."

And ye be beholden unto my lady for her good word, for she hath never praised you too much.[1]

Sir, like as I promised you, I am your man, and my good will ye shall have in word and deed, &c.

And Jesu have you in his merciful keeping, &c.

By your man,

THOMAS KELA.

February, 1476-7.
16 E. IV.

LETTER CCCLXXXII.—(LXXV. vol. ii. p. 221.)

We find by this letter that J. Paston was as desirous of having all obstacles to the match removed, as the lady could be, and now writes from the house where she was, and to which I suppose he went on the receipt of her last letter. He takes great pains to explain the reason for the meeting at Norwich to have been fixed by his desire, fearing his mother might have been displeased with any alteration in the original plan. [To us it rather appears that, not being able to get a larger fortune, and having been so repeatedly disappointed, he had made up his mind to accept of this, and to trust to future expectations; hoping that his future father-in-law would be kind to him, "though he be hard to me as yet." What could induce Sir. J. Fenn to say that he "was as desirous of having all obstacles removed as the lady could be," we cannot conceive. His care for his mother is, however, a redeeming trait in his character.]

To my right worshipful mother, Margaret Paston.

RIGHT worshipful mother, after all duties of recommendation, in as humble wise as I can I beseech you of your daily blessing. Mother, please it you to weet, that the cause that Dame Elizabeth Brews desireth to meet with you at Norwich, and not at Langley as I appointed with you at my last being at Mauteby, is by my means; for my brother Thomas Jermyn, which knoweth nought of the mate (*match*), telleth me that the Causey ere ye can come to Bokenham Ferry is so overflown that there is no man that may on ethe [*in ease*] pass it, though he be right well horsed; which is no meet way for you to pass over, God defend (*forbid*) it. But, all things reckoned, it shall be less cost to you to be at Norwich, as for a day or tweyn and pass not [*not beyond*], than to meet at Langley, where everything is dear; and your horse may be sent home again the same Wednesday.

Mother, I beseech you for diverse causes that my sister Anne may come with you to Norwich; mother, the matter is in a reasonable good way, and I trust with God's mercy, and with your good help, that it shall take effect better to mine advantage than I told you of at Mauteby; for I trow there is not a kinder woman living than I shall have to my

mother-in-law if the matter take; nor yet a kinder father-in-law than I shall have, though he be hard to me as yet.

All the circumstances of the matter, which I trust to tell you at your coming to Norwich, could not be written in three leaves of paper, and ye know my lewd (*poor*) head well enough, I may not write long, wherefore I fery over (*defer*) all things till I may await on you myself. I shall do tonnen (*cause to be tunned*) into your place a dozen ale, and bread according, against Wednesday. If Sym might be forborn (*spared*) it were well done that he were at Norwich on Wednesday in the morning at market. Dame Elizabeth Brews shall lie at John Cook's;[2] if it might please you, I would be glad that she might dine in your house on Thursday, for there should you have most secret talking.

And, mother, at the reverence of God beware that ye be so purveyed for that ye take no cold by the way towards Norwich, for it is the most perilous March that ever was seen by any man's days that now liveth; and I pray to Jesu preserve you and yours.

Written at Topcroft the 8th day of March.

Your son and humble servant,

JOHN PASTON.

Topcroft, Saturday,
8th of March, 1476-7. 17 E. IV.

[1] That is, deservedly praised you; for though she hath praised you much, her praise is not above your merit.

[2] John Cook was mayor of Norwich in 1484.

LETTER CCCLXXXIII.—(LXXVI. vol. ii. p. 225.)

[This letter, I suppose, accompanied one from J. Paston, in which the exact terms were specified, to his brother Sir John. Sir Thomas Brews seemed to expect that Sir John Paston would likewise do something for his brother on this occasion. [Sir Thomas seems certainly to be a "hard" determined man, but John Paston appears to have wrung at least the loan of a considerable sum from him. Sir Thomas died in 1482.]

To my right worshipful cousin, Sir John Paston, Knight, be this letter delivered, &c.

RIGHT worshipful, and my heartily well-be-loved cousin, I recommend me unto you, desiring to hear of your welfare, which I pray God may be as continually good as I would have mine own; and, cousin, the cause of my writing unto you, at this time, is I feel (*perceive*) well by my cousin John Paston your brother, that ye have understanding of a matter which is in communication touching a marriage, with God's grace, to be concluded betwixt my said cousin your brother and my daughter Margery, which is far communed and not yet concluded, nor neither shall nor may be till I have answer from you again of your good will and assent to the said matter; and also of the obligation which that I send you herewith; for, cousin, I would be sorry to see either my cousin your brother, or my daughter, driven to live so near a life as they should do, if the six score pounds should be paid (*out*) of their marriage money; and, cousin, I have taken myself so near in levying[1] of this said six score pounds, that whereas I had laid up an 100*l.* for the marriage of a younger daughter of mine, I have now lent the said 100*l.*, and 20*l.* over that, to my cousin your brother, to be paid again by such easy days as the obligation which I send you herewith specifies.

And, cousin, I were right loath to bestow so much upon one daughter that the other her sisters should fare the worse; wherefore, cousin, if ye will that this matter shall take effect under such form as my cousin your brother hath written unto you, I pray you put thereto your good will, and some of your cost, as I have done of mine more largely than ever I purpose to do to any two of her sisters, as God knoweth mine intent, whom I beseech to send you your levest (*dearest*) heart's desire.

Written at Topcroft, the 8th day of March, &c. By your cousin,

THOMAS BREWS, *knight.*

Topcroft, Saturday, 8th of March, 1476.- 17 E. IV.

LETTER CCCLXXXIV.—(XXXVII. vol. v. p. 165.)

[SIR JOHN PASTON here writes from Calais to his brother John about his marriage with Margery Brews, with which match he seems well content, saying, "Bykerton telleth me that she loveth you well; if I died, I had lever ye had her than the Lady Wargrave [*Walde-grave*], nevertheless she singeth well with an harp." The Lady Wargrave appears to have been another sought-for match of the indefatigable John Paston's, and even yet another is alluded to somewhat humorously in this same letter. Sir John Paston says, "as for this matter of Mistress Burley I hold it but a bare thing; I hold that it passeth not [*here the number is torn from the letter*] marks, I saw her for your sake; she is a little one, she may be a woman hereafter if she be not old now; her person seemeth thirteen years of age, her years men say be full eighteen; she knoweth not of the matter I suppose, nevertheless she desired to see me, as glad as I was to see her." The letter is dated Sunday, March 9, 1476-7.]

[1] Fenn has *leaving* in mistake, which he translates 'parting with.' *Levying* is used in the sense of *raising.*

LETTER CCCLXXXV.—(XXXVIII. vol. v. p. 167.)

[JOHN PASTON writes from Norwich to his brother Sir John at Calais, about his negociation for his marriage with Margery Brews, as to which he says, "I am yet at no certainty, her father is so hard; but I trow I have the good-will of my lady her mother and her:" he then proceeds to warn him of trusting J. Bykerton too far, as he is a man "at wild," and is sore endangered (*in debt*) to divers in this country; and that Perse Moody, one of Sir John's old retainers, is at Caister in great distress, but he adds in conclusion that "carpenters of my craft, that I use now, have not alderbest their wits their own." This seems to be some proverbial allusion to the distraction of thought in lovers, but we doubt if there was much fear of John Paston losing his wits through love. The letter is dated on the same day as the last, Sunday, March 9, 1476-7.]

NUMBER CCCLXXXVI.—(XXXIX. vol. v. p. 171.)

[THIS paper is headed "A determination of Sir Thomas Brews how much he would give with his daughter Margery in marriage." It contains several modifications of terms: first, if the dowry out of the manor of Sparham does not exceed ten marks, that then he will give 133*l*. 6*s*. 8*d*. in hand and board free for two or three years; or else 200*l*. without their board, payable by fifty marks (33*l*. 6*s*. 8*d*.) yearly; secondly, that he will give four hundred marks (266*l*. 13*s*. 4*d*.), 50*l*. on the day of marriage, and 50*l*. yearly, and lend John Paston 120*l*. "to pledge out the manor of Swainsthorp," provided he procures security for its repayment, "not paid of the marriage money, nor of the proper goods of my said cousin John;" thirdly, if the whole of the profits of Sparham are settled on them for their joint lives, he will give the said four hundred marks, and their board for a year or two; but this last clause about their board is struck through with a pen. The paper is dated March, 1467.]

LETTER · CCCLXXXVII.—(LXXVII. vol. v. p. 227.)

Under the direction of this letter, and in a hand of the time (I believe in Sir John Paston's hand) is written "Jon Pympe," "xvj die Mar' A⁰. E. 4. 17" (16th day of March, 17 E. IV.), being the date when the letter was received. I have given this letter merely as a specimen of the humour of the time, which, though indelicate, may I fear be matched by many a modern correspondence. Some amour seems to be couched under the simile of the sparrow, the barley, and the door, &c. The latter part of this epistle shows us what were the qualities of a horse at that time most esteemed. The writer was a person of some consideration, as he was to have had Sir J. Paston's lodgings in London, and was cousin to Sir J. Scot, deputy governor of Calais.

To Master Sir John Paston, be this letter delivered in Calais.

HONOUR and joy be to you, my right good master, and most assured brother; letting you know that all your well-willers and servants in these parts, that I know, fare well, and better would if they might hear of your well being, and forthwith some of your French and Burgundy tidings; for we in these parts be in great dread lest the French king with some assaults should in any wise disturb you of your soft, sote (*sweet*), and sure sleeps, but as yet we nothing can hear that he so disposeth him.

[Here follow some allusions to the women of Flanders, which, though possessing some humour, is of too coarse a nature to be given here.]

But in one thing we praise your sadnesses (*wisdoms*) and discretions right much, that is, in keeping of your truce and peace with the king of France as the king hath commanded; and a great reason why, for it were too much for you to have war with all the world at once, for the war aforesaid keepeth you blameless, for every reasonable man weeteth well, at it is too much for any people living to do oth at once. Sir, as for the more part of y thought, I pray you recommend me unto ourself, praying you that I may continue in ich case as your goodness hath taken me of ld, and if ye list to send any tidings or other iing to the parties that were wont to warm iem by your fire, in faith I shall do your crrand.

As for barley, it is of the same price that was wont to be of, and is the most sure corn nd best enduring that may be; and, Sir, here that some time was a little hole in a wall, s now a door large enough and easy passage, hereof ye were the deviser, and have thank or your labour of some parties, but nothing asteth ever; I mean that I trow my passage hall hastily fail me, and the door shall be hut up again; less then (*unless*) fortune be greeable to have my counsel kept; for not ong ago making my entry at that passage, I aw a sparrow that useth those eireys, and I aw her set so still that I could not endure nt I must needs shoot her, and so God me ielp I smote her I trow even to the heart; nd so I dread me lest either the barley will at the sparrow, or else the sparrow will eat he barley; but as yet all is well, but reason heweth me that it must needs fail by con- inuance, less then (*unless*) I forsake both the parrow and the barley also.

Sir, I have thank for the shew that I once nade of you and daily gramercy (*great hanks*), and ye their prayer.

Sir, furthermore I beseech you as ye will do anything for me, that ye see one day for my sake, and for your own pleasure, all the good horse in Calais, and if there be amongst them any prized horse of deeds that is to sell, in especial that he be well trotting of his own courage without force of spurs, and also a steering horse [1] if he be he is the better; I pray you send me word of his colour, deeds, and courage, and also of his price, feigning as ye would buy him yourself, and also I would have him somewhat large, not with the largest; but no small horse, as (*q. no?*) more than a double horse; praying you above all things to have this in remembrance, and that hastily as may be, for there is late promised me help to such an intent, and I wote not how long it shall endure; and therefore I beseech you send me word by time.

I trow the French men have taken up all the good horse in Picardy, and also they be wont to be heavy horse in labour, and that I love not; but a heavy horse of flesh, and light of courage I love well, for I love no horse that will always be lean and slender like greyhounds. God keep you.

Your JOHN PYMPE.

(*Recd.*) Sunday, 1 6th of March, 1476. 17 E. IV.

I pray you to recommend me to my cousin Sir John Scot and all his, in especial Mrs. Bedingfield. [2]

' NUMBER CCCLXXXVIII.—(XL. vol. v. p. 173.)

[THIS paper is headed "Notes touching the marriage between John Paston, Esq., and Margery Brews." They are written by John Paston, and seem to be intended for himself only. They are by no means clear, but, for whatever purpose, his mother was not to be informed of the conclusion of the treaty. The conditions here stated are those mentioned in Sir J. Brews' "Determination." Dated March, 1476-7.]

[1] Quære, a horse that obeys the rein? [We rather think an entire horse is meant. See also two passages at the end of Letter ccexci.]
[2] Margaret, daughter of Sir John Scot, and wife to Edmund Bedingfield.

LETTER CCCLXXXIX.—(XLI. vol. v. p. 177.)

[ANOTHER letter from John Pympe to Sir John Paston about his horse. The writer begins by saying, "I have written to you three long letters, which as yet be answerless;" and shortly after says, "this is the fifth letter I have sent you." There is nothing else but a renewal of the request for Sir John's assistance in procuring a horse, and a repetition of what he considers a good horse ought to be. Dated March, 1477.]

LETTER CCCXC.—(XLII. vol. v. p. 181.)

[SIR JOHN PASTON in this letter writes rather a stern answer to the exorbitant demands of his brother John for his own advantageous settlement. He says, "Ye have now written again. You need not to pray me to do that might be to your profit and worship that I might do, oftener than once, or to let me weet thereof, for to my power I would do for you, and take as much pain for your weal, and remember it when per case ye should not think on it yourself. I would be as glad that one gave you a manor of 20l. by the year as if he gave it to myself, by my troth. Item, where(as) ye think that I may with conscience recompense it again unto our stock of other lands that I have of that value in fee simple, it is so that Snailwell by my grandfather's will once, and by my father's will secondly, is entailed to the issue of my father's body. Item, as for Sporle 20l. by year; I had thereof but twenty marks (13l. 6s. 8d.) by year, which twenty marks by year, and the ten marks (6l. 13s. 4d.) over, I have endangered, as ye well know of that bargain; which, if it be not redeemed I must recompense some other manor of mine to one of my brethren for the said ten marks, and twenty marks that longeth to me, wherefore I keep the manor of Runham; then have I fee simple land, the manor of Winterton with Bastwick and Billys, which in all is not twenty marks by year, which is not to the value of the manor of Sparham. And as for Caister it were no convenient land to exchange for such a thing; nor it were not policy for me to set that manor in such case for all manner of haps. I need not to make this excuse to you, but that your mind is troubled; I pray you rejoice not yourself too much in hope to obtain a thing that all your friends may not ease you of, for if my mother were disposed to give me and any woman in England the best manor she hath to have it to me and my wife, and to the heirs of our two bodies begotten, I would not take it of her, by God. Stablish yourself upon a good ground, and grace shall follow; your matter is far spoken of, and blown wide, and if it prove no better I would it had never been spoken of. Also that matter noiseth me, that I am so unkind that I let (hinder) altogether. I think not a matter happy, nor well handled, nor politicly dealt with, when it can never be finished without an inconvenience, and to any such bargain I hope never to be condescending nor of counsel; if I were at the beginning of such a matter, I would have hoped to have made a better conclusion, if they mock you not. This matter is driven thus far forth without my counsel; I pray you make an end without my counsel: if it be well I would be glad, if it be otherwise it is pity. I pray you trouble me no more in this matter." There is no date to the letter, but it clearly belongs to this period.]

LETTER CCCXCI.—(LXXVII.* vol. ii. p. 235.)

I have here given a letter written to Sir John Paston in rhyme, as a specimen of the poetry of the age. By the writer's inquiry concerning a horse, and his referring back to his former letters, this appears to have been written in the latter end of March, or in April, 1477, 17 E. IV. [Pympe's horse, like John Paston's hawk, seems to have become a passion—rhyme and reason, and six letters in quick succession, to one who will neither " hear, nor see, nor say, nor send," seems a great deal to be wasted for such an object. There is but little in the poetry, but the stanza is curiously constructed, and there is considerable easiness in the versification and flow of thought.]

To Master Sir John Paston, Knight, be this letter delivered at Calais.

FRESH amorous sights of countries far and
    strange
Have all fordone your old affection;
In pleasures new, your heart doth scour and
    range
So high and far, that like as the falcon
Which is aloft, telleth (*q. taketh*) scorn to
    look a down
On him that wont was her feathers to pick
    and imp;
Right so forgotten ye have your poor Pymp;
That writeth, sendeth, and wisheth all day
    your weal
More than his own; but ye nor hear, nor see,
Nor say, nor send, and ever I write and seal
In prose and rhyme, as well as it will be;
Some evil tongue I trow mis-saith of me
And else your fast and faithful friendliness
Ye think mis-spent on such as I, I guess.

I will abate my customable concourse,
To you so costuous,[1] whensoever ye come
    again,
Which that I feel of reason, by the course
Of my proffered service, hath made you so
    unfain;
For verily the water of the fountain,
With bread only, forthwith your presence,
Me should content much more than your
    expense.

But aye deem I thus that fortune hath hired
    you,
For she but late of sorrows more than many
Hath raked unto my heart an heap more than
    a mow,
And would that ye should lay thereon on
    high
Your heavy unkindness to make it fast to lie,

And God know'th well it cannot long lie
    there
But it will bring me to the church bier.[2]

Take it away therefore, I pray you fair,
For hardily my heart beareth heavy enough;
For there is sorrow, at rest as in his chair,
Fixed so fast with his pricks (*prickles*) rough,
That in good faith I wot not when I love.[3]
For Master Paston, the thing whereon my
    bliss
Was wholly set, is all fordone, I wis.
            By your
              JOHN PYMPE.

This being the sixth letter that I have sent you.

Always praying you to remember the horse that I have in every letter written for; as thus, that it would please you to understand who hath the gentlest horse in trotting and steering that is in Calais, and if he be to sell to send me word of his price, largeness, and colour.

It is told me that the master porter hath a courageous roaned horse, and that he would put him away because he is dangerous in company,[4] and of that I force (*care*) not, so that he be not churlish at a spur, as plunging; and also I set not by him but if (*unless*) he trot somewhat high and genteelly. No more, but God keep you.

Latter end of March, or April,
    1477, 17 E. IV.

---

[1] Expensive.

[2] [Fenn, like other annotators of his day, undertakes to mend the metre of his original, and reads " *unto* the church bier." Certainly without any improvement.]

[3] [The original is "lowh," and the corresponding rhymes of this stanza are " ynowh," and " rowh." Lowh cannot certainly be *love*, which makes the line nonsense, for the poet goes on to describe how he loves " Master Paston:" it is probably *low* as a cow, used here for sigh, allowable enough to a poet in want of a rhyme, and would then mean that his sorrow makes him sigh so continually that he becomes unconscious of it.]

[4] [See Letter ccclxviii.]

LETTER CCCXCII.—(LXXVIII. vol. ii. p. 239.)

In this letter Sir John Paston shows himself a kind and generous brother, in permitting his mother to give the manor of Sparham, which appears to be entailed on him and his issue, to his younger brother; and though he cannot conscientiously permit the entail to be defeated, as the will of the dead by this means would not be performed, he very readily consents to enter into an engagement to debar himself from ever molesting his brother or his widow in their quiet possessions thereof. [Notwithstanding the late severe letter, Sir John appears to have relented towards his brother; indeed Sir John appears throughout as much the kindest and most disinterested man of the two. Still he will give nothing but his good wishes, and his reversionary interest in the manor of Sparham for his own life only.]

To my right worshipful mother, Margaret Paston.

PLEASE it you to weet that I have received your letter, wherein is remembered the great hurt that by likelihood might fall to my brother, if so be that this matter between him and Sir Thomas Brews's daughter take not effect; whereof I would be as sorry as himself reasonably; and also the wealthy and convenient marriage that should be if it take effect; whereof I would be as glad as any man; and am better content now that he should have her, than any other that ever he was heretofore about to have had.[1] Considered her person, her youth, and the stock that she is come of, the love on both sides, the tender favour she is in with her father and mother, the kindness of her father and mother to her in departing [*parting*] with her, the favour also and good conceit that they have in my brother, the worshipful and virtuous disposition of her father and mother, which prognosticateth that of likelihood the maid should be virtuous and good; all which considered, and the necessary relief that my brother must have, I marvel the less that ye have departed and given him the manor of Sparham in such form as I have knowledge of by W. Gurney, Lomner, and Skipwith; and I am right glad to see in you such kindness unto my brother as ye have done to him, and would by my troth lever (*rather*) than an 100*l.* that it were fee-simple land, as it is intailed, which by likelihood should prosper with him and his blood the better in time to

come, and should also never cause debate in our blood (*contention in our family*) in time to come, which God defend (*forbid*), for that were unnatural.

Item, another inconvenience is, whereas I understand that the manor is given to my brother, and to his wife, and to the issue between them begotten, if the case were so that he and she had issue together a daughter or more, and his wife died, and he married after another and had issue a son, that son should have none land, and he being (*although he be*) his father's heir; and for the inconvenience that I have known late inure [*take place*] in case like, and yet endureth in Kent between a gentleman and his sister, I would ye took the advice of your counsel in this point; and that that is past you by writing or by promise, I deem verily in you that ye did it of kindness, and in eschewing of a more (*a greater*) ill that might befall.

Item, whereas it pleaseth you that I should ratify, grant, and confirm the said gift unto my brother, it is so that with mine honesty I may not, and for other causes.

The pope will suffer a thing to be used, but he will not license nor grant it to be used nor done; and so I.

My brother John knoweth mine intent well enough heretofore in this matter; I will be found to him as kind a brother as I may be.

Item, if it be so that Sir Thomas Brews and his wife think that I would trouble my brother and his wife in the said manor, I can find no means to put them in surety thereof, but, if it need, to be bound in an obligation with a condition that I shall not trouble nor infet (*infest*) them therein.

Item, I think that she is made sure enough

---

[1] [In Fenn's translation this passage stands thus—"than any other, that ever he was heretofore about to have had considered. Her person," &c. This cannot be understood, the verb *considered* standing wholly unconnected. The original has neither points nor capital letters; we have therefore ventured on a slight alteration, which at least gives a meaning to the sentence. "Considered her person," &c., is "her person being considered," &c.]

in estate in the land, and that of right I deem they shall make none obstacles at my writing, for I had never none estate in the land, nor I would not that I had.

No more to you at this time, but Almighty God have you in keeping.

Written at Calais, the 28th day of March, in the 17th year of Edward IV.

By your son,

JOHN PASTON, *knight*.

Calais, Friday, 28th of March, 1477. 17 E. IV.

LETTER CCCXCIII.—(LXXIX. vol. ii. p. 245.)

[A kindly letter of Sir John to his brother, promising in generals, but saving his conscience and worship The value set upon Boulogne, and the superstitious expectation of the intervention of the Virgin Mary in its favour, are curious instances of the manners of the age ; but it must be remarked, to the credit of Sir John, that he does not seem infected with the superstition himself.]

To John Paston, Esq.

RIGHT worshipful and heartily-beloved brother, I recommend me to you ; letting you weet, that as by Perse Moody, when he was here, I had no leisure to send answer in writing to you, and to my cousin Gurney, of your letters, but for a conclusion ye shall find me to you as kind as I may be, my conscience and worship saved, which, when I speak with you and them, ye both shall well understand, and I pray God send you as good speed in that matter as I would ye had, and is I hope ye shall have ere this letter come to you ; and I pray God send you issue between you that may be as honourable as ever was any of your ancestors and theirs, whereof I would be as glad in manner as of mine own; wherefore I pray you send me word how ye do, and if God fortune me to do well, and be of any power, I will be to Sir Thomas Brews and my lady his wife a very son-in-law for your sake, and take them as ye do ; and do for them as if I were in case like with them as ye be.

No more, but Jesu have you in keeping.

Written at Calais, the 14th day of April, in the 17th year of Edward IV.

As for tidings here, the French king hath gotten many of the towns of the Duke of Burgundy, as Saint Quintin's, Abbeville, Montreuil ; and now of late he hath gotten Bethune and Hesden with the castle there, which is one of the royalest castles of the world; and on Sunday at even the Admiral of France laid siege at Boulogne ; and this day it is said that the French king shall come thither ; and this night it is said that there was a vision seen about the walls of Boulogne, as it had been a woman with a marvellous light; men deem that our lady there will show herself a lover to that town : God forefend [*forbid*] that it were French, it were worth 40,000l. that it were English.

JOHN PASTON, *knight*.

Calais, Monday, 14th of April, 1477. 17 E IV.

LETTER CCCXCIV.—(XLIII vol. v. p. 185.)

[THE difficulties attending the arrangement of the pecuniary matters appear to have destroyed, at least for a time, John Paston's most hopeful prospects of marriage. His mother now writes from Mauteby to Dame Elizabeth Brews, soliciting an early interview with her and Sir Thomas in order that they may, if possible, remove the difficulties, observing to her with some skill, " that with your advice and help, and mine together, we shall find some way that it shall not break ;

for if it did it were none honour to neither parties, and in chief to them in whom the default is, considering that it is so far spoken "

She speaks of her son's great inclinations towards the marriage, and concludes, " I beseech you that I may be recommended by this bill to my cousin your husband, and to my cousin Margery, to whom I supposed to have given another name ere this time." Dated Wednesday, June 11, 1477.]

LETTER CCCXCV.—(V. Appendix to vol. ii. p. 297.)

[This letter, as far as "xxɾj day of Aurill," is written by the secretary of the Lord Hastings, from thence to the end by that nobleman himself, in a hand almost illegible. John Paston appears here to have been in the service of, and so highly respected by, the Lord Hastings, as to be sent as a kind of deputy governor of the castle of Guisnes, during the illness of his brother, Sir Ralph Hastings. [We have placed it according to Fenn's chronological order, although we have no doubt that John Paston was not at Guisnes at this period. But as the original has no date of the year, it is much easier to discover that it is wrongly placed here than to decide where it would be properly placed. We are inclined to think, however, it may be guessed to belong to that earlier period when Sir John was exerting himself to get John Paston retained by Lord Hastings, he having probably succeeded, though it is not mentioned.]

To my right trusty and well-beloved servant, John Paston, Esq.

JOHN PASTON, I recommend me unto you. And whereas I appointed and desired you to go over unto Guisnes to give your attendance and assistance upon my brother, Sir Ralph Hastings, in all such things as concern the surety and defence of the castle of Guisnes during his infirmities; it is showed unto me that ye have full truly and diligently acquitted you unto my said brother, in all his businesses since your coming thither. Whereof I thank you heartily. And as I conceive to my great comfort and gladness my said brother is well recovered and amended, thanked be God. And so I trust he may now spare you. Whereupon I have written unto him, if he may so do, to licence you to come over unto me again.

Wherefore I will and desire you, the assent of my said brother had, to dispose you to come over in all goodly haste, as well for such great matters as I feel by your friends ye have to do here, as to give your attendance upon me. And (*at*) your return you shall be to me welcome. From London, the 26th day of April.

I pray you in nowise to depart as yet, without my brother Roaf's (*Ralph's*) assent and agreement; and recommend me to my sister, all my nieces, to the constable, and to all reeves.   Your true friend,
                                        HASTINGS.[1]

London, 26th of April, 147—.
    E. IV.

LETTER CCCXCVI.—(LXXX. vol. ii. p. 249.)

[John Paston's money affairs occupy the principal part of this letter. Money, indeed, seems to have been looked after pretty sharply, when the 15*l.* due on the 21st has been the subject of a negociation on or before the 23rd, and a "reasonable respite" granted, meaning, we suppose, for a "consideration."]

To John Paston, Esq.

I RECOMMEND me to you, letting you weet that I have spoken with Harry Colet,[2] and entreated him in my best wise for you, so that at the last he is agreed to a reasonable respite for the 15*l.* that ye should have paid him at Midsummer as he saith, and (*he*) is glad to do you ease or pleasure in all that he may; and I told him that ye would, as I supposed, be here at London here not long

to, and then he looketh after that ye should come see him, for he is sheriff, and hath a goodly house.

Item, my Lady of Oxford[3] looketh after you and Arblaster both.

My Lord of Oxford[4] is not come into England that I can perceive, and so the good lady hath need of help and counsel how that she shall do.

---

[1] William Hastings, Lord Hastings, was summoned to Parliament in 1461, 1 E. IV. He was Lieutenant of Calais, and enjoyed several high offices of trust and confidence, in the reign of Edward IV. He married Catherine, daughter of Richard Nevile, Earl of Salisbury, and was beheaded in the Tower, by the instant order of Richard Duke of Gloucester, on the 13th of June, 1483.

[2] Sir Henry Colet was lord mayor of London in 1486.
[3] Margaret, daughter of Richard Nevile, Earl of Salisbury; she was, during the imprisonment of her lord, in great distress.
[4] John de Vere, Earl of Oxford, was at this time a prisoner in the castle of Hammes.

No more at this time, but God have you in keeping.

Written at London on Saint Audrey's [*Etheldreda's*] day, in the 17th year of Edward IV.

Tidings but (*only*) that yesterday my Lady Marchioness of Dorset,[1] which is my Lady Hastings's daughter, had childed a son.

Item, my Lord Chamberlain is come hither from Calais, and ridden with the king to Windsor, and the king will be here again on Monday.

JOHN PASTON, *knight*.

London, Monday,
23rd of June, 1477. 17 E IV.

LETTER CCCXCVII.—(XLIV. vol. v. p. 189.)

THIS letter, or rather three letters in one, contains a curious display on the part of John Paston of what Sir John Fenn calls " good sense and address in managing a matter," " though some finesse appears " Perhaps the world now will be ill-natured enough to call it trickery, and indeed such is our opinion. Fenn chooses to assume that Sir Thomas Brews had failed in his promises, but this does not appear. His proposals, we have seen, were all conditional, and John Paston had been unable, from various causes, to comply with his terms. He now writes a short note to his mother, telling her that Dame Elizabeth Brews had been sick and not able till now to attend to business; that this day the matter had been communed, "but that other answer than she hath sent you in her letter closed herein can she not have of her husband." He therefore writes a letter in his mother's name which he begs her to have transcribed and sent to Dame Brews, together with "another letter to me, which I may show." In the first of these two he makes his mother say, " I am right sorry that John Paston is no more fortunate than he is in that matter, for, as I understand by your letter, my cousin your husband will give but in 100*l*., which is no money like for such a jointure as is desired of my son, though his possibility were right easy. But, madam, when I made that large grant in the manor of Sparham, that I have made to him and my

cousin your daughter, he told me of another sum that he should have with her than of an 100*l*. He hath before this been wont to tell me none untruth, and what I shall deem in this matter I cannot say, for methinketh if more than an 100*l*. were promised unto him by my cousin your husband, and you, that ye would not let to give it him, without so were that I or he abridged anything of our promise, which I wot well neither I nor he intend to do, if I may understand that his saying to me was truth, and that it may be performed ; but wist I that he told me otherwise than my cousin your husband and ye promised him, in order to deceive me of Sparham, by my troth if he have it he shall lose as much by it, if I live, and that shall he well understand the next time I see him." He next alludes to his brother Sir John's refusal to alter the entail of Sparham, and makes his mother express her dislike to " become a daily petitioner of his, sith he hath denied me once mine asking; peradventure he had been better to have performed my desire." This is certainly a masterly stroke to excite at once the hopes and fears of the opposite parties. She is then made to proceed thus : " but, madam, ye are a mother as well as I, where(*fore*) I pray you take it none otherwise but well that I may not do by John Paston as ye will have me to do, for, madam, though I would he did well, I have to purvey for more of my children than him, of which some be of that age that they can tell me well enough that I deal not evenly with them to give John Paston so large and them so little." John Paston here shows a most laudable interest in the welfare of his brethren, though it has not hitherto prevented his ex-

---

[1] Cecily, second wife to Thomas Grey, Marquis of Dorset, was daughter and heir of William Bonvile, Lord Bonvile and Harrington, by Katharine, daughter of Richard Nevile, Earl of Salisbury, who was now the wife of Lord Hastings, Lord Chamberlain, and governor of Calais.

torting all he could for himself. In the letter addressed to himself, he makes his mother express herself thus :—"I understand well by my cousin Dame Elizabeth Brews's letter, which I send you herewith, whereby ye may understand the same, that they intend not to perform those proffers that ye told me they promised you, trusting that ye told me none otherwise than was promised you; wherefore I charge you on my blessing that ye be well aware how ye bestow your mind without ye

have a substance whereupon to live, for I would be sorry to weet you miscarry, for if ye do, in your default, look never after help of me; and also I would be as sorry for her as for any gentlewoman living, wherefore I warn you beware in anywise." The cant of " bestowing his mind " is truly disgusting. His own letter is dated from Salle in Norfolk, June 28, and those intended for his mother from Manteby, June 29, 1477.]

LETTER CCCXCVIII.—(XLV. vol. v. p. 197.)

[THIS and the following letter contain more of the family disputes about money, and new attempts to get assistance from the widow's property. In this Sir John is the actor; he acquaints his mother that he has no means of paying a debt due to one Kokett, about which she had written to him, because of his expenses for the surety of the manor of Caister, "and the matter between Anne Hawte and me ;" he also announces that Sporle is mortgaged for four hundred marks (266l. 13s. 4d.) to Townshend, to be paid within three years, or the manor to be forfeited, which, if it should happen " ye were never like to see me merry after, so God help me." He then coolly adds :—" Ye gave me once 20l. towards it, and ye promised as much, which I received, and since of my money of said manor growing that came to your hands was received by you again the said 40l., which, when Kokett should be repaid was

not your ease to depart with; nevertheless ye may yet, when you liketh, perform your said gift and promise, and this sum owing to Kokett is not so much ; nevertheless I suppose that ye be not so well purveyed, wherefore if it please you at your ease hereafter to perform your said gift and promise, so that I may have it within a year, or two, or yet three, I should per case get your obligation again from Kokett an he pleased, wherefore I beseech you that I may have an assignment of such debts as be owing you payable at leisure of such money as is owing for the wood at Bassingham or elsewhere; for so God help me I should else wilfully undo myself." Respecting his brother John he says " I have granted him as much as I may; I would I were at one communication atween them for his sake;" but adds that the period of his return home is uncertain. Dated Thursday, Aug. 7, 1477.]

LETTER CCCXCIX.—(XLVI. vol. v. p. 201.)

[THIS is Margaret Paston's reply to the previous letter, at which she seems to have been justly indignant. Without any greeting, she begins at once upon the business, and says " I put you in certain that I will never pay him [Kokett] a penny of that duty that is owing to him, though he sue me for it, not of mine own purse, for I will not be compelled to pay your debts against my will; and though I would, I may [can] not; wherefore I advise ye to see me saved harmless

against him for your own advantage in time coming; for, if I pay it, at long way ye shall bear the loss. And whereas ye write to me that I gave ye 20l., and promised other 20l., that is not so, for I wot well if I had so done ye would not assigned me by your letters of your own hand-writing, the which I have to show, that I should refrain [retain] again the same sum of William Peacock, and of your farmers, and buyers of your wood of Sporle; and take this for a full conclusion in this matter, for it shall be none otherwise for me than I write here to you." She then reproaches him for his improvidence, for having again "so simply" mortgaged Sporle, and says it makes her doubt, "what your disposition will be hereafter for such livelihood as I have been disposed before this time to leave you after my decease, for I think verily that ye will be disposed hereafter to sell or set to mortgage the land that ye should have after me your mother, as gladly and rather than that ye have after your father." She concludes thus: —" And as for your brother William, I would ye should purvey for his finding, for as I told you the last time ye were at home, I would no longer find him at my cost and

charge; his board and his school-hire is owing since St. Thomas's day afore Christmas; and he hath great need of gowns and other gear, that were necessary for him to have in haste. I would ye should remember it and purvey them, for as for me I will not. I think ye set but little by my blessing, and if ye did you would have desired it in your writing to me: God make you a good man to his pleasance." The brother William here mentioned was at this time at Eton, and Sir John had the management of the property left for the education and support of his younger brothers. This letter is dated from Mauteby, Monday, Aug. 11, 1477.]

LETTER CCCC.—(LXXXI. vol. ii. p. 251.)

We have in this letter several anecdotes of a public nature, relative to the wars in France, and particularly concerning the hostilities committed by the French king on the possessions of the heiress of Burgundy.

Unto the right worshipful Sir John Paston, Knight.

MASTER PASTON; after all due recommendation and hearty desire to hear of your good hele (*health*), please it you to weet I have spoken with Sir John of Middylton as well as I could and it had been for myself for his hobby that ye desired, and told him he might well forbear him now in as much as Mrs. Jane was dead, and that it is a great cost for him to keep more horse than he needeth; and he answered me that he would sell him with good will, but there should no man buy him under 10*l*. Flemish; [1] and I offered him in your name 10 marks, for he would not hear of none other ambling horse that ye might give him therefore.

And also my lord desired to have bought him for the Lord Schauntrell [2] that is chief captain of St. Omers; and he would (*for*) no less let my lord have him than 10*l*., and so my lord bought another, and gave him the said lord, for he thought this too dear; never-

theless he will not sell him to no man under that money that he set him on, and so ye may buy your pleasure in him and ye list; for otherwise he will not do for you as I conceive.

And as for tidings in these parts, the French king lieth at siege at St Omers, on the one side of the town, a mile off, but he hath no great ordnance there; and they of the town skirmish with them every day, and keep a passage half a mile without the town; and the French king hath brenned (*burnt*) all the towns and fair abbeys that were that way about St. Omers, and also the corns which are there.

And also, as it is said for certain, the French king hath brenned Cassell, [3] that is my old Lady of Burgundy's [4] jointure, and all the country thereabout, whereby she hath lost a great part of her livelihood; and that is a shrewd token that he meaneth [5] well to the king our sovereign lord, when he intendeth to destroy her.

---

[1] Between 5*l*. and 6*l*. English, apparently a great price for a hobby.
[2] Ponton de Santrailles A nobleman of this name was taken prisoner by the Duke of Bedford, before Beauvais, and was exchanged for Lord Talbot when he was captured at the battle of Patae.

[3] A town situated about 10 miles N.E. of St Omers
[4] Margaret, sister to Edward IV.
[5] This seems to be spoken in irony.

Moreover, Sir Philip de Creveker[1] hath taken them that were in Fynes[2] within this four days to the number of fourteen persons, and the remanent were fled, and he had them to the French king, and he hath brenned all the place, and pulled down the tower and a part of the wall, and destroyed it.

And as it is said, if the French king cannot get St. Omers, that he intendeth to bring his army through these Marches into Flanders, wherefore my lord hath do broken (*caused to be broken*) all the passages except Newham Bridge, which is watched, and the turnpike shut every night.

And the said French king within these three days railed greatly of (*on*) my lord to Tyger Poursuivant, openly before two hundred of his folks; wherefore it is thought here that he would feign a quarrel to set upon this town if he might get advantage.

And as I understand, the emperor's[3] son is married at Ghent as this day; and there came with him but four hundred horse, and I can hear of no more that be coming in certain; and in money he bringeth with him an hundred thousand ducats,[4] which is but a small thing in regard for that he hath to do; wherefore I fear me sore that Flanders will be lost; and if St. Omers be won, all is gone in my conceit; nevertheless they say there should come great power after the emperor's son, but I believe it not because they have been so long of coming.

And I pray you to recommend me unto Sir Terry Robsart,[5] and that it please you to let him know of your tidings, and our Lord have you in his keeping.

At Calais, the Sunday next after the Assumption.

Your
EDMUND BEDYNGFELD.[6]

Calais, Sunday,
17th of August, 1477. 17 E. IV.

LETTER CCCCI.—(XLVII. vol. v. p. 207.)

[WILLIAM PEACOCK, the agent or steward at Manteby, writes to his master Sir John Paston of several matters connected with his employment. The first seems to be the collecting of evidence for some matter in which Sir John was only partly interested, for he calls it "Pickering's matter," and in this he appears to have been very unsuccessful, for on applying to a certain friar in Pickering's name, his messenger received for answer, that if he (the friar) "had a bushelfull of evidence, he should none have of them, for he (Pickering) had set the land in trouble, nor he could have no sight of none." Peacock then proceeds to remind his master of his right of wreck at Winterton. This right of wreck, a right still inherent in many manors, seems at this time to have been very extensive; as from the quantities of timber, &c., alleged to have been stolen, the wreck in this case must have been almost the entire ship and cargo. Peacock says "these are the men's names of Winterton, Robert Parker of West-Somerton, John Loneyard of Winterton, Thomas Woodknape of the same, William Wrantham and John Curteys of the same Winterton, that

---

[1] [This is the Count of Crevecœur, rendered so celebrated by Walter Scott's novel of 'Quentin Durward.']

[2] [Furnes in West Flanders.]

[3] Maximilian, son of the emperor Frederick, married Mary, daughter and heir of Charles the Bold, Duke of Burgundy.—She was the richest heiress of her time, and had been promised by her father to many princes, and amongst the number to this prince, whom she now chose for herself.—She was about 19 years of age at the time of her marriage, in August, 1477, and lived only five or six years after it.

[4] A ducat of gold is worth about 10s.—Of silver, nearly 5s.

[5] Sir Terry Robsart, knight, of Sidistern, in Norfolk, by the marriage of his daughter Lucy to Edward Walpole, Esq., became an ancestor to the Earls of Orford.

[6] Edmund Bedyngfeld married Margaret, daughter of Sir John Scott, comptroller of Calais, and was created a Knight of the Bath at the coronation of Richard III. He was highly in favour with Henry VII., who paid him a royal visit at Oxburgh, in Norfolk; which fine seat he built.—He died in 1496.

carried off your several ground twenty-two cartsfull of stuff, eight score bow-staves, three score and seven wainscoats, fourteen hundred clepalde,[1] five barrels of tar, four couple of oars, and great plenty of wreck of the ship, as ye shall understand the truth after this." The rest of the letter is of minor matters : he informs Sir John that the "herrings that should into Essex, are there by the grace of God," the cost having been 4l. 3s. 4d. beside other costs; this sum must have purchased a

very large quantity of herrings at this time, the price of a horse-load being stated to be 4s. 6d. in Letter lxxv. (vol. i. p. 57). Fenn guesses they were for winter provisions, but Paston had no residence in Essex. Swans are also promised to be sent into Essex by the Lady-day following; and he complains that "I sold yet no barley, nor none can above fourteen pence the comb." The letter is written at Mauteby on Sunday, November 30, 1477.]

LETTER CCCCII.—(LXXXII. vol. ii. p. 257.)

[John Paston is at length married, and to Margery Brews; who is living, not with her parents according to one of the proposed arrangements, but at Oxnead, one of the residences of the family, and part of the jointure of Agnes Paston, her husband being at this time in London. It is a pretty simple letter, very characteristic of a young wife. Sir John Fenn queries whether the date assigned to it is right, or whether "our Lady's day" and "Saint Thomas's day" may not mean the visitation of the Virgin Mary, July 2, and the translation of St. Thomas à Becket, July 7. 1478. We think the present date right from the following circumstances; the next letter is from her husband, mentioning her removal to the house of her father and mother on account of her situation, and is dated Jan. 21, 1477-8 ; and though Sir John does not write till August, 1478, to congratulate his brother on the birth of an heir, yet he complains of the delay which had taken place in informing him of the event.]

To my right reverend and worshipful husband, John Paston.

RIGHT reverend and worshipful husband, I recommend me to you, desiring heartily to hear of your welfare, thanking you for the token that ye sent me by Edmund Perys, praying you to weet that my mother sent to my father to London for a gown cloth of mustyrddevyllers[2] to make of a gown for me; and he told my mother and me when he was come home, that he charged you to buy it after that he was come out of London. I pray you, if it be not bought, that you will vouchsafe to buy it and send it home as soon as ye may, for I have no gown to wear this winter but my black and my green a lyer,[3]

and that is so cumbrous that I am weary to wear it.

As for the girdle that my father behested (*promised*) me, I spake to him thereof a little before he yed (*went*) to London last, and he said to me that the fault was in you that ye would not think thereupon to do make it (*to have it made*), but I suppose it is not so, said it but for a skeusacion (*an excuse*); I pray you, if ye dare take it upon you, that ye will vouchsafe to do make it against ye come home, for I had never more need thereof than I have now, for I have waxed so fetys (*prettily*) that I may not be girt[4] in no bar of no

---

[1] [Wainscoats were planks (probably oak) for lining the walls of rooms; clepaldes or clapboards were boards cut ready for making casks.]

[2] This word occurs more than once in these letters, but the meaning of it I cannot ascertain to my own satisfaction; though perhaps it refers to some place in France where the cloth was manufactured. The following, however, appears the most satisfactory explanation : Musterdevelers — mustyrddevyllers, *moittie*, or (as sometimes anciently and erroneously spelt) *mestier de velours*, French, a half-velvet; or *mestis de velours*, a bastard-velvet. *Mestoyant* is also an old French word, signifying *between both*. On the present occasion, a proper allowance must be

made for the imperfections of female spelling, in an age of unsettled orthography. [In vol. i. p. 83, the word is spelt *musterdevelers*. In Rymer's ' Fœdera,' in a list of articles shipped from England for the use of the King of Portugal and the Countess of Holland in 1428, two pieces of *mustrevilers* and two pieces of russet *mustrevilers* are enumerated.]

[3] Qu. grenouilliere, frog-colour ?

[4] The same very natural thought occurs in the ancient ballad of ' Child Waters.' See Percy's Collection, 3rd edit. vol. iii. p. 55.

"My girdle of gold that was too longe,
Is now too short for mee."

girdle that I have but of one. Elizabeth Peverel hath lain sick fifteen or sixteen weeks of the sciatica, but she sent my mother word by Kate that she should come hither when God sent time, though she should be crod (*carried*) in a barrow.

John of Damme was here, and my mother discovered me to him, and he said by his truth that he was not gladder of nothing that he heard this twelvemonth than he was thereof.

I may no longer live by my craft (*cunning*), I am discovered of all men that see me.

Of all other things that ye desired that I should send you word of, I have sent you word of in a letter that I did write on our Lady's day[1] last was; the Holy Trinity have you in his keeping.

Written at Oxnead, in right good haste, on the Thursday next before Saint Thomas's day.[2]

I pray you that ye will wear the ring[3] with the image of Saint Margaret that I sent you for a remembrance till ye come home. Ye have left me such a remembrance that maketh me to think upon you both day and night when I would sleep.

Yours,

MARGERY PASTON.

Oxnead,
Thursday, 18th of December,
1477. 17 E. IV.

LETTER CCCCIII.—(XLVIII. vol. v. p. 209.)

[JOHN PASTON in this letter advises his brother Sir John to conclude his matters now, if possible, with the Duke of Suffolk, probably matters relating to the contested property at Heylesdon and elsewhere, because "an hundred marks (66*l.* 13*s.* 4*d.*) will do more in their need than ye shall peradventure do with two hundred marks in time coming," some of the Duke of Suffolk's folks having "let me in secret wise have knowledge that he (the Duke) must make a shift for money, and that in all haste;" and the Duchess is said to be the person to treat with, "as for my lord, he needeth not to be moved till it shall be as good as ready for the sealing." John Paston next informs his brother that the priest of the newly-founded chapel at Caister had written by an attorney for an account and payment of his profits, and suggests that as "ye said unto me that ye would assay to make a bargain with him so that ye might have a priest to sing in Caister; Sir, methink ye cannot have so good a season to move him with it as now this parliament time, for now I think he shall be awaiting on the queen;[4] and also if ye might compound with him ere he wist what the value were, it were the better." He says, "We would fain hear of all your royalty at London, as of the marriage of my Lord of York." This was the marriage of the younger son of Edward IV. to Ann Mowbray, the daughter and heiress of John Duke of Norfolk, who died very young, and which took place on Jan. 15, 1477-8, and fixes the correctness of the date of this letter. He then concludes, "And, Sir, as for my housewife, I am fain to carry her to see her father and her friends now this winter, for I trow she will be out of fashion (*shape*) in summer." The letter is written from the house of Playters, where he stayed in his progress "from my father Brews unto Mauteby," and is dated Jan. 21, 17 Edward IV., 1477-8.]

---

[1] Conception of our Lady, 8th of December.
[2] [Dec. 21.]
[3] This ring, bearing the image of her favourite saint, being worn by her husband as a remembrance, might be looked upon as a guardian to her in her then situation, and be a means of preserving her from any disagreeable accident.
[4] [The priest of Caister chapel was Dr. Yotton, chaplain also to the queen.]

LETTER CCCCIV.—(XLIX. vol. v. p. 213.)

IOHN PASTON writes to his mother from
Swainsthorp, informing her of his having
made an appointment for her with James
Hubbart and Dr. Pykenham at Norwich
during the week after Midlent Sunday, for
the purpose of advising her on certain matters
relating to her property; and in a postscript
tells her she ought to be in Norwich five or
six days before the lawyers, to look up her
evidences and all other things; probably her
title-deeds connected with the property disputed between her and the Duke of Suffolk.
Being now married himself, John Paston
seems to have been employing his talents for
match-making in favour of his brother Edmund; and he writes to his mother—"I
heard while I was in London where was a
godly young woman to marry, which was
daughter to one Seff, a mercer, and she shall
have 200l. in money to her marriage, and
twenty marks (13l. 6s. 8d.) by year of land,
after the decease of a step-mother of hers,
which is upon fifty years of age; and ere I
departed out of London I spake with some of
the maid's friends, and have gotten their good
wills to have her married to my brother Edmund, notwithstanding those friends of the
maid's that I communed with advised me to
get the good will of one Sturmyn, which is in
Master Pykenham's danger (debt) so much
that he is glad to please him. And so I
moved this matter to Master Pykenham, and
incontinently he sent for Sturmyn, and delivered his good will for my brother Edmund;
and he granted him his good will, so that he
would get the good will of the remanent that
were executors to Seff as well as the said
Sturmyn was; and thus far forth is the
matter." He then requests a letter from his
mother in favour of Edmund to Dr. Pykenham, and he says—"and, for I am acquainted
with your conditions of old, that ye reck not
who inditeth more letters than ye, therefore I
have drawn a note to your secretary's hand,
Friar Peise, which letter we must pray you
to send us by the bearer hereof, and I trust it
shall not be long from Master Pykenham."
John Paston seems to have been possessed
with a most active spirit of intrigue. Edmund Paston was at this time staying at
Swainsthorp, which, however, his brother says
"for none interest that his hostess your
daughter nor I could intreat him, might not
keep him but that he would have been at
home with you at Mauteby on Sunday last
past at night; and as he was departing from
hence had we word from French's wife that,
God yeld (thank) you, mother, ye had given
him leave to disport him here with us for a
seven or eight days, and so the drevyll (simple-
ton) lost his thank of us and yet abode nevertheless. Your daughter sendeth you part of
such poor stuff as I sent her from London,
beseeching you to take it in gree (favour),
though it be little plenty that she sendeth
you; but as for dates, I will say truth, ye
have not so many by two pounds as were
meant unto you, for she thinks at this season
dates right good meat, whatsoever it meaneth,
I pray God send good tidings." Fenn says
that dates were formerly considered wholesome for ladies in Margery Paston's situation,
and at any rate the notice is curious. The
letter is dated Ash Wednesday, Feb. 4,
1477-8.]

LETTER CCCCV.—(XXII. vol. i. p. 297.)

This letter combines very curiously an account of the writer's schoolboy studies and progress with that of
his courtship and a description of his mistress. Besides an interesting picture of the domestic manners of
the time, it proves, as is remarked by Hallam in his 'State of Europe during the Middle Ages,' vol. iii.
p 597, " that Latin versification was taught at Eton as early as the beginning of Edward the IVth's reign. It is
true that the specimen he (Master Wm Paston) rather proudly exhibits, does not much differ from what we
denominate nonsense verses. But a more material observation is, that the sons of country gentlemen living at

a considerable distance were already sent to public schools for grammatical education." We may add, W. Paston was apparently not on the foundation, but sent as a boarder. Fenn says he was " at this time I suppose about eighteen or twenty, a time of life when he might have been better employed than in learning to make verses." True: and he might have been worse employed,—at any rate his letter proves that his attention was not by any means solely directed to this one object. His eyes are open to the charms of youth and beauty, and he seems to have adopted the aristocratic feeling in favour of slender hands ; while he is by no means dull to the dictates of worldly prudence.]

To his worshipful brother, John Paston, be this delivered in haste.

RIGHT reverend and worshipful brother, after all duties of recommendation I recommend me to you, desiring to hear of your prosperity and welfare, which I pray God long to continue to his pleasure and to your heart's desire; letting you weet that I received a letter from you, in the which letter was 8*d*. with the which I should buy a pair of slippers.

Farthermore certifying you as for the 13*s*. 4*d*. which ye sent by a gentleman's man for my board, called Thomas Newton, was delivered to mine hostess, and so to my creancer (*creditor*), Mr. Thomas Stevenson; and he heartily recommended him to you; also ye sent me word in the letter of 12lb. of figgs[1] and 8lb. of raisins; I have them not delivered, but I doubt not I shall have, for Alweder told me of them, and he said that they came after in another barge.

And as for the young gentlewoman, I will certify you how I first fell in acquaintance with her; her father is dead, there be two sisters of them, the elder is just wedded; at which wedding I was with mine hostess, and also desired (*invited*) by the gentleman himself, called William Swan, whose dwelling is in Eton. So it fortuned that mine hostess reported on me otherwise than I was worthy,[2] so that her mother commanded her to make me good cheer, and so in good faith she did; she is not abiding where she is now, her

dwelling is in London ; but her mother and she came to a place of hers five miles from Eton where the wedding was, for because it was nigh to the gentleman which wedded her daughter ; and on Monday next coming, that is to say, the first Monday of Clean Lent,[3] her mother and she will go to the pardon at Sheene, and so forth to London, and there to abide in a place of hers in Bow Churchyard ; and if it please you to inquire of her, her mother's name is Mistress Alborow, the name of the daughter is Margaret Alborow, the age of her is, by all likelyhood, eighteen or nineteen years at the farthest; and as for the money and plate, it is ready whensoever she were wedded ; but as for the livelihood, I trow (*I believe*) not till after her mother's decease, but I cannot tell you for very certain, but you may know by inquiring.

And as for her beauty, judge you that when you see her, if so be that ye take the labour ; and specially behold her hands, for and if it be as it is told me, she is disposed to be thick.

And as for my coming from Eton, I lack nothing but versifying, which I trust to have with a little continuance.

Quare, Quomodo. Non valet hora, valet mora.

Unde dî |o|

Arbore jam videas exemplum. Non die possunt

Omnia suppleri, sed tû illa mora.[4]

---

[1] These were for his subsistence in Lent.

[2] [Beyond what I was worthy of.]

[3] In 1479 the first Sunday in Lent fell on the 28th of February, which agrees with the date, St. Mathias being on the 24th of February. Sheen is now called Richmond, so named by Henry VII.

[4] Of these verses I can make nothing ; but an ingenious friend has attempted the following solution :—

Quære, Quomodo non valet hora, valet mora ?
    Unde dictum vel deductum ?
Arbore jam videas exemplum. Non die possunt
   Omnia suppleri; sed tamen illa mora.

Perhaps the words preceding young Paston's attempt at a distich exhibit only a common theme given out at school, with some formulary query annexed to it. On this theme the hexameter and pentameter appear to have been written. It is needless to particularise their defect in quantity, &c. That versification, however, was attended to in our public schools, at this early period, may be ascertained by such imperfect lines, as well as by a more correct performance.

nd these two verses aforesaid be of mine
own making.

Io more to you at this time, but God have
you in his keeping.

Eton,
Wednesday, 23d of February,
1478-9. 18 E. IV.

Written at Eton the even of Saint Mathias
the Apostle, in haste, with the hand of your
brother.

WILLIAM PASTON, *junior.*

LETTER CCCCVI.—(L. vol. v. p. 221.)

THIS is a very strange letter. The writer,
fter recommending herself in the usual style,
roceeds thus : " Touching the cause of my
vriting to your mastership is, forasmuch
is I appointed with you to have been with
rou by the day that ye assigned me of, the
vhich, without your good supportation, I
:annot well have mine intent, without it
)lease you to send one of your men to me,
ind I shall provide a letter in mine uncle's
iame, the which he shall deliver to my
:ousin as (*if*) he were my uncle's mes-
ienger; and by this mean I will come at your
·equest, for my cousin would I should not
lepart with him (*leave him*), without it were
:o mine uncle's service; his and all others I
refuse for yours, if my simple service may be
to your pleasure ; and of an answer hereof I
beseech you by the bringer of my bill, and I
will conform me to your intent by the grace
of God, the which mot (*may*) preserve you at
all hours." Signed " By your woman and
servant, CONSTANCE RENNYFORTH," Cobham,
Saturday, March 21, 1477-8. By this lady
Sir John had a natural daughter, to whom her
mother left ten marks, by will, dated Feb. 4,
1481, on her coming of age ; she afterwards appears to have resided with her uncle John Paston, then Sir John, between 1495 and 1500, and
to have been sought in marriage by John Clip-

pesby, of Oby, Esq., as appears from another
letter given in the Fifth Vol. of the quarto
edition, of the reign of Henry VII. Sir John
Fenn says " The style of this letter is artless
and simple, but the lady's contrivance by a
forged letter, as from her uncle to her cousin,
to leave him and to go to Sir John, shows she
understood what she had undertaken, and that
her attachment to him got the better of every
other consideration." Artless and simple !
He adds " no one can read this letter without
feeling an interest in the welfare of her writer."
To us the style of language, so obscure and
involved, and the spelling, which is not very
good in the original, seems rather that of a
bold and perhaps vulgar woman; and Sir John
is here strangely at issue with his own remarks,
upon which we made a few observations in
Letter ccxlvii. vol. i. p. 199.]

LETTER CCCCVII.—(LXXXIII. vol. ii. p. 261.)

It appears by this letter that Sir John Paston feared that his mother would not send the cloth of gold to him
lest he should sell it, and not apply the money to the purpose of erecting a tomb to the memory of his

father, who had now been dead twelve years. He was buried very sumptuously in Bromholm Priory; and probably a suitable tomb should have been immediately erected, but had been deferred by Sir John from time to time on account of the expense.

To my right worshipful mother, Margaret Paston, be this delivered.

PLEASE it you to weet, that whereas I intended to have been at home this Midsummer, and purposed with your good help to have begun upon my father's tomb so that it might have been ended this summer; it is so, that for such causes as are now begun between my Lord of Suffolk and me for the manors of Heylesdon, Drayton, &c., for which matters I must needs be here this next term; therefore I deem it would be after Midsummer ere than (*before*) I can see you.

Please it you also to weet that I communed with Master Pykenham to weet if he would buy the cloth of gold for so much as he desired once to have bought it, and he offered me once 20 marks (13*l.* 6*s.* 8*d.*) therefor, nevertheless it cost me 24*l.*; yet now, when that I spake to him thereof, he refused to buy it; and said that he had now so many charges that he may not.

But it is so that the king doth make certain copes and vestments of like cloth, which he intendeth to give to the college of Fotheringay where my Lord his father is now buried, and he buyeth at a great price; I communed with the vestment maker for to help me forth with twelve yards, and he hath granted to do as Wheatley can tell you; wherefore if it please you that it be bestowed for to make a tomb for my father at Bromholm, if ye like to send it hither, if it be sold I undertake ere

Michaelmas that there shall be a tomb and somewhat else over my father's grave, on whose soul God have mercy, that there shall none be like it in Norfolk; and as ye shall be glad hereafter to see it; and God send me leisure that I may come home, and if I do not, yet the money shall be put to none other use, but kept by some that ye trust till that it may be bestowed according as is above written, and else I give you cause never to trust me while ye and I live.

When I was last with you, ye granted that the said cloth of gold should be bewared (*expended in exchange*) about this work that is above written, which, if ye will perform, I undertake that there shall be such a tomb as ye shall be pleased at, though it cost me 20 marks (13*l.* 6*s.* 8*d.*) of mine own purse beside, if I once set upon it.

No more, but I beseech God have you in his keeping.

Written at London the Wednesday in Whitsun-week, in the 18th year of Edward IV.

Please it you to send me word by Wheatley of your pleasure herein.

By your son,
JOHN PASTON, *knight.*

London,
Wednesday, 13th of May,
1478. 18 E. IV.

LETTER CCCCVIII.—(LI. vol. v. p. 225.)

[WALTER PASTON writes to his mother Margaret from Oxford relative to his expenses there. He says, "I marvel sore that you sent me no word of the letter which I sent to you by Master William Brown at Easter. I sent you word that time that I should send you mine expenses particularly; but as at this time the bearer hereof had a letter suddenly that he should come home, and therefore I could have no leisure to send them you on that wise, and therefore I shall write to you in this letter the whole sum of my expenses since I was with you till Easter last past, and

also the receipts, reckoning the twenty shillings that I had of you to Oxon wards with the bishop's finding:—

	£.	s.	d.
The whole sum of receipts is	5	17	6
And the whole sum of expenses is	6	5	5¾
And that [*what*] cometh over my receipts and my expenses I have borrowed of Master Edmund, and it draweth to	0	8	0

and yet I reckon none expenses since Easter,

at as for them they be not great." Fenn says, "Had this letter contained a particular account of Walter Paston's expenses at Oxford it would have been more curious; we must, however, take it as we find it, and be content with knowing that he had expended *l.* 5s. 5¾d. from the time he left his mother to Easter last, which this year fell on the 22nd March, from which time it was now two months, and of the expenses 'since incurred' he says 'they be not great.' We may therefore conclude the former account was from the Michaelmas preceding, and a moderate one; if so we may fairly estimate his university education at 100*l.* a-year of our present money. I mean that 12*l.* 10s. 11½d. would then procure as many necessaries and comforts as 100*l.* will at this day." This letter is dated Tuesday, May 19, 1478, and is signed "By your sonn and scoler, Walter Paston." We add the autograph.

LETTER CCCCIX.—(LII. vol. v. p. 229.)

J. WHETLEY (or Wheatley) here writes a long letter to Sir John Paston, "lodged at the sign of the George at Paul's Wharf in London," about divers matters connected with the litigated titles to Heylesdon and Drayton manors. He says, "First, your subpœna to Denton was delivered by me on Trinity Sunday in his parish church at matins time, before all the substance of the parish." The serving of a subpœna on a Sunday in service time, and publicly, is a very curious circumstance, and it is not mentioned as being at all out of the ordinary course: when personal feelings or interests were involved the clergy seem to have been treated with as little ceremony as the laity. He then proceeds to describe the proceedings at Drayton and Heylesdon, and gives us a lively sketch of the Duke of Suffolk's blustering bearing and manners, seeming to have out-Heroded Herod. "As for Drayton wood it is not all down yet, but it draws fast toward. I have the names of all the ministers (*servants or agents*) of and in that wood, and more shall know ere I come if there be any more dealing, &c. And as for Heylesdon, my Lord of Suffolk[1] was there on Wednesday in Whitsun week (13*th May*), and there dined, and drew a stew, and took great plenty of

'Gentleman's Magazine,' as there quoted. By the favour of a gentleman resident at Wingfield, we learn that there exists, on vellum, " an exact account of the Delapoles, collected 1684 by William Bedford, perpetual curate of Wingfield," which formerly hung in a frame in the church. It is there stated of Duke William, that " his body was cast up at Dover, and buried at the Charter-house at Hull; but after, the body was translated, and honourably interred in the church of Wingfield in Suffolk. This Duke William is represented by the figure that lieth alone on the north side of the chancel of Wingfield." Weever, in his 'Ancient Funeral Monuments,' 1631, says, on the authorities of Hall and the 'Catalogue of Honours,' by Brooke, that Duke William was " brought to this college, and here honourably interred;" but he makes no mention of the monument. Gough, in his 'Sepulchral Monuments,' 1786 and 1796, thus describes it:—

'In the north wall of the chancel at Wingfield, without the rails, under a purfled arch with a bouquet on the point, and a quatrefoil in the pediment, on a freestone altar tomb, lies a freestone figure of an armed knight, with whiskers, pointed helmet, gorget of mail, gauntlets, square-toed shoes, no sword or dagger, lion at his feet, and under his head a helmet without a crest; four plain quatrefoils, with shields on the front of the tomb."

Stothard has given this figure in his ' Monumental Effigies,' but calls it the effigies of a Wingfield of Letheringham; and in a second engraving, representing the " details, with the figure as originally painted," he has depicted on the sword-belt the arms of Wingfield in conformity with this idea, but for which the monument itself gives not the slightest authority; for the correspondent to whom we have already acknowledged our obligation says, " I can discover no appearance of arms of any kind on any part of the figure, nor can I see anything

---

[1] John de la Pole, Duke of Suffolk, married Elizabeth, third daughter of Richard Plantagenet, and sister of Edward IV. They both lie buried at Wingfield, in Suffolk. [In the previous volume, at page 19, we have stated that Fenn was in error as to the monuments of the De la Poles; but we are glad to be able to do him the justice to say that the error is not in his statement, but in those of Stothard and the

fish; yet hath he left you a pike or two again ye come, the which would be great comfort to all your friends and discomfort to your enemies; for at his being there that day there was never no man that played Herod in Corpus Christi play[1] better, and more agreeable to his pageant, than he did; but ye shall understand that it was afternoon and the weather hot, and he so feeble for sickness that his legs would not bear him, but there was two men had great pain to keep him on his feet; and there ye were judged. Some said 'slay,' some said 'put him in prison;' and forth come my lord, and he would meet you with a spear, and have none other mends (*amends*) for that trouble as ye have put him to but your heart's blood, and that will he get with his own hands; for and (*if*) ye have Heylesdon and Drayton ye shall have his life with it; and so he comforted your enemies with that word that they have dealed and dealeth with the wood; and (*the*) most principal now is Nicholas Ovy, for as for Farrer[2] the mayor he deals not without it be under covert; for it is said that he besought my lord that he might have other assignments for his money that he had paid, for plainly he would deal no more with the wood; and so my lord hath set in the bailiff of Cossey: and all is done

in his name; and as for his servants, they daily threat my master your brother and me to slay for coming on their lord's ground; and they say that we made aventure, and they be answered as ye commanded me, for many a great challenge make they to Master John, both Master Wodehouse, Wiseman, with other divers that I know not their names, but he holdeth his own that they get no ground of him; and this he lets them know, that if they beat him or any of his they shall abide (*suffer*) six for one, and so they deal not but with their tongues; and as yet, since Farrer was at London, there passes not three acres of wood down, but they carry fast for fear of rain." It is also added, farther on, that Farrer is said to have denied being aware that Sir J. Paston had an interest in the manors, and also that " Wiseman was bound to Farrer to save him harmless, and he had for bringing that matter about, that Farrer should have the wood, twenty shillings." This we suppose was on account of the difficulty of getting a customer from the generally-known disputed title to the property. Wheatley then mentions that he had applied to one Popy for money claimed from him by Paston, "which as he (Popy) saith is a strange thing to him," for as it appears the person who owed the debt was his uncle; but he was, it seems, not unwilling to pay a part for a release from the whole, like a wise man, rather than be probably involved in a law-suit. Wheatley next states that Worcester (or Botoner) is again moving as to Sir J. Fastolf's affairs, but he does not write fully, as he expects to be with Sir John in about a week, "without I may have more comfort of money than I have yet." He adds, " And as for my mistress, your mother, (*she*) hath been greatly diseased and so sick that she weened to have died, and hath made her will, the which ye shall understand more when I come, for there is every man for himself; I know not the circumstance of every thing as yet, and therefore I write no more to you therein, but I am promised to know ere I depart from thence." This will never took effect, as the one proved after her death was dated Feb. 4, 1481. This long and interesting letter is dated from Norwich, May 20, 1478.]

---

like an inscription." Stothard has also added, on the authority of Weever, a mutilated inscription, as belonging to this tomb: "Hic jacet Dominus Wingfield de Letheringham . . . . . cujus anime." But both Weever and Gough distinctly separate the monument and the inscriptions. Weever says, some sentences after mentioning the three Dukes of Suffolk, "In the *parish church* are these *inscriptions* or *epitaphs*:—

Ric. de la Pole } sons of Mich.
Johan. de la Pole } de la Pole.
Dom. Wingfield de Letheringham," &c.

This, however, has probably been the foundation of the mistake; and we are not aware that the writer of the article in the 'Gentleman's Magazine' had any other authority than Stothard's. That the effigy is in truth that of the unfortunate William de la Pole is still farther confirmed, as our correspondent observes, by the use of the lion at the feet, as in the other De la Pole monuments.]

[1] [The old mysteries or miracle plays. Corpus Christi day is the Thursday after the octave of Whitsuntide, a time when the mysteries were frequently performed.]

[2] [Richard Farrer, or Ferriour, was five times mayor of Norwich, in 1473, 1478, 1483, 1493, and 1498.]

LETTER CCCCX.—(LXXXIV. vol. ii. p. 265.)

the following is indorsed, " Lrã Johi Paston mil p. quã patet." " Se fore in magno favore Regis." This letter is in answer to that of Sir John Paston to his mother, dated 13th of May, 1478, and shows the desire that she had that some tomb should be erected over her husband's grave. [The mention of Clere expending 100l. upon the desks in the choir is very curious: the sum is large, but was probably for the rich though sometimes grotesque carvings so profusely lavished on some of our ancient religious edifices. Her advice regarding the marriage is also noticeable, if only for the kindly womanly feeling that breaks out through the other selfish motives suggested by her, " if ye can find in your heart to love her."]

To the right worshipful Sir John Paston, Knight.

GREET you well, and send you God's blessing and mine; letting you weet that I have sent you by Wheatley the cloth of gold, charging you that it be not sold to none other use than to the performing of your father's tomb as ye send me word in writing; if ye sell it to any other use, by my troth, I shall never trust you while I live.

Remember that it cost me 20 marks (13 . 6s. 8d.) the pledging out of it, and if I were not glad to see that made, I would not depart from it. Remember you what charge I have had with you of late, which will not be for my ease this two years; when ye may, better, I trust ye will remember it.

My cousin Clere [1] doth as much cost at Bromholm as will draw an 100l. upon the desks in the choir, and in other places, and Heydon in likewise, and if there should nothing be done for your father it would be too great a shame for us all, and in chief to see him lie as he doth.

Also as I understand it, my cousin Robert Clere thinketh great unkindness in dealing with him of Peacock, for certain pasture that ye granted him to have, and Peacock hath let it to others, such as he list to let it to, notwithstanding my cousin hath laid the pasture with his cattle, and Peacock hath distrained them. I think this dealing is not as it should be: I would that each of you should do for other, and live as kinsmen and friends; for such servants may make trouble betwixt you, which were against courtesy, so nigh neighbours as ye be. He is a man of substance and worship, and so will be taken in this shire; and I were

loath that ye should lose the good will of such as may do for you.

Item, whereas ye have begun your claim in Heylesdon and Drayton, I pray God send you good speed and furtherance in it; ye have as good a season as ye would wish, considering that your adversary stands not in best favour with the king.

Also ye have the voice in this country, that ye may do as much with the king as any knight that is belonging to the court; if it be so, I pray God continue it; and also that ye should marry right nigh of the queen's blood;[2] what she is we are not as certain, but if it be so that your land should come again by the reason of your marriage, and to be set in rest, at the reverence of God forsake it not if ye can find in your heart to love her, so that she be such one as ye can think to have issue by, or else by my troth I had rather that ye never married in your life.

Also, if your matter take not now to good effect, ye and all your friends may repent them that ye began your claim, without that ye have taken such a sure way as may be to your intent, for many inconveniences that may fall thereof; God send you good speed in all your matters.

Written at Mauteby, the day after Saint Austin,[3] in May, the 18th year of King Edward IV.

By your mother.

Mauteby,
Tuesday, 26th of May,
1478. 18 E. IV.

---

[1] William or Thomas Clere; they both died without issue, and were succeeded by Robert their next brother, who was knighted in 1494 and died in 1529. The advice which she gives her son respecting his

behaviour towards this gentleman shows her to be a woman of sense and discernment.

[2] Some lady of the Woodvile or Widvile family.

[3] St. Augustine, 25th of May.

LETTER CCCCXI.—(LXXXV. vol. ii. p. 271.)

We see by this account the methods practised by the great men of the time to get possession of estates and benefices; and we are informed of the king's intention of sitting as a judge to try a criminal. The anecdotes likewise of the Earl of Oxford are curious.

To John Paston, Esq., be this letter delivered, or to my mistress, his wife, at Norwich, to deliver to him.

BROTHER JOHN, I recommend me to you, and I thank God, my sister your wife, and you, of my fair nephew Christopher, which I understand ye have, whereof I am right glad, and I pray God send you many if it be his pleasure; nevertheless ye be not kind that ye send me no weeting thereof; I had knowledge by footmen or ever ye could find any messenger on horseback to bring me word thereof.

Sir, it is so that the Duke of Buckingham [1] shall come on pilgrimage to Walsingham, and so to Bokenham Castle to my lady his sister :[2] and then it is supposed, that he shall to my Lady of Norfolk,[3] and mine uncle William cometh with him; and he telleth me that there is like to be trouble in the manor of Oxnead; wherefore I pray you take heed lest that the Duke of Suffolk's council play therewith now at the vacation of the benefice,[4] as they did with the benefice of Drayton, which by the help of Master John Salett and Donne his man, there was a quest made by the Donne, that found that the Duke of Suffolk was very patron, which was false, yet they did it for an evidence; but now if any such prat (*practice*) should be laboured it is I hope in better case, for such a thing must needs be found before Master John Smyth, who is our old friend; wherefore I pray you labour him, that, if need be, he may do us a friend's turn therein.

Item, both ye and I must needs take this matter as our own, and it were for none other cause but for our good grandam's sake; nevertheless ye wrote well, that there is another entress (*interest*) longing to us after her decease; if there be any such thing begun there by such a fryer or priest, as it is said, I marvel that ye sent me no word thereof: but ye have now wife and child, and so much to care for that ye forget me.

As for tidings here, I hear tell that my cousin Sir Robert Chamberlain hath entered the manor of Scolton upon your bedfellow Conyers,[5] whereof ye send me no word.

Item, young William Brandon [6] is arrested for that he should have by force ravished an old gentlewoman, and yet was not therewith eased, but ravished her eldest daughter, and then would have ravished the other sister both; wherefore men say foul of him, and that he would eat the hen and all her chickens; and some say that the king intendeth to sit upon him, and men say he is like to be hanged, for he hath wedded a widow.[7]

---

[1] Henry Stafford. He was beheaded in 1483, 1 Richard III.

[2] Joan, sister to Henry Duke of Buckingham, was the second wife of Sir William Knevet, knight, of Bokenham Castle, Norfolk.

[3] Elizabeth, widow of John Mowbray, Duke of Norfolk.

[4] Agnes Paston, grandmother to Sir John, presented Thomas Everard to the rectory of Oxnead in 1475, and in 1479 she again presented William Barthulmew, so that the Duke of Suffolk either did not attempt to disturb her right, or at least did not succeed if he endeavoured to do it.

[5] [The custom of sleeping together seems not to have been uncommon in this or even a later age, and to have generally implied a great degree of confidence and friendship. Shakspere has more than once alluded to the custom, and Malone characterised it as "unseemly;" but, as the editor of the 'Pictorial Shakspere' truly observes, "customs are unseemly, for the most part, when they are opposed to the general usages of society, and to the state of public opinion. The necessity for two persons occupying one bed belonged to an age when rooms were large and furniture scanty."—*Histories*, vol. i. p.341.]

[6] We are not told who this William Brandon was, therefore it must remain uncertain whether he was related to Sir William Brandon or not. [Jas. Pettit Andrews, in his 'Anecdotes,' alludes to this as an instance of the early existence of the class of silly and profligate young men who, at different periods, under the names of bucks, bloods, mohawks, and swells, have endeavoured to attain notoriety by sacrificing all common sense and decency, and publicly committing follies and crimes alike mean and mischievous; and for which many, we have no doubt, have no taste whatever, and no motive but a morbid vanity craving for public attention.]

[7] His being already a married man was certainly an aggravation of his crime.

Item, as for the pageant that men say that the Earl of Oxford hath played at Hammes, I suppose ye have heard thereof; it is so long ago, I was not in this country when the tidings came, therefore I sent you no word thereof; but for conclusion, as I hear say, he leaped the walls, and went to the dyke, and into the dyke to the chin; to what intent I cannot tell; some say to steal away, and some think he would have drowned himself, and so it is deemed.

No more, but I am not certain whether I shall come home in haste or not.

Written at London, the day next St. Bartholomew,[1] in the eighteenth year of Edward IV.

JOHN PASTON, *knight*.

London, Sunday or Tuesday,
23rd or 25th of August,
1478. 18 E. IV.

LETTER CCCCXII.—(LIII. vol. v. p. 237.)

[WILLIAM PASTON, a younger brother of John's, was born in 1459, and was now about nineteen years of age, and pursuing his studies at Eton. He writes to inquire as to his brother's health, and to thank him for a "noble in gold" which he had received, but goes on to state that "my creauser (*creditor*) Master Thomas (Stevenson) heartily recommendeth him to you, and he prayeth you to send him some money for my commons, for he saith ye be twenty shillings in his debt, for a month was to pay for when he had money last; also

I beseech you to send me a hose cloth, one for the holy days of some colour, and another for the working days (how coarse soever it be it maketh no matter), and a stomacher, and two shirts, and a pair of slippers: and if it like you that I may come with Alweder by water, and sport me with you at London a day or two this term-time, then ye may let all this be till the time that I come, and then I will tell you when I shall be ready to come from Eton by the grace of God, who have you in his keeping." Dated from Eton, Nov. 7, 1478.]

LETTER CCCCXIII.—(LIV. vol. v. p. 239.)

[WILLIAM DE PYKENHAM, who was afterwards chancellor of Norwich and archdeacon of Suffolk, writes in this letter as a friend to Margery Paston, discouraging an attempt apparently desired to be made to force Walter Paston into the church before he was legally eligible. The opinion given seems a sincere and honest one, and the postscript is curious, showing that though bribery in endeavouring to obtain church preferment was common enough to render its offer no matter of surprise or offence, it was not always effectual. He says, " I have received your letter and understand your desire, which is against the law for three causes; one is, for your son Walter is not tonsured, in mother tongue called Benett; another cause, he is not twenty-four years of age, which is required complete; the third,

he ought of right to be priest within twelve-months, after that he is parson,[2] without so were he had a dispensation from Rome, by our Holy Father the Pope, which I am certain cannot be had; therefore I present not your desire unto my lord, lest he would have taken it to a displeasure; or else to take a great simpleness in your desire, which should cause him, in such matters as shall fortune you to speed with him another time, to show unto you the rigour of the law, which I would be loth; therefore present another man able; ask counsel of Master John Smyth, and cease of your desire in this part, for it is not goodly

---

1 24th of August.
[2 This refers to his serving as a curate as a qualification for orders.]

VOL. II.

K

neither godly, and let not your desire be known after my advice: be not wroth, though I send unto you thus plainly in the matter, for I would ye did as well as any woman in Norfolk, that is, with right, to your honour, prosperity, and to the pleasure of God, with you and all yours, who have you in his blessed keeping. From Hoxne on Candlemas-day.

" I send you your present again in the box.
WILLIAM PYKENHAM."]

Hoxne,
Tuesday, Feb. 2, 1478-9.

LETTER CCCCXIV.—(LV. vol. v. p. 243.)

[FROM this letter Walter Paston appears to have removed to Oxford, and his tutor, Edmund Alyard, writes to his mother, Margery Paston, from Oxford, Thursday, March 4, 1478-9, giving certainly a very favourable account of the young man, as follows :—" As for your son Walter, his labour and learning hath been, and is, in the faculty of art, and is well sped therein: and may be bachelor at such time as shall like you, and then to go to law, I can think it to his preferring, but it is not good he know it unto the time he shall change; and as I conceive there shall none have that exhibition to the faculty of law, therefore move ye the executors that at such time as he shall leave it ye may put another in his place, such as shall like you to prefer. If he shall go to law, and be made bachelor of arts before, and ye will have him home this year, then may he be bachelor at Midsummer, and be with you in the vacation, and go to law at Michaelmas."]

LETTER CCCCXV.—(LVI. vol. v. p. 245.)

[WALTER PASTON writes to his brother Sir John for money for his expenses at Oxford; he says,—" I sent a letter to my brother John, certifying my costs, and the causes why that I would proceed, but as I have sent word to my mother, I purpose to tarry now till it be Michaelmas, for, if I tarry till then, some of my costs shall be paid; for I supposed, when that I sent the letter to my brother John, that the queen's brother should have proceeded at Midsummer, and therefore I beseeched her to send me some money, for it will be some cost to me, but not much." The queen's brother here mentioned was no doubt Lionel Wideville, afterwards Bishop of Salisbury, in 1482; Fenn says, "It appears from this letter that when any person related to the royal family took any degree in the university, a part of the expenses of those who became graduates at the same time were borne by such personage. It does not appear whether the university fees were so discharged, or whether it related only to the expense attending the feasts given at such time. It most probably related only to the expenses attending the good cheer; and if so, it might be confined to those of the same college only." An inceptor is one admitted to an university degree previous to the usual time, up to which period he is so termed. Walter Paston concludes his letter by inquiring " what is done with the horse I left at Tottenham, and whether the man be content that I had it of or not?" It is dated from Oxford, Saturday, May 22, 1479.]

LETTER CCCCXVI.—(LVII. vol. v. p. 249.)

[THIS is another letter from Walter Paston to his brother John, announcing his being made a B.A., and noticing a reproach of his brother as to not complying with his request of writing how he got on. The letter, he says, did not contain such a request, and was not received till too late if it had. The delay is thus accounted for :—" Master Brown had that same ime much money in a bag, so that he durst not bring it with him, and that same letter was in that same bag, and he had forgotten to ake out the letter, and he sent all together by London, so that it was the next day after that I was made bachelor ere then the letter came, and so the fault was not in me. And if ye will know what day I was made bachelor, I was made on Friday was se'nnight (18*th June*),

and I made my feast on the Monday after (21*st June*). I was promised venison against my feast of my Lady Harcourt, and of another person too, but I was deceived of both; but my guests held them pleased with such meat as they had, blessed be God, who have you in his keeping." Dated Oxford, June 30, 1479.]

LETTER CCCCXVII.—(LVIII. vol. v. p. 251.)

[THIS letter, dated from Norwich, Saturday, August 21, 1479, has neither address nor signature, but is supposed to have been written by John Paston. Walter Paston died at Norwich, and was buried at St. Peter's, Hungate; Agnes Paston died about the same time, and was buried in Norwich Cathedral. The "uncle William" is always spoken of with ill feeling, and seems now to be suspected of having some sinister designs upon his mother's property, to a part of which, however, if even he had no previous right, he might naturally expect to succeed under her will or settlement : " Sure tidings are come to Norwich that my grandam is deceased, whom God assoil! my uncle had a messenger yesterday

that she should not escape, and this day came another at such time as we were at mass for my brother Walter, whom God assoil! My uncle was coming to have offered, but the last messenger returned him hastily, so that he took his horse incontinent to inform more of our heaviness. My sister is delivered, and the child passed to God, who send us of his grace. [This sister was probably Anne, wife of W. Yelverton.] Docking told me secretly that for any haste (*in all haste*) my uncle should ride by my Lady of Norfolk to have a threescore persons, whether it is to convey my grandam hither or not he could not say; I deem it is rather to put them in possession of some of her lands."]

LETTER CCCCXVIII.—(LXXXVI. vol. ii. p. 277.)

This is the last letter from Sir John Paston, who died on the 15th of November following, but whether of the sickness which he seems in this letter so much to fear, I cannot discover. He here complains of sickness of body, and seems to have likewise much uneasiness of mind. The lands at Caister, Heylesdon, &c. were a constant trouble to him from the claims of the Dukes of Norfolk, Suffolk, &c. [His whole life, from his coming of age, seems to have been one game of law. Even in this his last letter he boasts of his skill in checking " uncle William " in the prosecution of his suits. The passion for holding land seems to have been very intense. the Pastons submit to almost any sacrifice rather than alienate land, and " uncle William " and others seem equally ardent for its acquisition]

To the right worshipful Mistress Margaret Paston, be this delivered.

PLEASE it you to weet that I have been here at London a fortnight, whereof the first four days I was in such fear of the sickness, and also found my chamber and stuff not so clean as I deemed, which troubled me sore ; and as I told you at my departing I was not well moneyed, for I had not past ten marks (6*l.* 13*s.* 4*d.*), whereof I departed 40*s.* to be delivered of my old bedfellow ; and then I rode beyond

Dunstable, and there spake with one of my chief witnesses, which promised me to take labour and to get me writings touching this matter between me and the Duke of Suffolk,[1] and I rewarded him (*with*) 20*s.*, and then, as I informed you, I paid five marks (3*l.* 6*s.* 8*d.*) incontinent (*immediately*) upon my coming

---

[1] John de la Pole, Duke of Suffolk.

here to repledge out my gown of velvet and
other geer; and then I hoped to have borrowed
some of Townshend, and he hath ffoodyd [1]
not forth ever since, and in effect I could have
at the most and at the soonest yesterday 20s.;
wherefore I beseech you to purvey me an 100s.,
and also to write to Peacock that he purvey
me as much, 100s., which I suppose that he
hath gathered at Paston and other places by
this time; for without I have this 10l., as God
help me, I fear I shall do but little good in no
matter, nor yet I wote not how to come home
but if (unless) I have it.

This geer hath troubled me so that it hath
made me more than half sick, as God help me.

Item, I understand that my uncle William
hath made labour of the escheator, and that he
hath both a writ of essend. closeth extr. and
also a supersedeas. I have written to the escheator therein of mine intent; if my uncle had
his will in that, yet should he be never the
nearer the land, but in effect he should have
this advantage, which is behoveful for a weak
matter, to have a colour, or a cloak, or a but-
tress; but on Tuesday I was with the Bishop
of Ely,[2] who showeth himself good and wor-

shipful, and he said that he should send to
mine uncle William that he should not proceed in no such matter till that he speak with
him, and moreover that he should cause him to
be here hastily; in which matter is no remedy
as now, but if (unless) it were so that the escheator, if he be entreated to sit by mine uncle
William, which percase he shall not, that if
my brother John and Lomnor have knowledge
of the day, and they might be there, Lomnor
can give evidence enough in that matter without the book; and moreover that they see both
the letter and the other note that I sent to the
escheator, and with help of the escheator all
might be as best is; and if my brother and
Lomnor take labour herein I shall recompense
their costs.

Written in haste with short advisement on
the Friday next St. Simon and Jude, in the
nineteenth year of Edward IV.

Let my brother John see this bill, for he
knoweth more of the matter.

JOHN PASTON, knight.

London,
  Friday, 29th of October.
  1479. 19 E. IV.

LETTER CCCCXIX.—(LIX. vol. v. p. 253.)

[THIS is merely a bill of the receipts and
expenses of a manor-court at Cressingham,
held before John Paston, on Nov. 25, 1479;
and the amount for a few sums paid on account of the sickness and burial of his brother
Walter.]

LETTER CCCCXX.—(LX. vol. v. p. 255.)

[JOHN PASTON here writes a detailed answer
to his brother's letter (ccccxviii). He informs
him that Lomnor and himself had drawn a
bill, and sent it by their brother Edmund,
who chanced to have another errand to that
part of the country, namely, to get the good-
will of H. Spilman "towards the bargain like
to be finished hastily betwixt Mistress Clippesby and him," afterwards still more detailed.
John Paston goes on to relate that Edmund
had found the escheator a more zealous friend
than was desired. At the desire of the
Bishop of Ely both parties were to refrain
from litigation, and this was urged by Edmund on the escheator as a reason why Sir
John Paston's inquisition should not be moved
in unless Wm. Paston first moved for his;
"but the escheator answered him that he
would find it for you, after your bill, of his
own authority; and so it was found." The
opinions and advice conveyed in the following

---

[1] Qy. footed, i.e., set foot out of his own house;
or fooded, i.e., eat out of his own house, for fear of
the sickness mentioned at the beginning of this letter?
[2] John Morton, afterwards Archbishop of Canterbury.

extracts are very creditable to John Paston's honesty, as well as talent; he appears to have been greatly improved by marriage, and to have shaken off something of his selfishness and greediness :—"But, sir, ye must remember that my Lord of Ely desired mine uncle as well as you to surcease, as I put mine uncle in knowledge, and mine uncle at the first agreed that he would make no more suit about it, in trust that ye would do the same, according to my Lord of Ely's desire; wherefore ye had need to beware that the escheator skips not from you, when he cometh to London, and certify it, ere ye speak with him. * * * * Sir, your tenants at Cromer say that they know not who shall be their lord; they marvel that ye nor no man for you hath not yet been there. Also when I was with mine uncle, I had a long pystyl (*letter*) of him, that ye had sent Peacock to Paston, and commanded the tenants there that they should pay none arrearages to him but if (*unless*) they were bound to him, by obligation, for the same; mine uncle saith it was otherwise appointed before the arbitrators; they thought, he saith, that as well my master Fitzwalter as other, that he should receive that as it might be gathered; but now he saith that he weeteth well some shall run away, and some shall waste it, so that it is never like to be gathered, but lost; and so I trow it is like to be of some of the debtors, what for casualty of death and these other causes before rehearsed; wherefore me thinketh, if it were appointed before the arbitrators that he should receive them, as he saith, it were not for you to break it, or else, if he be pleyn [full] executor to my grandam, then also he ought to have it. I speak like a blind man, lo ye as ye think (*best*), for I was at no such appointment before the arbitrators, nor I know not whether he is executor to my grandam or not, but by his saying." This is a very curious passage : so much employed as John Paston had been, it is scarcely possible to imagine that he could be wholly ignorant of so important a provision of his grandmother's will. He then proceeds with another, and, as we know, a favourite subject—a marriage, and for his brother Edmund : this was to be done by procuring the wardship of a young widow's son, and he urges Sir John to use his influence "that mine uncle Sir George (Brown)

may get to my brother Edmund of the king the wardship of John Clippesby, son and heir to John Clippesby, late of Oby, in the county of Norfolk, esquire, during the nonage of my Lord and Lady of York, though it cost four or five marks (2*l.* 13*s.* 4*d.*, or 3*l.* 6*s.* 8*d.*) the suit; let mine uncle Sir George be clerk of the hanaper, and keep the patent, if it be granted, till he have his money, and that shall not be long to. Mine uncle Sir George may inform the king for truth that the child shall have no land during his young mother's life, and there is no man [this means no father will marry his daughter to him] here that will marry with him without they have some land with him, and so the gift shall not be great that the king should give him, and yet I trow he should get the mother by that mean." This lady was the widow of William Clippesby (not John, says Fenn) of Oby; she shortly after became the wife of Edmund Paston, by whom she had one son, and died in 1491. The postscript of this letter shows the nature of John Paston's pecuniary and domestic troubles. "Sir, it is told me that Nicholas Barley, the squire, hath taken an action of debt against me this term; I pray you let Wheatley or somebody speak with him, and let him weet that, if he sue me softly this term, that he shall be paid ere the next term be at an end; it is about six pounds, and in faith he should have had it ere this time and (*if*) our threshers of Swainsthorp had not died; and if I might have paid it him a year ago, as well as I trust I shall soon after Christmas, I would not for twelve pounds have broken him so many promises as I have. Also, sir, I pray you send me, by the next man that cometh from London, two pots of treacle of Genoa; they shall cost 16*d.*, for I have spent out that I had with my young wife, and my young folks, and myself; and I shall pay him that shall bring them to me, and for his carriage; I pray you let it be sped. The people dieth sore in Norwich, and specially about my house, but my wife and my women come not out; and flee farther we cannot, for at Swainsthorp, since my departing thence, they have died, and been sick nigh in every house of the town." Much sickness and mortality are recorded as having happened in England in this year. The letter is dated from Norwich, Nov. 6, 1479.]

LETTER CCCCXXI.—(LXI. vol. v. p. 263.)

[WILLIAM LOMNOR writes to John Paston an account of the death of Sir John, his brother; and of what had been done to defend his interests against the old foe, "uncle William," who was endeavouring to get possession, and was, there is little doubt from the tenor of many preceding letters, a creditor to a very considerable amount:—"Your brother Edmund, on Sunday next before St. Andrew, rode to Marlingford, and before all the tenants examined one James, keeper there for William Paston, where he was the week next before Saint Andrew, and then he said that he was not at Marlingford from the Monday unto the Thursday at even, and so there was no man there but your brother's man at the time of his decease; so by that your brother died seized; and your brother Edmund bade your man keep possession to your behest, and warned the tenants to pay no man till you had spoken (to) them; so meseemeth that is a remitter to your old tailed title [*your original title under the entail*] : commune with your counsel. Further, at afternoon he was at Oxnead, to understand how they had done; and Perys kept your brother's possession at that time, and your uncle's man was not there, but he assigned another poor man to be there, whether that continued the possession of William Paston or not be remembered, &c. And after the decease, &c., W. Paston sent the man, that kept possession before, to enter and keep possession, which was no warrant by that appointment, for ye stand at your liberty as for any appointment or combination had before, and so men seem it were good for you to stand at large till ye hear more : if ye might have my Lord Chamberlain's good favour and lordship it were right expedient; as for my Lord of Ely, deal not with him by our advice, for he will move for treaty, and else be displeased. Your brother Edmund sent to John Wymondham, and he sent word he would be a mean of treaty, but would take no part, and as I suppose that was by Heydon's advice, for your uncle sent to me to be with him, and also the same man rode to Heydon and Wymondham, &c., the bringer of this letter can tell you, for he was with your brother Edmund at these places." Lomnor concludes by informing him that his brother Edmund " doth his diligence and part for you full well and sadly in many behalves, and hath brought my mistress your wife to Topcroft," which was her father's residence. This seems rather a singular arrangement at such a time. The letter is dated from Norwich, Saturday, Nov. 28, 1479.]

LETTER CCCCXXII.—(LXXXVII. vol. ii. p. 281.)

On the back of this letter is written in an ancient hand, " a Lr'e sent from Jo Paston ar.[*arm*] to his mother, touching the buryall of his Brother Sir John Paston in London." Sir John Paston died on the 15th of November, 1479, 19 Edward IV., aged between thirty and forty years : I should suppose nearly forty. This letter therefore was written in November, 1479.

To my right worshipful mother, Margaret Paston, at St. Peter's of Hungate [Norwich].

RIGHT worshipful mother, after all duties of humble recommendation, as lowly as I can, I beseech you of your daily blessing and prayers; and, mother, John Clement, bearer hereof, can tell you, the more pity [*it*] is if it pleased God, that my brother is buried in the White Fryers at London,[1] which I thought should not have been; for I supposed that he would have been buried at Bromholm, and that caused me so soon to ride to London, to have purveyed his bringing home; and if it had been his will to have lain at Bromholm, I had purposed all the way as I have ridden to have

[1] [Fenn points this passage so as, we think, to destroy all meaning whatever : " John Clement, bearer hereof, can tell you the more pity is, if it

pleased God that my brother," &c. The word *it* which we have inserted, though it makes the sense clearer, is not indispensable, as such elisions frequently occur in old writers.]

rought home my grandam[1] and him together, ut that purpose is void as now; but this I hink to do when I come to London, to speak ith my Lord Chamberlain,[2] and to win by is means my Lord of Ely[3] if I can; and if I aay, by any of their means, cause the king to ake my service and my quarrel[4] together, I ill; and I think that Sir George Brown,[5] ir James Radcliff, and others of mine acquaintance, which wait most upon the king, nd lie nightly in his chamber,[6] will put to heir good wills: this is my way as yet.

And, mother, I beseech you, as ye may get r send any messengers, to send me your advice and my cousin Lomnor's, to John Lee's ouse, tailor, within Ludgate.

I have much more to write, but my empty ead will not let me remember it.

Also, mother, I pray that my brother Edmund may ride to Marlingford, Oxnead, Paston, Cromer, and Caister, and all these manors to enter in my name; and to let the tenants of Oxnead and Marlingford know that I sent no word to him to take no money of them, but their attornment; wherefore he will not till he hear from me again ask them none, but let him command them to pay to[7] servants of mine uncle, nor to himself, nor to none other to his use, in pain of payment again to me. I think if there should be any money asked in my name, peradventure it would make my Lady of Norfolk against me, and cause her to think I deal more contrary to her pleasure than did my brother, whom God pardon of his great mercy!

I have sent to enter at Stansted and at Orwellbury; and I have written a bill to Anne Montgomery and Jane Rodon, to make my Lady of Norfolk if it will be.

Your son, and humble servant,
JOHN PASTON.

November, 1479.
19 E. IV.

LETTER CCCCXXIII.—(LXII. vol. v. p. 267.)

JOHN PASTON writes from London to "his ight worshipful and most kind mother, Margaret Paston," apparently in reply to her advice o him to leave London on account of some revalent sickness. His resolute determination not to leave important business undone hrough fear of death is markedly characterstic both of the man and the times, when, for he attainment of almost any object of ambiion or earnest desire, and sometimes even hrough mere love of excitement, life was isked, both actively and passively, with a eadiness that was not indifference, and a :ourage that was seldom rashness, and it was felt as a "shame" to abandon an undertaking through fear of death. Paston continues to complain of his "unkind uncle." He says,— "Please it you to understand that, whereas ye willed me by pains to haste me out of the air that I am in, it is so that I must put me in God, for here must I be for a season; and in good faith I shall never, while God sendeth me life, dread more death than shame; and thanked be God, the sickness is well ceased here; and also my business putteth away my fear. I am driven to labour in letting of (hindering) the execution of mine unkind uncle's intent, wherein I have as yet none other discourage but that I trust in God he shall fail of it." He then proceeds to explain his hopes of assistance from the support of the Lord Chamberlain and the Bishop of Ely, the latter of whom he says hath put him in certainty by his words "that he will be with me against my uncle;" but acknowledges he hath not had much as yet from them. He then concludes thus:—"Mother, I beseech you that Peacock may be sent to purvey

[1] Agnes, daughter and coheir of Sir Edmund Berry, knight, and widow of Sir William Paston, knight, died in 1479.
[2] William Lord Hastings.
[3] John Morton, afterwards Archbishop of Canterbury, and Lord Chancellor.
[4] This must relate to his dispute with the Duchess of Norfolk, relative to Caister, or to some disputes with his uncle, William Paston, concerning other manors and estates. [It must mean all his quarrels, his cause generally. It would be impossible to guess he one among his numerous disputes.]
[5] Of Beechworth Castle, in Surrey.
[6] These seem to have been the "esquires of the king's body," who lay in his chamber.

[7] [This to should evidently be no, or no must be inserted after it.]

me as much money as is possible for him to make against my coming home, for I have much to pay here in London, what for the funeral costs, debts, and legacies, that must be content in greater haste than shall be mine ease. Also I would the farm barley in Fleg, as well as at Paston, if there be any, were gathered, and if it may be reasonably sold, then to be sold, or put to the malting; but I would at Caister that it were out of the tenant's hands, for things that I hear: keep ye counsel this from Peacock, and from all folks, which matter I shall appease, if God will give me leave." Dated Dec. 1479.]

LETTER CCCCXXIV.—(LXIII. vol. v. p. 273.)

[This letter, though not subscribed, is no doubt from John Paston to some person unknown. The first part of the letter relates to his brother's tombstone, or rather effigy, as it would seem by the objection that the "man at St. Bride's is no cleanly portrayer." The remainder of the letter is occupied with directions as to the transacting of some business at Rome respecting a bull, but the nature and cause of it is not stated. We give the passage respecting the effigy as a curious notice of the state of art in England at the time, having one artist to make the drawing, and another to carve it:—"Sir, I pray you that ye will send some child to my Lord of Buckingham's place, and to the Crown, which, as I conceive, is called Gerard's Hall, in Breadstreet, to inquire whether I have any answer of my letter sent to Calais, which ye know of; and that ye will remember my brother's stone, so that it might be made ere I come again, and that it be cleanly wrought. It is told me that the man at Saint Bride's is no cleanly portrayer, therefore I would fain it might be portrayed by some other man, and he to grave it up." It has no date, but must have been written in 1479-80.]

LETTER CCCCXXV.—(LXIV. vol. v. p. 277.)

[This curious letter is from Edmund Paston to his mother, Margaret Paston, and was probably written soon after his marriage with the widow Clippesby, as he apologizes apparently for not having yet introduced her. His notion of setting off the value of a horse which died while at livery against the keep of the other horses, alleging it was put to grass and to work, reminds us of the horse causes of the present day. He writes as follows:—"Right worshipful and most especial good mother, in my most humble wise, with all my duty and service, I recommend me to you, beseeching you of your blessing, which is to me most joy of earthly thing; and it please you to be so good and kind mother to me to forgive me, and also my wife, of our lewd (rude) offence, that we have not done our duty, which was to have seen and have waited upon you ere now. My huswife trusteth to lay to you her huswifery for her excuse, which I must beseech you not to accept, for in good faith I deem her mind hath been otherwise occupied than to huswifery, which seemeth well by the lacheness (negligence) of the tilth of her lands. I beseech God for the furtherance of them as now, reward you, and the good parson of Mauteby, who I weened would not have balked this poor lodging to Norwich ward.[1] I understand by the bringer hereof that ye intend to ride to Walsingham; if it please you that I may weet the season, as my duty is, I shall be ready to await upon you.

---

[1] [This sentence is very obscure, but we think it is intended to read thus:—" I beseech God for the furtherance of them as [from] now," that is, the tilth of the lands from this time; " reward you, and the good parson of Mauteby, and also Master Baily," &c., i. e., and to reward you, that is, he beseeches God for all these objects.]

'lease it you that the bringer hereof came to
ae for 10s. 8d. which I should owe his father;
:ue it was at my last departing from him I
wed him so much, but certainly ere I came at
'hetford homewards I thought of conscience
e ought to have restored me as much; I had
1y horses with him at livery, and, among all,
ne of them was put to grass and to labour, so
1at he died of a lax by the way; I paid for
ard meat ever to him. Please it you to de-
:ver Katharine 5s. which I send you in this
ill. I am not ascertained how she is purveyed of money towards her journey. If her
father could not have claimed one penny of
me, I would not see her dispurveyed (*unprovided*) if I might, nor the poorest child that is
belonging to his lodging. Mother, my wife
is bold to send you a token. I beseech you
pardon all things not done according to duty.
I beseech God send you the accomplishment
of your most worshipful desires. At Oby, the
Saturday next before Candlemas. Jan. 29,
1179-80.]

LETTER CCCCXXVI.—(LXV. vol. v. p. 281.)

This is one of the few letters of William
'aston, the "uncle William," who is so often
omplained of by the other members of the
imily. This letter shows that he was at least
s much sinned against as sinning, for he
1ust have inherited Harwelbury[1] from his
1other, who retained it till her death, and
pon which his elder brother and his de-
:cendants could scarcely have had any just
laim, although they appear to have endea-
oured to obtain possession of it. Then, as
ow, the ties of relationship had but small
ifluence when any right, or fancied right,
2 property was concerned. The letter to
is tenant at Harwelbury, John King, is
rank and well written, and, containing no
mputations upon the motives of his relatives,
1ough asserting the justice of his own claim,
y no means gives us such an impression of
is character as is conveyed by the frequent
ccusations and complaints of his kinsfolk.
le says, "John Kyng, I greet you heartily
'ell, and I understand, as well by my friend
iir William Storar, as by Richard Browne,
hat as well my kinsman Sir John Paston that
lead is, as my kinsman John Paston that now
iveth, have been with you, and given you
many great threats for that ye, according to
the truth, told unto them that ye occupied my
manor of Harwelbury by my lease and by my
right; and furthermore I understand, notwithstanding the said great threats, that ye, like a
full, true, hearty friend, have dealed and
fastly abiden in my title, and would not re-
tourn (*attourn*) to none of them; wherefor I
heartily thank you; and furthermore to courage (*encourage*) you in your fast dealing, I
show unto you that I have right both in law
and in conscience, whereby I promise you on
my faith to defend you and save you harmless for the occupation of the land, or anything that ye shall do in my title against him,
and (*if*) it should cost me as much as the
manor is worth, and also another time to do
as much for you and (*if*) it lie in my power,
if ye have any matter to do there as I may do
for you. And also I hear say by my said
friend Sir William Storar, and by Richard
Browne, that ye are of such substance, and of
such trust, and such favour, in the country
there, that it lieth in your power to do a good
turn for your friend." The letter is dated
from London, Thursday, Feb. 24, 1179-80.]

LETTER CCCCXXVII.—(LXVI. vol. v. p. 283.)

This is another letter on wife-procuring, from
2dmund Paston to his brother William. In
7rose's Local Proverbs (given at the end of
his Provincial Glossary) he gives the following under Norfolk:—"There never was a
Paston poor, a Heydon a coward, or a Corn-
wallis a fool." In this correspondence the
Pastons certainly appear not willing to belie
the proverb, and particularly by marriage.

[1] Harwelbury, in other instances spelled Horwel-
1ury and Orwelbury, is in the parish of Harfield,
:ear Royston, in Hertfordshire.

The one here proposed, however, did not take effect, and William died unmarried. The date of the letter is uncertain; it is here guessed at Jan. 13, 1480-1, but it might have been a few years later, which would reduce the seniority of the lady.

"I heartily recommend me to you; here is lately fallen a widow in Worsted, which was wife to one Bolt, a worsted-merchant, and worth a thousand pound. and gave to his wife an hundred marks (66*l.* 13*s.* 4*d.*) in money, stuff of household, and plate to the value of an hundred marks, and ten pounds by the year in land; she is called a fair gentlewoman. I will for your sake see her. She is right sister, of father and mother, to Harry Ingloss; I purpose to speak with him to get his good will. The gentlewoman is about thirty years, and has but two children, which shall be at the dead's charge; she was his wife but five years; if she be any better than I write for, take it in woothe [*take it in good part*]. I show the least; thus let me have knowledge of you as shortly as ye can, and when ye shall moun [*be able to*] be in this country." Written from Norwich.]

LETTER CCCCXXVIII.—(LXVII. vol. v. p. 285.)

[JOHN PASTON having desired the attendance at Norwich of a certain Thomas Cryne, the latter here writes to excuse himself, as he is about to attend the courts and leets of "Master Heydon," to whom he seems to have been bailiff. He writes: "My Lord Rivers in his own person hath been at Hickling, and his counsel learned, and searched his fees for his homages, among which ye be for Begvile's pasture in Somerton, and I suppose Winterton, late Sir John Fastolf's. My mistress, your mother, for Mautebys, in Waxham; wherein I beseech you provide, for I have done therein heretofore as far as I might, &c. What (*ever*) it meaneth, my lord is set sore to approvement and husbandry; his counsel hath told him he may set his fines for respite of homage at his pleasure, &c." This is a curious feature in the character of Earl Rivers; history shows him to us as a chivalrous knight, and a protector and patron of literature; here we have him as an encourager of agriculture, "set sore to approvement and husbandry" beyond the conception even of a country bailiff. The letter is dated from Thorpland, Wednesday, April 14, 1482.]

LETTER CCCCXXIX.—(LXVIII. vol. v. p. 289.)

[MARGERY PASTON writes from Norwich to her husband John Paston about the state of his tenantry, in consequence of having their implements seized, under legal process, in part by "uncle William." The whole letter displays, not the lawlessness, but the rude methods of legal process, at the time, and the very imperfect state of agriculture:—"Right reverend and worshipful sir, in my most humble wise I recommend me unto you as lowly as I can, &c. Please you to weet, John Howes, Alexander Warden, John Tille, with the parson and the new miller of Marlingford, have gotten Thomas at Well's cart of East Todenham, farmer; and mine uncle William Paston, Harry Hervy of Melton Magna, farmer, and bailiff to my said uncle, Richard Barker's cart of the said town of Melton, late farmer, and yet is in danger (*debt*) to my said uncle; and William Smyth's cart of Brandon juxta Barnham Broom, late farmer and bailiff, and also in danger to my said uncle, on Monday and Tuesday last past carried away from Marlingford into the place at Saint Edmund's at Norwich twelve of your great planks, of the which they made six loads, hearing about the said carts bows and glaives (*bows and bills*) for fear of taking away. Sir, as for your tenants of Marlingford, they withhold their cattle and themselves both from the court, and come not within the lordship, nor make none attournment, except Thomas Davy and John Wake, which absenting of the tenants is to them a great hurt and loss for lack of seeding their lands with their winter corn; beseeching you for God's sake to remember some remedy for them." The letter then proceeds to state that some negotiation was being carried on by Lady Calhorpe with William Paston, when he promised to abide by a proposal of his "touching the manor of Sporle," and to "write and seal is largely as any man will desire him." But Margery Paston adds, showing the feeling of suspicion entertained towards him,—"At his departing from my lady he was not merry; what the cause was I wot not. My Lady Calthorpe desireth me to write to you to have end, for he intends largely to have a peace with you, as he saith; but trust him not too much, for he is not good. My mother-in-law thinketh long she hear no word from you; she is in good health, blessed be God, and all your babies also. I marvel I hear no word from you, which grieveth me full evil; I sent you a letter by (*the*) brasier's son of Norwich, whereof I hear no word." Her postscript is in her usual affectionate style. "Sir, I pray you, if ye tarry long at London, that it will please (*you*) to send for me, for I think long since I lay in your arms." Dated Nov. 2, about 1482 or 1483.]

LETTER CCCCXXX.—(LXIX. vol. v. p. 293.)

[ANOTHER of the prudent and affectionate letters of Margery Paston to her husband, about the same disputes with his uncle William mentioned in the last. The Duchess of Norfolk seems to have hitherto favoured William, but to be now weary of so doing, and Margery hopes to win her to her husband's side if she be allowed to attempt it, but will not do so without his consent. From her frequent complaints of not receiving answers, her husband does not appear to have been a very punctual correspondent, at least with her, though, as we have seen, a good and ready letter-writer. "Mine own sweet heart; in my most humble wise I recommend me unto you, desiring heartily to hear of your welfare, the which I beseech Almighty God preserve and keep to his pleasure and your heart's desire. Sir, the cause of my writing to you at this time; on Friday at night last past came Alexander Wharton, John Howes, and John Fille, with two good carts well manned and horsed with them to Marlingford, and there at the manor of Marlingford, and at the mill, loaded both carts with mestlyon (*mesling*) and wheat, and betimes on Saturday in the morning they departed from Marlingford towards Bungay, as it is said; for the said carts came from Bungay, as I suppose, by the sending of Bryon, for he goeth hastily over the sea, as it is said, and as I suppose he will have the mestlyon over with him, for the most part of the cartloads was mestlyon, &c. Sir, on Saturday last past I spake with my cousin Gurney, and he said, if I would go to my lady of Norfolk and beseech her good Grace to be your good and gracious lady, she would so be, for he said that one word of a woman should do more than the words of twenty men, if I could rule my tongue, and speak none harm of mine uncle; and if ye command me so for to do, I trust I shall say nothing to my lady's displeasure but to your profit; for me thinketh by the words of them, and of your good farmer of Oxnead, that they will soon draw to an end, for he curseth the time that ever he came in the farm of Oxnead, for he saith that he weeteth well that he shall have a great loss, and yet he will not be aknowyn (*let it be known*) whether he hath paid or not; but when he seeth his time he will say truth. I understand by my said cousin Gurney that my lady is near weary of her part; and he saith my lady shall come on pilgrimage into this town, but he knoweth not whether afore Christmas or after; and if I would then get my Lady Calthorpe, my mother-in-law, and my mother, and myself, and come before my lady beseeching her to be your good and gracious lady, he thinketh ye shall have an end, for fain she would be rid of it with her honour saved, but yet money she would have. No more to you at this time, but I marvel sore that I have no letter from you, but I pray God preserve you, and send me good tidings from you, and speed you well in your matters. And as for me, I have gotten me another lodging fellow, the first letter of her name is Mistress Bishop; she recommendeth her to you by the same token that ye would have had a token to my Master Bryon." Written from Norwich, Sunday, November, about 1482 or 1483.]

LETTER CCCCXXXI.—(LXXI. vol. v. p. 297.)

[This letter is from John Paston to his mother Margaret, who, he has heard from his wife, is about making her will. The letter is remarkably characteristic of the man; smooth, plausible, cunning, selfish, and jealous even of the influence of his wife. Of the manner in which the provisions of wills were fulfilled by the Pastons we have already had frequent specimens, and therefore, if he means that he must put from him all that she might bequeath orally, we may guess how well his word would have been kept. The will, however, was made, dated February 4, 1481-2, and proved December 18, 1484. After thanking his mother for her kindness to himself and his wife, he says—"It pleased you to have certain words to my wife at her departing, touching your remembrance of the shortness that ye think your days of, and also of the mind that ye have towards my brethren and sister your children, and also of your servants, wherein ye willed her to be a mean to me that I would tender and favour the same. Mother, saving your pleasure, there needeth not ambassadors nor means betwixt you and me, for there is neither wife nor other friend shall make me to do that (that) your commandment shall make me to do, if I may have knowledge of it; and if I have no knowledge, in good faith I am excusable both to God and you; and, well remembered, I wot well, ye ought not to have me in jealousy for one thing nor other that ye would have me to accomplish, if I overlive you; for I wot well not one man alive hath called so oft upon you as I to make your will and put each thing in certainty that ye would have done for yourself, and to your children and servants. Also at the making of your will, and at every communication that I have been at with you touching the same, I never contraried anything that ye would have done and performed, but always offered myself to be bound to the same; but, mother, I am right glad that my wife is anything (in) your favour or trust, but I am right sorry that my wife, or any other child or servant of yours, should be in better favour or trust with you than myself, for I will and must forbear and put from me that that all your other children, servants, priests, workmen, and friends of yours, that ye will ought bequeath to, shall take to them; and this have I and ever will be ready unto while I live, on my faith, and never thought other, so God be my help; whom I beseech to preserve you and send you so good life and long that ye may do for yourself and me after my decease; and I beshrew (curse) their hearts that would other, or shall cause you to mistrust or to be unkind to me or my friends." Written from Norwich, between 1482 and 1484.]

LETTER CCCCXXXII.—(II. of Appendix to vol. ii. p. 291.)

This letter shows the friendly disposition of the Lord Cromwell, and seems to hint his suspicions that some disagreeable circumstance might attend the strangeness alluded to if both parties did not obey his injunctions. Humphrey Bourchier, Lord Cromwell, was third son of Henry Earl of Essex : and marrying Joanna, co-heiress of Maud, sister of Ralph Lord Cromwell, had summons to parliament as Baron Cromwell in 1461, 1 E. IV. This letter therefore was written in this reign.

To my right trusty friend, John Paston, Esq.

TRUSTY and well-beloved friend, I greet you well; and forasmuch as it is done me to understand that there is a great strangeness betwixt my right trusty friend John Radcliff[1] and you, without any matter or cause of substance as I am learned, wherefore, inasmuch as I love you well both, I am not content it should so be.

Praying you heartily to forbear the said strangeness on your part to such time as I speak with you next myself, letting you weet I have written to him to do the same. And that ye fail not hereof, as I may do anything for you hereafter.

And our Lord have you in his keeping. Written at London the tenth day of February.

CROMWELL.

London.
10th of February. E. IV.

[1] John Radcliff was afterwards Lord Fitzwalter.

LETTER CCCCXXIII.—(III. of Appendix to vol. ii. p. 293.)

The whole of this letter (of which, for its curiosity, I have had a fac-simile engraved) is written by Elizabeth, third daughter of Richard Plantagenet, Duke of York, and Cecily, daughter of Ralph Nevile, Earl of Westmorland. She was sister to Edward IV. and Richard III., by the latter of whom her son, John Earl of Lincoln (after the death of his own son), was declared heir to the crown. She married John de la Pole, Duke of Suffolk, and lies buried with him in Wingfield church in Suffolk. Under the direction is written (I believe) in the hand of Sir John Paston, ... "Littrâ Ducisse Suff." If so, this letter was written in the reign of Edward IV., for Sir John died in 1479, 19 E. IV.; but if this memorandum be the handwriting of Sir John Paston's brother, then this letter might be written in the reign of Richard III., or even of Henry VII. The curiosity of this letter consists in the rank of the lady, and in being perhaps the only one extant of her writing. It shows likewise the simplicity of the times, when a princess of the blood royal, coming to London unprovided of a lodging, petitions for the use of that of a friend for a few days, in the humblest terms: "for God's sake, say me not nay." As to exterior form, this is rather a note than a letter, being only folded, without turning in the edges of the paper. A silken twine had been passed through every fold of it, the ends of which were afterwards united, and secured under the seal. The direction seems not to be in the hand of the Lady Elizabeth, but of some secretary in attendance on her. Perhaps she did not choose to trust him with the singularity of her request, but employed him only to superscribe it.

Unto John Paston, in haste.

MASTER PASTON, I pray you that it may please you to leave[1] your lodging for three or four days, till I may be *purveyed*[2] of another, and I shall do as much to your pleasure; | for God's sake, say me not nay, and I pray you recommend me to my Lord Chamberlain.[3]

E. IV.

Your friend, ELIZABETH.

[1] Leve, or lend : I believe it is leve, but it is so written that it is very difficult to determine.
[2] Porred, purveyed.
[3] William Lord Hastings was Lord Chamberlain to Edward IV.

LETTER CCCCXXXIV.—(IV. of Appendix to vol. ii. p. 295.)

This letter from John Paston to Mrs. Annes, or Anne, is either to a Mrs. Anne Hawte, or to some lady abroad at Calais, from which place he was at this time returning. His saying, "I am prowd that ye can reed Inglyshe." seems to imply that some other language was her native one; and therefore she was most probably some foreign lady. [The date of the year is not ascertainable, and the letter is therefore placed here, though it certainly comes much earlier in chronological arrangement.]

To Mistress Anne.

SINCE it is so that I may not as oft as I would be there, as I might do my message myself, mine own fair Mistress Anne, I pray you to accept this bill for my messenger, to recommend me to you in my most faithful wise, as he that fainest of all other desireth to know of your welfare, which I pray God increase to your most pleasure.

And, mistress, though so be that I as yet have given you but easy (*little*) cause to remember me for lack of acquitation,[1] yet I beseech you let me not be forgotten, when ye reckon up all your servants, to be set in the number with other.

And I pray you, Mistress Anne, for that service that I owe you, that in as short time as ye goodly may that I might be ascertained of your intent, and of your best friends, in such matters as I have broken to you of; which both your and mine right trusty friends John Lee, or else my mistress his wife, promised

before you and me at our first and last being together, that as soon as they or either of them knew your intent, and your friends, that they should send me word, and if they so do I trust soon after to see you.

And now farewell, mine own fair lady, and God give you good rest, for in faith I trow ye be in bed.

Written in my way homeward, on Mary Magdalen's day at midnight.

Your own,   JOHN PASTON.

Mistress Anne, I am proud that ye can read English, wherefore I pray you acquaint you with this my lewd (*uncouth*) hand, for my purpose is that ye shall be more acquainted with it, or else it shall be against my will; but yet and when ye have read this bill, I pray you burn it, or keep it secret to yourself, as my faithful trust is in you.

22nd of July,
St. Mary Magdalen.

LETTER CCCCXXXV.—(VI. Appendix to vol. ii. p. 301.)

We are here furnished with a curious though imperfect catalogue of the library of a gentleman in the reign of Edward IV. It is written on a strip of paper about seventeen inches long, and has been rolled up, by which means one end, having been damp, is entirely decayed, so that the names of some of the books are imperfect; and the then price or value of all of them is not now to be discovered, that having been uniformly written at the end which is now destroyed. It contained an account of all the books he had, as it mentions those which were lent out at the time the catalogue was made; and though the name of the owner is gone, yet, by comparing the list with the account of William Ebesham, in Letter CCLXIV. v. ii. p. 15, it fixes it to the library of John Paston. It contained only one book in print, the rest being manuscripts, and appear to have been bound together as numbered 1, 2, 3, &c., in the inventory. An account of most of the books mentioned is to be found in Mr. Warton's 'History of English Poetry,' and some of them, when afterwards printed, in Mr. Herbert's improved edition of Ames's 'History of Printing.' To these, therefore, I refer the reader. [Much of the original is torn or obliterated, and the titles of the works in each volume are run on together; but the deficiencies have been supplied by Fenn in all those cases where sufficient of the titles have been left to identify the works.]

The Inventory of English books, of John (Paston), made the 5th day of November, in the . . . year of the reign of Edward IV.

1 A BOOK had of my hostess at the George, ... of the Death of Arthur, beginning at Cassibelan

Guy Earl of Warwick
King Richard Cœur de Lyon
A Chronicle to Edward the III.   Price

[1 In the original *aqueytacōn*, which Fenn translates *acquaintance*, but this gives a very obscure meaning. We believe we have given the right word, meaning that he has not acquitted himself regularly as a correspondent.]

2 Item, a Book of Troilus, which William
  Br...... hath had near ten years, and
  lent it to Dame ...... Wyngfeld,
  and there I saw it ...... worth
3 Item, a black Book, with the Legend of
  Lad¹ ...... sans Mercy.
  The Parliament of Birds.
  The Temple of Glass
  Palatyse and Scitacus
  The Meditations of ......
  The Green Knight ...... worth
4 Item, a Book in print of the Play of the ..
5 Item, a Book lent Midelton, and therein is
  Belle Dame sans Mercy.
  The Parliament of Birds
  Ballad of Guy and Colbrond,
  ..... of the Goose, the ......
  The Disputation between Hope and Despair.
  ...... Merchants.
  The Life of Saint Chrystopher.
6 A red Book that Percival Robsart gave me;
  of the Meeds of the Mass.
  The Lamentation of Child Ipotis.
  A Prayer to the Vernicle,
  called the Abbey of the Holy Ghost.
7 Item, in quires, Tully de Senectute in
  whereof there is no more clear writing.
8 Item, in quires, Tully or Cypio² (*Scipio*)
  de Amicitia,³ left with William Worcester ..... worth

9 Item, in quires, a Book of the Policy of
  In....
10 Item, in quires, a Book de Sapientiâ,
   wherein the second person is likened to
   Sapience.
11 Item, a Book de Othea⁴ (*Wisdom*), text
   and gloss, worth in quires
   Memorandum; mine old Book of Blazonings of Arms.
   Item, the new Book portrayed and
   blazoned.
   Item, a Copy of Blazonings of Arms, and
   the   names to be found by
   Letter (*alphabetically*).
   Item, a Book with Arms portrayed in
   paper.
   Memorandum; my Book of Knighthood;
   and the manner of making of Knights;
   of Justs, of Tournaments; fighting in
   Lists; paces holden by Soldiers;
   and Challenges; Statutes of War; and
   de Regimine Principum ..... worth
   Item, a Book of new Statutes from Edward the IV.

5th of November. E. IV.

---

¹ May not the chasm be thus supplied? *The Le-*
ende off Ladys, and la bele Dame, as la bele Dame
nunce m'eye is never called by the name of Legend
i any edition of Chaucer that I have seen.
² Query, if Cypio is not a mistake for "Somnium
cipionis," a piece which is usually printed with the
De Amicitiâ,' and probably accompanied it in this
manuscript?
³ It is a curious circumstance that this book should

be here mentioned as left with William Worcester,
who, with the assistance of John Tiptoft, Earl of
Worcester, and John Phrea, or Free, a monk of
Bristol, translated it.
⁴ This book, ' De Othea,' is a poetical epistle, if
I remember right, from Hector to Othea, probably
Minerva or Wisdom, who is addressed in the 'Iliad'
frequently by the title of Ω Θεα. This circumstance
is laid hold of by some French antiquary (for the
original of this book is in French) to prove that
Greek was understood in France earlier than is
usually imagined.

LETTER CCCCXXXVI.—(VII. of Appendix to vol. ii. p. 305.)

These verses are inserted as a specimen of the poetry of a lady, sent as a letter to a nobleman who was absent from her, and for whom she appears to have had a sincere affection. The thoughts contained in them are, many of them, natural and tender, and some of them pretty and affecting. They are certainly originals, as in several places the words first written are struck out, and words more to the writer's satisfaction inserted above them : thus the sixth line in the fifth stanza was originally written—

" Er *then may I* but *thys* ye shall not mysse."

And then thus altered :—

" Er I my sylf but yett ye shall not mysse."

Several others have similar alterations. They were written either in the reign of Henry VI. or Edward IV., the writing and paper being both of that age, and the paper-mark is used upon two other letters in this collection, of the former reign.

Verses written by a Lady, in the reign of Henry VI. or Edward IV., to an absent Lord with whom she was in love.

My right good lord, most knightly gentle
    knight,
Unto your grace in my most humble wise
I me commend, as it is due and right,
Beseeching you at leisure to advise [1]
Upon this bill, and pardon mine emprize,
Grounded on folly, for lack of providence,
Unto your Lordship to write without licence.

But when a man is with a fever shake,
Now hot, now cold, as falleth by adventure,
He in his mind conjecture will, and take
The nighest mean to work his cure,
More patiently his paines to endure ;
And right so I, so it you not displease,
Write in this wise my paines to appease.

For when I count and make a reckoning
Betwixt my life, my death, and my desire,
My life, alas ! it serveth of nothing,
Since with your parting departed my pleasure; [2]
Wishing your presence setteth me on fire,
But then your absence doth my heart so cold,
That for the pain I not [3] me where to hold.

O out on absence, there fools have no grace,
I mean myself, nor yet no wit to gwye [4]
Them out of pain, to come unto that place;
Where as presence may shape a remedy
For all disease, now fie on my folly,
For I despaired am of your soon meeting,
That God, I pray, me to your presence bring.

Farewell, my lord, for I may write no more,
So troubled is my heart with heaviness ;
Envy also, it grieveth me most sore,

That this rude bill shall put himself in press, [5]
To see your lordship of his presumptuousness
Ere I myself ; but yet ye shall not miss
To have my heart tofore [6] my bill I wis.

Which I commit, and all my whole service,
Into your hands, demean it as you list,
Of it, I keep [7] to have no more franchise
Than I heartless surely me wist,
Saving only that it be as trist [8]
And to you true as ever was heart, and plain,
Till cruel death depart [9] it upon twain.

Adieu, disport ; farewell, good company ;
In all this world there is no joy I ween,
For there as whilom I see with mine eye
A lusty [10] lord leaping upon a green ;
The soil is sole, no knights there be seen,
No ladies walk there they were wont to done ;
Alas ! some folk departed hence too soon.

Some time also men might a wager make,
And with their bows [11] afield have it tried,
Or at the paume [12] their pleasure for to take,
Then were they loose that now stand as tied.
I not [13] whereto this world may be applied ;
For all good cheer, on even and on morrow,
Which then was made, now turneth me to
    sorrow.

---

[1] Consider, reflect.
[2] As spelt in the original, plesyer, it rhymes exactly with desyer and fyer.
[3] [*Not* is used here for *know not*. It is used in the same way in the last stanza.]
[4] Guide.

[5] Readiness. [Rather in the *crowd* or *press*.]
[6] [In the original—
" To have my hert to for my byll I wys."
Meaning, we think, " to have my heart too before my bill."]
[7] I care.
[8] Query, whether this means *sorrowful* or *trusty* ?
[9] [*Depart* for *divide*. It is frequently used in the same sense by Shakspere.]
[10] Lively, and active in his exercises.
[11] [In original, *bowys*, which completes the rhythm.]
[12] Some place of resort for the game of tennis.
[13] [*I know not.* See preceding column.]

EDWARD V.
From a MS. in the Archbishop's Library at Lambeth.

EDWARD V.—1483.

THE only letter given by Sir John Fenn under this reign is not from the Paston Collection, but was furnished by Mr. Brand, who found it in a MS. collection of pedigrees belonging to Sir Walter Blackett of Newcastle, under the title of 'A Coppie of some letters which were found in Rabie Castle [in Durham] after the Rebellion, to show the fashion . . . . . of those times.' The date of the MS. is of James I. The letter is addressed by Richard Duke of Gloucester to a Lord Nevile, whose identity is not ascertained; there was a Nevile Lord Abergavenny, but no Lord Nevile, at the period. The letter is of no importance, merely inviting the said Lord Nevile to come in haste, "defensibly arranged," and is dated 11th June, 1483. It has therefore been omitted.]

RICHARD III.
From a Painting on Glass belonging to Trinity College, Cambridge.

RICHARD III.—1483 to 1485.

LETTER CCCCXXXVII.—(I. vol. ii. p. 315.)

This letter refers to the commotions excited in different parts of the kingdom by the Duke of Buckingham, who from discontent conspired against Richard. He failed in his enterprise, however, and, being deserted by his forces, fled, was treacherously betrayed, taken, and beheaded. John Lord Howard (descended from Margaret, daughter and coheir of Thomas Mowbray, Duke of Norfolk) was created Duke of Norfolk in 1483, 1 R. III., and was slain at the battle of Bosworth in 1485.

To my right well-beloved friend, John Paston, be this delivered in haste.

RIGHT well-beloved friend, I commend me to you. It is so that the Kentishmen be up in the Weld,[1] and say that they will come and rob the city, which I shall let if I may.

Therefore I pray you that with all diligence ye make you ready and come hither, and bring with you six tall fellows in harness; and ye shall not lyse (*lose*) your labour, that knoweth God, who have you in his keeping.

Written at London, the tenth day of October.

Your friend,

J. NORFOLK.

London,
Friday, 10th of October,
1483. 1 R. III.

LETTER CCCCXXXVIII.—(II. vol. ii. p. 317.)

We have here an order of the Duke of Suffolk upon a tenant, for the payment of a sum of money which the Duke had promised on his honour should be paid. This is a common occurrence, and certainly not worth recording, if it had not been for the threat at the end of it, under his own hand, which shows the despotism of the Duke, and that the farm was let at will, and not on lease.

The Duke of Suffolk to Thomas Jeffreys, our farmer of Maundevills, greeting.

WE will and straitly charge you that ye content and pay unto the bringer hereof, for money employed in our household, three pounds thirteen shillings and four pence, for such stuff as we our own person have promised, and not to be failed, upon our worship.

Of the which sum of 73s. and 4d. so by you contented and paid, we will and also straitly charge our auditors for the time being, by virtue of this our writing, signed with our hand, to make you due and plein (*full*) allowance at your next account.

At Wingfield, the first day of May, in the first year of King Richard III.

SUFFOLK, and fail not on pain (*of*) losing of your farm.

Wingfield,
Saturday, 1st of May,
1484. 1 R. III.

---

[1] [The Weald of Kent.]

NUMBER CCCCXXXIX.—(III. vol. ii. p. 319.)

This address of King Richard to his people is drawn up in the most artful manner, in order to inflame the minds not only of the multitude, but of the peers, bishops, dignitaries, and great men, and to induce them to resist the attempts of the Earl of Richmond upon the crown with all their power.

On the back of the paper in an ancient hand is written,

Kent Sheriffs.

The copy of a Letter of King Richard III., persuading his subjects to resist Henry Tydder (Tudor), *afterwards King of England, and declaring from whom the said Henry was descended.*

RICHARD R.

Richard, &c., wisheth health : we command you, &c.

Forasmuch as the king our sovereign lord hath certain knowledge that Piers Bishop of Exeter,[1] Jasper Tydder[2] (*Tudor*) son of Owen Tydder, calling himself Earl of Pembroke, John late Earl of Oxford,[3] and Sir Edward Wodevile,[4] with other diverse his rebels and traitors, disabled and attainted by the authority of the High Court of Parliament, of whom many be known for open murderers, advowterers (*adulterers*), and extortioners, contrary to the pleasure of God, and against all truth, honour, and nature, have forsaken their natural country, taking them first to be under the obeisance of the Duke of Bretagne,[5] and to him promised certain things, which by him and his council were thought things too greatly unnatural and abominable for them to grant, observe, keep, and perform, and therefore the same utterly refused.

The said traitors, seeing the said duke and his council would not aid nor succour them nor follow their ways, privily departed out of his country into France, and there taking them to be under the obeisance of the king's ancient enemy, Charles,[6] calling himself King of France, and to abuse and blind the commons of this said realm, the said rebels and traitors have chosen to be their captain one Henry Tydder[7] (*Tudor*), son of Edmund Tydder, son of Owen Tydder, which of his ambitious and insatiable covetise encroacheth and usurpeth upon him the name and title and royal estate of this realm of England; whereunto he hath no manner interest, right, title, or colour, as every man well knoweth; for he is descended of bastard blood, both of father's side and of mother's side; for the said Owen the grandfather was bastard born, and his mother was daughter unto John Duke of Somerset, son unto John Earl of Somerset, son unto Dame Katherine Swynford, and of their indouble avoutry[8] gotten; whereby it evidently appeareth that no title can nor may in him, which fully intendeth to enter this realm, proposing a conquest; and if he should achieve his false intent and purpose, every man's life, livelihood, and goods, shall be in his hands, liberty, and disposition; whereby should ensue the disheriting and destruction of all the noble and worshipful blood of this realm for ever, and to the resistance and withstanding whereof every true and natural Englishman born must lay to his hands for his own surety and weal.

And to the intent that the said Henry Tydder might the rather achieve his false intent and purpose by the aid, support, and assistance of the king's ancient enemy of France, (*he*) hath covenanted and bargained with him and all the council of France, to give up and release in perpetuity all the right, title, and

[1] Peter Courtney, Bishop of Exeter, after the miscarriage of the Duke of Buckingham's conspiracy, fled into Bretagne to the Earl of Richmond, who, after he became Henry VII., promoted this prelate to the see of Winchester in 1486, in which he died in 1492.

[2] Jasper Tudor de Hatfield, half-brother to Henry VI., created Duke of Bedford in 1485.

[3] John de Vere, Earl of Oxford, who had escaped from the castle of Hammes.

[4] Sir Edward Wodevile, brother to the queen of Edward IV.

[5] Francis II., the last Duke of Bretagne, was overthrown by Charles VIII. King of France, and died in 1488.

[6] Charles VIII. ascended the throne in 1483, and died in 1498.

[7] Henry Tudor, Earl of Richmond, who, in 1483, became King of England, &c., by the title of Henry VII. He died in 1509.

[8] This either means double adultery, that is adultery on both sides; or indubitable, undoubted adultery.

laim that the Kings of England have had and ought to have to the crown and realm of France, together with the duchies of Normandy, Anjou and Maine, Gascony and Guisnes Cassell,[1] and the towns of Calais, Guisnes, Hammes, with the Marches appertaining to the same, and dissever and exclude the arms of France out of the arms of England for ever.

And in more proof and showing of his said purpose of conquest, the said Henry Tydder hath goven (given), as well to divers of the said king's enemies as to his said rebels and traitors, archbishoprics, bishoprics, and other dignities spiritual; and also the duchies, earldoms, baronies, and other possessions and inheritances of knights, esquires, gentlemen, and other the king's true subjects within the realm; and intendeth also to change and subvert the laws of the same, and to induce and stablish new laws and ordinances amongst the king's said subjects.

And over this, and besides the alienations of all the premises into the possession of the king's said ancient enemies, to the greatest mytishment[2] (annihilation), shame, and rebuke that ever might fall to this said land, the said Henry Tydder and others, the king's rebels and traitors aforesaid, have extended (intended)[3] at their coming, if they may be of power, to do the most cruel murders, slaughters, and robberies, and disherisons that ever were seen in any Christian realm.

For the which and other inestimable dangers to be eschewed, and to the intent that the king's said rebels, traitors, and enemies may be utterly put from their said malicious and false purpose and soon discomforted, if they enforce[4] (endeavour) to land, the king our sovereign lord willeth, chargeth, and commandeth all and every of the natural and true subjects of this his realm to call the premises to their minds, and like good and true Englishmen to endower (furnish) themselves with all their powers for the defence of them, their wives, children, and goods, and hereditaments, against the said malicious purposes and conspirations, which the said ancient enemies have made with the king's said rebels and traitors for the final destruction of this land, as is aforesaid.

And our said sovereign lord, as a wellwilled, diligent, and courageous prince, will put his most royal person to all labour and pain necessary in this behalf for the resistance and subduing of his said enemies, rebels, and traitors, to the most comfort, weel, and surety of all his true and faithful liege men and subjects.

And over this, our said sovereign lord willeth and commandeth all his said subjects to be ready in their most defensible array to do his highness service of war, when they by open proclamation or otherwise shall be commanded so to do, for resistance of the king's said rebels, traitors, and enemies. And this under peril, &c.

Witness myself at Westminster, the twenty-third day of June,[5] in the second year of our reign.

Westminster,
Wednesday, 23rd of June,
1483. 2 R. III.

[1] [Query, if this does not mean the castle of Guisnes? The original has Guyne Cascell.]
[2] Aneantisement—anientised is used by Chaucer, in his tale of Melebeus, for reducing to nothing.
[3] [Extended may perhaps mean here given out—made known.]
[4] Or rather, make good their landing by force.

[5] Some of our historians say, that King Richard was proclaimed on the 20th, and others, on the 22nd of June, 1483; the 23rd of June, in the second year of his reign, must therefore be in 1484.—[The 26th of June is the date now generally received as the actual time of his accession: see 'Pictorial History of England,' vol. ii. p. 122. Dr. Shaw's famous sermon was preached on Sunday, June 22, 1483, at Paul's Cross; on the following Tuesday the assembly at the Guildhall of London took place, at which Richard presented himself and was hailed by a few as king; and on the 26th he took upon himself the office of king in Westminster Hall. He, however, afterwards himself dated from the 22nd June, and his accession is so given in Sir N. H. Nicolas's 'Chronology of History.' The date of the letter in any point of view must, however, be an error, and it may have been that of the copyist; but it is most probable it is the date of the year, which should be 1484.]

[The Autograph is taken from an original in the possession of Thomas Astle, Esq.

LETTER CCCCXL.—(IV. vol. ii. p. 327.)

John Paston, Esq., was Sheriff of Norfolk and Suffolk on the accession of Henry VII.; he most probably therefore entered upon that office at Michaelmas, 1484, 2 R. III., this letter being dated on the 20th of October.

To our trusty and well-beloved John Paston, Sheriff of Suffolk and Norfolk.

The Duke of Suffolk.

Right well-beloved, we greet you well; and forasmuch as the king our sovereign lord hath late addressed his letters of commission under his seal unto us, reciting by the same that his highness understanding certain of his rebels associate to his old enemies of Scotland, intending not only to trouble his peace, the nobles and subjects of this realm to destroy, their goods and possessions to spoil, and reward at their liberties, but also the laws of this land and holy church to subvert.

Our said most dread sovereign lord, as a Christian prince . . . . . .[1] his said enemies and rebels to resist, hath assigned and commanded us to do all manner . . . . . . and others defensible able to labour, as well archers as hobbellers,[2] to come before us and charge them . . . . . . armed and arrayed every man after his degree and power, to attend upon his person and upon us, to do him service, in defence as well of the church as of the said nobles and subjects of this realm, against his said enemies and rebels. We therefore will and in our said sovereign lord's name straightly charge and command you, that in all possible haste ye do (*cause*) this to be proclaimed : and that all manner men able to do the king service, as well knights, esquires, and gentlemen, as townships and hundreds, as well within franchises and liberties as without, within the counties of Suffolk and Norfolk; and that they be charged to be ready at all times, upon an hour's warning, and ordered, according to the last commission afore this, to attend upon his grace and upon us to do him service, whatsoever they shall be commanded; not failing hereof, as ye will answer at your peril.

Given at Long Stratton,[3] the 20th day of October.

And furthermore that ye give credence unto our servant this bringer, as this same day we received the king's commission at four in the afternoon.

Suffolk, your friend.

Long Stratton,
Wednesday, 20th of October,
1484. 2 R. III.

LETTER CCCCXLI.—(V. vol. ii. p. 331.)

We are here acquainted with the diversions and amusements allowed in the houses of the nobility and gentry during the joyous season of Christmas. We see likewise the respect paid to the memory of the head of a family, when, at the Christmas following his death, none of the more merry or noisy disports were permitted.

To my right worshipful husband, John Paston.

Right worshipful husband, I recommend me unto you : please it you to weet that I sent your eldest son to my Lady Morley,[4] to have knowledge what sports were used in her house in Christmas next following after the decease of my lord her husband; and she said that there were none disguisings, nor harping, nor luting, nor singing, nor none loud disports; but playing at the tables, and chess, and cards; such disports she gave her folks leave to play and none other.

Your son did his errand right well, as ye

---

[1] The letter is defective in those places where dots are used.

[2] Hoblers, or hobilers, so called from the hobbies, or diminutive horses on which they rode : or more probably from *hobilles*, the short jackets they wore. They were light horsemen, and proved of considerable service to Edward III. in his French expeditions. By the tenure of their lands they were obliged to maintain their nags, and were expected to be in readiness, when sudden invasions happened, to spread immediate intelligence of the same throughout the country.

[3] In Norfolk.

[4] Widow of William Lovel, Lord Morley, who died the 23rd of July, 1475.

all hear after this. I sent your younger m to the Lady Stapleton,[1] and she said ac- rding to my Lady Morley's saying in that; id as she had seen used in places of worship ereas (*where*) she hath been.

I pray you that ye will assure to you some an at Caister to keep your buttery, for the an that ye left with me will not take upon m to breve[2] daily as ye commanded; he ith he hath not used to give a reckoning ither of bread nor ale till at the week's end, id he saith he wot (*knows*) well that the ould not condeneth (*give content*), and there-

fore I suppose he shall not abide, and I trow ye shall be fain to purvey another man for Symond, for ye are never the nearer a wise man for him.

I am sorry that ye shall not at home be for Christmas.

I pray you that ye will come as soon as ye may; I shall think myself half a widow, be- cause ye shall not be at home, &c. God have you in his keeping. Written on Christmas even.

By your servant and beadwoman, MARGERY PASTON.

Friday, 24th of December, 1484. 2 R. III.

LETTER CCCCXLII.—(I. vol. v. p. 305.)

THIS letter is from Dame Elizabeth Browne (formerly Poynings), the daughter of Sir Wil- am Paston the judge, to her nephew John aston. Fenn supposes it to have been written to disprove some assertion of William Pas-

ton concerning the matters in dispute between him and his nephew." As W. Paston is in no way alluded to throughout the letter, we do not see the value of this guess, but Fenn ad- mires so indiscriminatingly the chief contri- butors to his Collection, that he enters, on too many occasions, into the petty feelings of dis- like which they appear to have entertained for William Paston. Except compliments, the following is the letter :—" Whereas ye desire me to send you word whether my brother John Paston, your father, was with my father and his, whom God assoil, during his last sickness and at the time of his decease at St. Bride's or not. Nephew, I ascertain you upon my faith and poor honour, that I was fourteen, fifteen year, or sixteen year old, and at St. Bride's with my father and my mother, when my father's last sickness took him, and till he was deceased ; and I dare depose be- fore any person honourable that, when my fa- ther's last sickness took him, my brother your father was in Norfolk, and he came not to London till after that my father was deceased ; and that can Sir William Cooting and James Gresham record, for they both were my fa-

---

[1] Sir Miles Stapleton died in 1466.

[2] To breve is to make up an account. How ictly this custom of *breving* was formerly observed great houses may be known from one of the *daily* les enforced in the family of the fifth Earl of orthumberland. "Furst, that the said clerkis be yly at the *brevynge* every day by vii of the cloke in e mornynge. And theire to *breve* every officer ac- rdynge as the custome is unto half howre after viii the cloke. And that theire be no brackfasts dely- ret unto the tyme that all the officers have *breved*." See *Household Book*, p. 59. As this letter has no te of the year, I have some doubts where to place unless we may suppose that the same respect uld be paid to the memory of Margaret, mother of Paston, who was an heiress, and died in 1484, and use will was proved on the 18th of December in at year. If I could have placed it earlier, I should ive fixed upon the death of Sir John Paston, in ovember 1479, as the time of its being written ; but e present J. Paston was not married till 1477, and s eldest son being born in 1478, was now only in s seventh year, which might be the case, as the ex- ession that he "dede hese heyrne ryght wele" iplies his being very young.

ther's clerks at that time." There are two
dates to the letter, "the Thursday next before
Whitsunday, the second year of King Richard
the Third" (May 19, 1485), which is scratched
through with a pen; and then "the 23rd

of September, the first year of the reign of
King Henry the Seventh." It was probably
written on the first date, but not transmitted
till the second, a proof that its contents were
not considered very urgent.]

LETTER CCCCXLIII.—(VI. vol. ii. p. 335.)

Henry, Earl of Richmond, landed upon Saturday the 6th of August, 1485, at Milford Haven in South Wales;
this letter therefore could not be written before the Friday or Saturday following (12th or 13th of August),
Richard appears not to have regarded the landing of the Earl as a matter of that great importance which it
soon became; for, as a valiant prince, he certainly would have set forwards to meet his competitor as soon as
possible; and however great his veneration might have been for the day of "the Assumption of our Lady,"
yet his fears of losing a crown, for the possession of which he had ventured everything, would have been
still greater, and would have prompted him to break in upon the services due to our Lady. The Duke of
Norfolk survived the writing of this letter only a few days, for he joined his royal master, and commanded
the vanguard of his army in the field of Bosworth, where he fell on Monday the 22nd of August, valiantly
fighting for his sovereign lord and benefactor.

To my well-beloved friend John Paston, be this bill delivered in haste.

WELL-BELOVED friend, I commend me to you;
letting you to understand that the king's
enemies be a-land, and that the king would
have set forth as upon Monday, but only for
our Lady-day;[1] but for certain he goeth forward as upon Tuesday, for a servant of mine
brought to me the certainty.

Wherefore I pray you that ye meet with
me at Bury,[2] for, by the grace of God, I purpose to lie at Bury as upon Tuesday night;

and that ye bring with you such company of
tall men as ye may goodly make at my cost
and charge, besides that which ye have promised the king; and, I pray you, ordain
them jackets[3] of my livery, and I shall content you at your meeting with me.

       Your lover,

           J. NORFOLK.

Between the 8th and 15th of August,
1485. 3 R. III.

---

[1] The Assumption of our Lady, 15th of August.
[2] Bury St. Edmund's, in Suffolk.

[3] From this it appears that the royal army, when
embodied, was clothed in jackets of the livery of the
respective great lords and commanders.

/E have now brought down our correspondence to the close of the reign of Richard III.
effect this in an unbroken chronological series, we have introduced abstracts of several
ters from the fifth quarto volume, of which the copyright is yet unexpired, and upon the
hts of which we should be sorry to trespass. There are only two letters in the fourth quarto
ume belonging to the reign of Henry VII.; but the fifth quarto contains many of that
gn of a most interesting character. To all to whom expense is not an object, we can
ommend the volume as a desirable one to possess.

Taking it for granted that the reader, who has been admitted so freely into the family
irs and secrets of the Pastons, will feel some interest in their further fortunes, we have
led the pedigree of the family to its final extinction.]

PEDIGREE OF THE FAMILY OF PASTON, OF NORFOLK.

Clement Paston, of Paston, died 1419. = Beatrice, daughter of John de Somerton, died before 1419. Buried at Paston. Buried at Paston.

Sir William Paston, Kt., born 1378. Brought up to = Agnes, daughter and coheir of Sir Edmund Berry, the law, and became a judge of the Common Pleas. of Harlingbury Hall, in Therfield, Herts, by Alice, His will is dated 20th June, 1443, and he died 13th daughter and heir of Sir Thomas Gerbridge. Died August, 1444, aged 66. He was called the Good Judge. 1479. Both she and Sir William are buried at Norwich Cathedral, in Our Lady's Chapel.

| John Paston, Esq., born 1420. = Margaret, daughter and heir of John Mauteby, Esq., by Margaret, daughter of John Berney, Esq., of Reedham. Her will is dated 4th Feb., 1484, and proved 18th Dec. 1484. She was buried at Mauteby. | Edmund Paston, Esq., born 1425. His will is dated 21st March, 1448. | William Paston had disputes with his nephews concerning their estates, &c. | Clement Paston, born 1442. Was at London under the care of Master Grenfeld in 1457. | Elizabeth Paston, born about 1429. She lived with Lady Pole in 1457, and was alive in 1485. Married, first, Robert Poynings; second, Sir George Browne, Kt., of Beechworth Castle, in Surrey. |

John Paston, Esq., born before 1440, when he studied the law in the Inner Temple. He was one of the executors of the will of Sir John Fastolf, to which his cousin Hugh Fenn was supervisor. His estates were seized by Edward IV., and he was committed to the Fleet just before his death, which happened in London on 26th of May, 1466. He was buried very sumptuously at Bromholm Priory in Norfolk.

Walter Paston.

| Sir John Paston, Kt., born about 1440. He took possession of his father's estates by a warrant from Edward IV., dated 6 July, 1464; was a brave soldier; performed many gallant actions in the French wars, and was the king's champion at Eltham. He died unmarried on 15 November, 1479, 19 Edward IV., aged nearly forty years, and was buried in London. He left a natural daughter, named Constance. | John Paston, Esq., appears to have been brought up in the family of the Duke of Norfolk; was a soldier, and engaged in the French wars. He attended the Princess Margaret to Bruges in 1468; was heir to his brother in 1479, and in 1485 High Sheriff of Norfolk. He was knighted, and made a knight banneret at the battle of Stoke, by Henry VII. in 1487. = Margery, daughter of Thomas Brews, of Stinton Hall, in Salle, by Elizabeth, daughter of Sir Giles, and sister and heir of Sir Gilbert Debenham. She was married in 1477, and, dying in 1495, was buried in the White Friars in Norwich, where her husband was afterwards interred. | William Paston was at Eton in 1467. | Clement Paston. | Walter Paston took a degree, and died at Oxford in 1479. | Edmund Paston was in the garrison at Calais in 1473. He was twice married, and died about 1504. | Anne Paston, married Wm. Yelverton, son of John, son of Sir William Yelverton, the judge. | Margery Paston, married Richard Calle. |

Erasmus Paston, died during his father's life, in 1538, and was buried at Paston. == Mary, daughter of Sir Thomas Windham, of Felbrig, Kt., died in 1596, and was buried at Paston.

Clement Paston, Esq., a great sea commander. He built Oxnead Hall, and, dying in 1597, was buried at Oxnead.

Sir William Paston, Kt., was born in 1528, died in 1610, aged 82, and was buried at North Walsham. He was heir to his uncle, Clement Paston. == Francis, daughter of Sir Thomas Clere, of Stokesby, Kt.

Christopher Paston, Esq., born in 1554. Married in 1577. Adjudged an idiot in 1611, 9 Jac. I., when the jury found that he had been so from about 1587. == Anne, daughter of Philip Audley, Esq. of Palgrave, near Swaffham.

Sir Edmund Paston, Kt., born 1585. Married 1603. Died 1632, aged 48. Buried at Paston. == Catharine, daughter of Sir Thomas Knevet, of Ashwelthorpe, Kt. She died in 1628, and lies buried at Paston.

Sir William Paston, Bart., an antiquary and collector, was High Sheriff of Norfolk in 1636, created a baronet in 1641, and, dying in 1662, was buried at Paston. == Catharine, daughter of Robert Bertie, Earl of Lindsey, died 1636, and is buried at Oxnead, where there is an elegant mural monument with her bust, &c.

Robert Paston, Earl of Yarmouth, &c., born 1631, created Baron Paston and Viscount Yarmouth, 1673, and Earl of Yarmouth in 1679. He was shot at in his coach in 1676; and, dying in 1682, was buried at Oxnead. == Rebecca, daughter of Sir Jasper Clayton, Kt., a citizen of London.

William Paston, Earl of Yarmouth, &c., encumbered his inheritance, and having survived all his male issue, died in 1732, when his titles became extinct, leaving his estates to be sold for the payment of his debts, &c. == First wife, Lady Charlotte Boyle, alias Fitzroy, a natural daughter of Charles II. by Elizabeth Viscountess Shannon. She died in 1684. Second wife, Elizabeth, daughter of Dudley Lord North.

Charles Lord Paston, born 1673. Died unmarried.

William, born 1677. Died an infant.

William Lord Paston, born 1682. Died unmarried.

Charlotte, married Thos. Hyrne, Esq., of Heverland.

Rebecca, married Sir John Holland, Bart. of Quidenham.

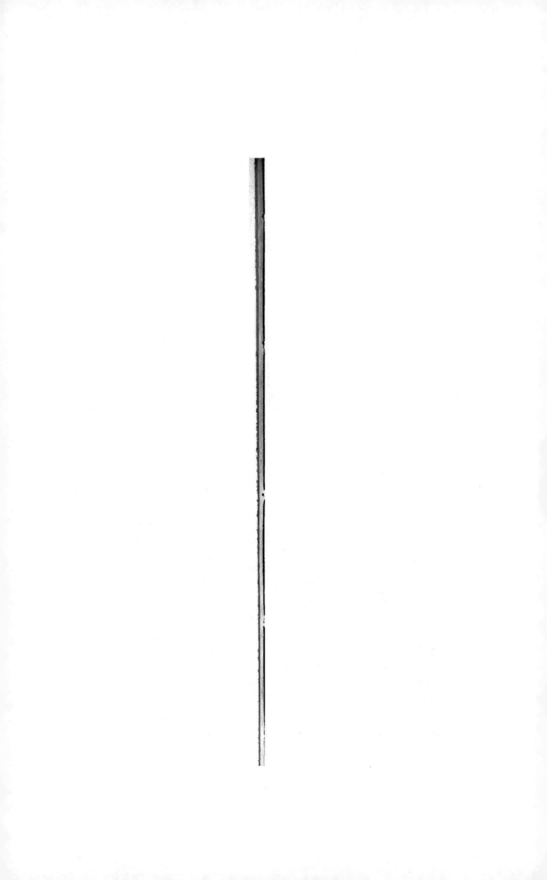

INDEX.

London : Printed by WILLIAM CLOWES and SONS, Stamford Street.

CPSIA information can be obtained at www.ICGtesting.com
Printed in the USA
LVOW09*1228130716

R11113700001B/R111137PG496099LVX3B/1/P

9 781296 569136